PUBLIC OPINION AND THE TEACHING OF HISTORY IN THE UNITED STATES

A Da Capo Press Reprint Series

CIVIL LIBERTIES IN AMERICAN HISTORY

GENERAL EDITOR: LEONARD W. LEVY

Brandeis University

PUBLIC OPINION AND
THE TEACHING OF HISTORY
IN THE UNITED STATES

BY BESSIE LOUISE PIERCE

DA CAPO PRESS • NEW YORK • 1970

A Da Capo Press Reprint Edition

This Da Capo Press edition of *Public Opinion and the Teaching of History in the United States* is an unabridged republication of the first edition published in New York in 1926.

Library of Congress Catalog Card Number 71-107416

SBN 306-71883-9

Published by Da Capo Press
A Division of Plenum Publishing Corporation
227 West 17th Street, New York, N.Y. 10011
All Rights Reserved

Manufactured in the United States of America

PUBLIC OPINION
AND THE
TEACHING OF HISTORY

Public Opinion and
The Teaching of History
in the United States

BY

BESSIE LOUISE PIERCE, Ph.D.

Associate Professor of History, University of Iowa
Head of the Department of Social Studies
University High School

NEW YORK
ALFRED A. KNOPF
1926

PREFACE

Many influences have conditioned the teaching of history in the public schools — local and national, statutory and constitutional, ephemeral and enduring, religious, educational, racial and patriotic.

It is the purpose of this study to give an historical account of some of the attempts to control the teaching of history in the public schools. The first four chapters trace the legislative control that has been exerted in all periods of our history, beginning with the educational enactments of the early colonies and following the development of the curriculum to the present time.

Such statutory control falls into fairly definite periods. The first embraces the earliest statutes relating to public education. During this period history was introduced into the school curriculum as a separate subject specified by law. The next stage, 1860 to 1900, was characterized by the influences set in motion by the Civil War and the Economic Revolution. In the years from 1900 to 1917, the history curriculum reflected the new interest of the American people in the social and economic conditions that had developed. From 1917 to the present, the dominant note has been a dynamic patriotism growing out of the World War.

Besides the legislative aspects of the subject, I have endeavored to set forth the propagandist influences on textbook-making exerted by religious, patriotic, racial and other organized groups. Within the last five years attention to an unprecedented degree has been focused upon history and its allied subjects. Although much interest has been attached to the agitation carried on since the World War, similar movements marked earlier periods. A chapter on Disloyalty Charges against Teachers since 1917 has been included as pertinent to the discussion in general.

Because of their kinship with history, the other social studies have been considered. The term *social studies* has been used to embrace history, economics, government and sociology. Geography has not been included, because it but recently acquired a place in the curriculum as a social study. More attention, furthermore, has been paid to the subject of history, since it has been the chief social study in the public school curriculum. There has been no attempt to portray the extent to which laws have been enforced. Throughout it has been my desire to narrate without partiality or prejudice the facts relating to the subject under discussion.

In the preparation of this volume I am indebted to many friends for advice and coöperation in obtaining material. In the search for present-day conditions I have drawn heavily upon many correspondents including school superintendents, textbook authors and publishers, as well as those engaged in criticising school histories. To all who have aided, I would here express my sincere gratitude. I have particularly profited by the guidance and constructive criticism of Professor Arthur M. Schlesinger of Harvard University, who first called the subject to my attention, and who is chiefly responsible for whatever merit there is in this study. I am indebted for many helpful suggestions to Professor Ernest Horn of the University of Iowa, to Professor Carl Wittke of Ohio State University, and to Dr.

Richard J. Purcell of the Catholic University of America. These acknowledgments would not be complete without mentioning my obligation to my sister, Anne E. Pierce, for assistance at all stages in the preparation of the manuscript, and to my mother, whose spirit of coöperation has proved a constant source of inspiration.

B. L. P.

CONTENTS

PART I

STATUTORY REGULATION OF THE TEACHING OF HISTORY

PART II

THE ACTIVITIES OF PROPAGANDIST AGENCIES

PART I

STATUTORY REGULATION OF THE TEACHING OF HISTORY

" The law is only a memorandum . . . and as fast as the public mind is opened to more intelligence, the code is seen to be brute and stammering. It speaks not articulately and must be made to. . . . The history of the State sketches in coarse outline the progress of thought, and follows at a distance the delicacy of culture and of aspiration."

EMERSON, *Essays and English Traits.*

PART I

STATUTORY REGULATION OF THE TEACHING
OF HISTORY

CHAPTER I

THE PERIOD OF BEGINNINGS

Statutory prescriptions of history as a specific subject in the American public school had their beginning in the years between 1827 and 1860; yet the way for such enactments had been charted by earlier educational legislation. For example, in 1642 the Massachusetts Puritans provided that every child be taught enough " to read and understand the principles of religion and the capital laws of the country," [1] and returning to the subject in 1647, expressed their belief that education would serve to "thwart that auld deluder Sathan " whose " cheife project [was] to keep men from ye knowledge of ye Scriptures." [2]

In the course of time it was natural that the function of education should enlarge. From the religious conception inevitably sprang a belief in education as a means of imparting an understanding of the principles of " right living." The individual as a virtuous, polite, and exemplary force in the community became the objective of the law-maker. Closely allied with this conviction was a faith in education as an instrument for teaching patriotism and for training in the fundamentals of government. Thus, in 1732, New York justified the establishment of her schools on the

[1] Shurtleff, N. B., ed., *Records of the Governor and Company of the Massachusetts Bay in New England*, 5 v. (Boston, 1853), Vol. II, p. 6.

[2] *Ibid.*, p. 203. Connecticut in 1650 expressed a similar purpose for the establishment of her schools. *The Code of Connecticut*, 1650, p. 90.

3

ground that "good Learning is not only a very great Accomplishment but the properest Means to Attain Knowledge, Improve the Mind, Morality and good Manners and to make Men better, wiser and more useful to their Country as well as to themselves." [3]

In 1780 Massachusetts took a similar stand,[4] perceiving in her schools a method of directing the masses in the great undertaking of self-government, — a function recognized by Washington, John Adams, Jefferson and other men of the

[3] *Laws of the Colony of New York, 1720–1737*, Vol. II, p. 813.

[4] "Wisdom and knowledge, as well as virtue, diffused generally among the body of the people being necessary for the preservation of their rights and liberties; and as these depend on spreading the opportunities and advantages of education in the various parts of the country, and among the different orders of the people, it shall be the duty of legislatures and magistrates, in all future periods of this commonwealth, to cherish the interests of literature and the sciences, and all seminaries of them; . . . especially public schools and grammar schools in towns; . . . ." Thorpe, Francis Newton, editor, *The Federal and State Constitutions, Colonial Charters, and other Organic Laws of the States, Territories, Now or Heretofore Forming the United States of America.* 7 v. (Government Printing Office, Washington, 1909), Vol. II, p. 1907. Similar statements were placed in the constitutions of neighboring New Hampshire, Vermont and Maine. Indiana, Arkansas, Mississippi, Missouri, Rhode Island, South Dakota, Tennessee, Kansas and North Dakota have likewise pinned their faith to "knowledge and learning" as an agent for democratizing the government as well as for the encouragement of "the principles of humanity, industry, and morality." *Ibid.*, Vol. IV, p. 2487; Vol. II, pp. 1069, 1086; Vol. I, pp. 283, 322, 353; Vol. IV, p. 2080; p. 2212; Vol. VI, p. 3233; p. 3373; p. 3469; Vol. II, p. 1232; Vol. V, p. 2872. In constitutions adopted at a much later time the same purposes of education are often expressed. In 1789 a Massachusetts law charged "instructors of youth" that they should "take diligent care, and to exert their best endeavors to impress on the minds of children and youth committed to their care and instruction, the principles of piety, justice, and a sacred regard to truth, love to their country, humanity, and universal benevolence, sobriety, industry, and frugality, chastity, moderation and temperance, and those other virtues which are the ornament of human society, and the basis upon which the Republican Constitution is structured. And it shall be the duty of such instructors to endeavor to lead those under their care (as their ages and capacities will admit) into a particular understanding of the tendency of the above mentioned virtues, to preserve and perfect a Republican Constitution, and to secure the blessings of liberty, as well as to promote their future happiness; and the tendency of the opposite

day.[5] Other commonwealths also accepted education as a means to "preserve and perfect a Republican Constitution" and to "secure the blessings of liberty."[6]

These early laws thus paved the way for those of a later time. They laid the foundation of an education directed toward the development of civic efficiency. Yet their influence was circumscribed by the virtual absence of free, public schools. This lack, however, the second quarter of the nineteenth century was destined to remedy; for such was the democratic awakening of the 'twenties and 'thirties that nearly every field of human activity was transformed. Trade associations attested a quickened consciousness in the laboring man; reform movements bore testimony to a new social point of view; and an aroused electorate chose for the highest office of the land that exponent of democracy, Andrew Jackson.[7]

---

vices to slavery and ruin." *Statutes* of Massachusetts, 1780–1807, sec. 4, Vol. I, pp. 470–471. On the statute books in 1823. Also *Statutes*, 1826, ch. 143, p. 180; also *General Statutes*, 1860, ch. 38, sec. 10, p. 216; also *Public Statutes*, 1882, ch. 44, sec. 16. This law became the source of many similar in character.

[5] In 1784, Jefferson took occasion to declare, " In every government on earth is some trace of human weakness, some germ of corruption and degeneracy, which cunning will discover, and wickedness insensibly open, cultivate and improve. Every government degenerates when trusted to the rulers of the people alone. The people themselves are its only safe depositories; and to render even them safe, their minds must be improved to a certain degree." Jefferson, Thomas, *The Writings of Thomas Jefferson*. Paul Leicester Ford, ed. (New York, 1894), Vol. III, p. 254.

[6] See footnote 4 for the Massachusetts law of 1789. *Statutes* of New Hampshire, 1830, title XCII, ch. 1, sec. 8, p. 431; also *Compiled Statutes*, 1853, sec. 20, p. 179. *Statutes* of Maine, 1821, Vol. II, sec. 2, p. 504, also *Revised Statutes*, 1840, ch. 17, p. 170. *Supplement to Revised Statutes*, 1885–1895, ch. 11, sec. 91; *Acts and Resolves*, 1917, ch. 228, p. 263. *Revised Code* of Mississippi, 1824, ch. 82, sec. 14, p. 407; *Ibid.*, 1840, ch. 9, sec. 12, p. 124. *Statutes* of Indiana, 1806, p. 17. *Revised Statutes* of Illinois, 1833, p. 556.

[7] An illuminating discussion of " Jacksonian Democracy " is found in Arthur M. Schlesinger's *New Viewpoints in American History* (New York, 1922).

In the states outside of New England little had been accomplished in the early years of the century toward the establishment of tax-supported schools. With the extension of manhood suffrage, however, came the realization that the functions of government were safe only in the hands of an enlightened electorate — a conviction which had come only after much agitation and bitter argument. Gradually and inevitably the public school, supported by public funds, became the embodiment of the democratic ideal in which " intelligence is the grand condition." [8]

The year 1827 signalized the entrance of United States history into the school curriculum as a study required by law. At this time both Massachusetts and Vermont made the teaching of national history compulsory. The Massachusetts law provided that " every town, containing five hundred families or householders, shall maintain a school to be kept by a master of competent ability and good morals, who shall . . . give instruction in the history of the United States, book-keeping, surveying, geometry, and algebra; and such last mentioned school shall be kept for the benefit of all the inhabitants of the town, ten months at least, exclusive of vacations each year . . . ; and in every town containing four thousand inhabitants, the said master shall, in addition to all the branches of instruction before required in this chapter be competent to instruct in the Latin and Greek languages, and history, rhetoric and logic." [9] The Vermont statute, designed for the elementary school, required that " each organized town in this state shall keep and support a school or schools, provided with a

[8] Mann, Horace, *Annual Reports on Education* (Boston, 1868), pp. 523–558.

[9] *Laws of Massachusetts*, 1827, ch. 148, p. 180; also *Revised Statutes*, 1836, ch. 23, p. 218. In the *Revised Statutes* " general history," not " history," is required.

teacher or teachers, of good morals, for the instruction of youths in . . . the history of the United States, and good behavior." [10]

Counterparts of these laws presently appeared in other states. In 1846 New Hampshire prescribed history as a subject in high schools,[11] and shortly after it was sanctioned by Rhode Island.[12] In 1857 the Massachusetts legislature placed United States history in her elementary schools, and added general history, the " civil polity " of the commonwealth and political economy to the required subjects for high schools.[13] Three years later, she again committed herself in favor of the social studies in the curriculum. " In every town," the law read, " there shall be kept for at least six months in each year, a sufficient number of schools for the instruction of all the children . . . in orthography, reading, writing, English grammar, geography, arithmetic, the history of the United States and good behavior. . . ." This law further required in every town of five hundred families or householders the maintenance of a school in which instruction in general history and the " civil polity " of the commonwealth and of the United States should be given,[14] and also permitted the teaching of political economy.[15]

[10] *Laws of Vermont* . . . to 1834, ch. 50 (1827), sec. 1, p. 136; also *Revised Statutes*, 1840, ch. XVIII, sec. 1, p. 111; also *Compiled Statutes*, 1851, p. 144.

[11] *Laws of New Hampshire*, 1845, ch. 220, sec. 6; also *Compiled Statutes*, 1853, ch. 79, sec. 6, p. 183. This law was retained in 1863.

[12] *Revised Statutes* of Rhode Island, 1857, ch. 67, sec. 3, p. 173.

[13] *Acts and Resolves* of Massachusetts, 1857, ch. 206, sec. 1, p. 542.

[14] *General Statutes of Massachusetts*, 1860, ch. 38, sec. 1, p. 215; *Public Statutes*, 1882, ch. 44, sec. 1, p. 299. According to a table in A. J. Inglis' *The Rise of the High School in Massachusetts* (Columbia University, New York, 1911), p. 90, history was offered in six out of seven towns in 1860, with a per cent of 200 with algebra as a base of 100 per cent. This would indicate an interest in history to a considerable extent.

[15] *Political economy* as a term included *political science* as we understand it today. *Cf.* Inglis, *op. cit.*, p. 141.

The South did not awaken to the needs of public education at this early period because of its institutional and economic development. Virginia was the only state of that section to enact legislation relating to the teaching of history before the Civil War. In 1849 she provided that in district schools "shall be thoroughly taught, . . . history, especially that of the United States and of Virginia." [16]

None of the states of the Middle West followed the example set by Massachusetts and Vermont in 1827; but California, still in a pioneer stage of development, required instruction in the federal and state constitutions in her grammar schools, as well as political economy in the high schools.[17] This provision constitutes one of the first attempts by statute to place the subject of government in the curriculum, although several of the older states had at an early time emphasized the necessity of a knowledge of the state law.[18] In fact, such was the lack of systematic instruction in " political morals " at this time, that foreign travelers commented upon it, and Harriet Martineau stig-

---

[16] *Laws of Virginia*, 1848–49, ch. 110. An act establishing free schools in the county of Albemarle, p. 60.

[17] *Laws of California*, 1851, ch. 126, art. VII, sec. 2, p. 499.

[18] Connecticut, as early as 1796, had emphasized the necessity of inculcating a knowledge of the state law, prescribing that "all parents and masters of children, shall by themselves or others teach and instruct . . . , all such children as are under their care and government, according to their ability, and to read the English tongue well, and to know the laws against capital offenses. . . ." *Statutes* of Connecticut, 1796, p. 60. The law further stated that in case it was impossible to comply with the statement quoted above the children should at least be instructed to answer certain parts of the catechism. To enforce the law, a fine of $3.34 to be used for the poor of the town was imposed upon all parents who failed in compliance. Also *cf.* law of Massachusetts of 1642, page 3. Massachusetts also in 1789 had emphasized the necessity of training the youth of the commonwealth "to preserve and perfect a Republican Constitution and to secure the blessings of liberty as well as to promote their future happiness." *Laws* of Massachusetts, 1780–1807, sec. 4, Vol. I, pp. 470–471. Again in 1826, ch. 143, p. 180.

matized it as " an enormous deficiency in a republic," where participation in government was a birthright of all.[19]

By 1860, only six states had passed laws requiring the teaching of the social studies. To the east lay Massachusetts, Vermont, New Hampshire, and Rhode Island; to the south, Virginia; and to the far west, California. To the first requirement of United States history had been added provisions necessitating the presentation of general history, political economy and civil government, and Virginia had prescribed a study of the history of the state.[20] It was not until after the Civil War that history acquired a real place in the public school curriculum.

THE CERTIFICATION OF TEACHERS

The interest awakened in public education led also to the passage of laws for the certification of teachers. Often legislation of this type indirectly describes the character of the curriculum, for, in general, the teacher was examined in those subjects which he was expected to teach. At an early time, the chief qualifications for teachers seemed to be " good morals " and " competency," but with the expansion of the curriculum, there were added, in many cases, specifically named subjects.[21]

[19] Martineau, Harriet, *Society in America* (London, 1837), Vol. III, p. 165.

[20] The year in which the Virginia law was passed, 1849, was a time of sectional discord. Sectional interest may have entered into the passage of the law.

[21] In the discussion of the qualifications of teachers, in each period there is a neglect of all laws in which history or some other social study is not specifically named. Regulations often are quite definite regarding the qualifications of teachers in rural and elementary schools, with no statement or with no definitely named qualifications for high school teachers. In some states the superintendent of public instruction or some other official prescribes the subjects in which the examination is held. The tendency of recent legislation has been to accept graduation from reputable colleges or universities giving training in methods of teaching, in lieu of examination.

Thus a Connecticut law of 1841 provided that " the board of visitors [of the schools] . . . shall . . . examine all candidates for teachers . . . and shall give to these persons with whose moral character, literary attainments, and ability to teach, they are satisfied, a certificate, setting forth the branches he or she is found capable of teaching; provided that no certificate shall be given to any person not found qualified to teach reading, writing, arithmetic, and grammar, thoroughly, and the rudiments of geography and history." [22]   In 1857 in the *Revisions* of their laws, Maine and Rhode Island specified a knowledge of history as a necessary qualification for a teacher.[23]   Illinois, in her *Revised Statutes* of 1845, included a law which made it the duty of the school commissioner to examine " any persons proposing to teach a common school, in any township in his county," on the candidate's ability to teach the usual branches, including " the history of the United States." [24]

[22] *Acts* of Connecticut, 1841, p. 47; *Revised Statutes*, 1849, sec. 22, p. 300; *Statutes,* 1854, p. 414; *General Statutes,* 1866, p. 132; *ibid.,* 1875, ch. 4, sec. 1; *ibid.,* 1888, sec. 2135, p. 466; *ibid.,* 1902, par. 2245, p. 584; *ibid.,* 1918, ch. 56, par. 1007, Vol. 1, p. 349. Additions and slight changes have been made in the regulations for the social studies. With modifications the law has been on the statute books from 1841 to the present.

[23] *Revised Statutes* of Maine, 1857, sec. 49; *ibid.,* 1871, ch. 11, sec. 54; *Acts and Resolves,* 1873, ch. 120, p. 76; *ibid.,* 1891, ch. 32, p. 20; *ibid.,* 1895, ch. 155, p. 173. *Revised Statutes* of Rhode Island, 1857, ch. 67, sec. 3, p. 173.

[24] In 1845 the law was slightly modified to distinguish between grades of certificates, but in all cases United States history was prerequisite to certification, and in 1905, Illinois history was added to the qualifications necessary for a license. In 1913, in the requirements for a state certificate she included sociology among the subjects for examination, and for the first, second and third grade certificates, United States history, civics and the history of Illinois. *Revised Statutes* of Illinois, 1845, ch. XCVIII, sec. 12, p. 498. The law is substantially the same, *Statutes,* 1856, ch. 198, sec. XLVI, Vol. II, p. 1098; *ibid.,* 1858, sec. 50, p. 449. *Laws,* 1865, sec. 19, p. 119; *Revised Statutes,* 1874, ch. 122, 51, p. 963; *Annotated Statutes,* 1885, ch. 122, sec. 51, p. 2229; *Revised Statutes,* 1903, ch. 122, 187, par. 3, p. 1683; *ibid.,* 1906, 187, par. 3, p. 1820. During this period these subjects were to be taught in the schools. *Revised Statutes* of Illinois, 1913, ch. 122, 541, par. 2, p. 2270; *Laws,* 1913, p. 588 (Senate Bill No. 355, approved

In 1846, during the period of her earliest legislation, Iowa prescribed the history of the United States as a requirement for a teacher's license. This state is an example of those states which have passed little legislation defining the content of the curriculum, but have secured the same end by specifying subjects for the examination of their teachers. The law appeared again in the *Code* of 1851, but history was dropped from the required list of subjects in 1858.[25] Legislation in Nebraska took much the same course as had that in Iowa. In 1855, the territorial laws placed United States history among the subjects required in a teacher's examination, but the laws of 1856 ignored it as a prescribed subject.[26]

June 28, 1913); the same for the social studies in the laws of 1903 and 1905, also in 1917 and in 1919. See *Revised Statutes,* 1917, ch. 122, p. 2216; and *Laws,* 1919, ch. 122, p. 900.

[25] *Acts* of Iowa, 1846, sec. 72, p. 105; *Code* of Iowa, 1851, sec. 1148, p. 181; *Acts,* 1858, p. 72; *Code,* 1873, sec. 1766, p. 325; *Acts,* 1878, ch. 143, p. 130. In 1882, regulatory provision requiring for a state certificate a knowledge of civil government, the constitution and laws of Iowa, besides history of the United States, passed the legislature, and economics and civics were added to the subjects required for certification in 1896; *Acts,* 1882, ch. 167, sec. 4, p. 153. *Acts,* 1896, ch. 39 (H. F. 135), p. 44. *Supplement to Code,* 1902, sec. 2736, p. 315, for first grade certificate, civics, elementary economics besides the requirements of second grade, which included history of the United States; also *Acts,* 1906, ch. 122, sec. 4, p. 88.

[26] *Laws* of Nebraska, 1855, par. 61, p. 220; *ibid.,* 1858, p. 292; *ibid.,* 1872, p. 55; *ibid.,* 1881, sec. 5, pp. 359, 366; *ibid.,* 1885, sec. 5, p. 327. The same subjects as in 1881 in *Laws,* 1901, ch. 66, p. 448; *ibid.,* 1903, ch. 135, p. 559. Also *Consolidated Statutes,* 1891, ch. 44, 3624, p. 792; *ibid.,* 1903, 5542, sec. 5. In 1891, there is a distinction made in the grades of certificates, requiring civil government and United States history in all but the lowest grade, *Revised Statutes,* 1913, ch. 71, art. XIII, 6857, sec. 158, p. 1913, 6859, sec. 160, p. 1914. In 1881 United States history and civics were added to the prescribed subjects for a second grade certificate, and for a professional state certificate general history, political economy, civil government and American history were required. In the forty years intervening between 1881 and 1921, there is no change in the prerequisites for county certificates, state certificates, and the additional certificates of more recent origin — city certificates — so far as the social studies are concerned, with the exception of the dropping of political economy from the required list by 1919. *Laws* of Nebraska, 1919, 1921, ch. 70, sec. 2, p. 262.

CHAPTER II

NATIONALISM AND LOCALISM IN HISTORY LEGISLATION, 1860–1900

THE CURRICULUM

The Civil War marked a turning point in American history. Forces undreamed of before 1860 conspired to change the whole tenor of American life. From isolated rural communities of simple tastes and unexploited resources, the United States emerged into a growing urbanization of multifarious activities. Prior to 1860 there had been little change from the days of George Washington, when nine-tenths of the people had been engaged in agriculture; by 1890, however, the population had so shifted that more than one-third dwelt in towns of over two thousand inhabitants.

These vast and far-reaching changes were brought about by an expansion particularly in the fields of transportation, agriculture, and manufacturing. Steam, electricity, progress in invention, the growth of an immigrant population, and the opening of new lands to settlement, all served as contributing factors. It was a period characterized by a strong national sentiment. The theory of state rights had been settled forever by the victory of the Union in 1865, and a realization of the great opportunities of America bore the fruit of patriotic fervor. Nationalism expressed itself in the nationalization of industry, in the organization of national labor units, in the nationalization of the financial resources of the country, and in a deepened interest in the public school system. It led inevitably to a new appreciation of the distinctive contributions of local communities to the new national spirit, and was, in a sense, responsible for a strong reaction toward deep-seated local interests in the 'nineties.

These vast changes necessitated new aims and purposes in education. The preceding period had witnessed the educational system transformed from an instrument of the church into one of the state. By 1860 the theory of tax-supported schools had become established, and most states provided at least elementary instruction. By 1880, legal and legislative objections to the establishment of high schools had succumbed to the conviction that education was essential in the new social and industrial order. There came to be an abiding faith in the power of education to regenerate society. The " knowledge aim " of the preceding decades was followed by the desire for a citizenship trained to active participation in the society of which it was the warp and woof. As a result, those subjects in the curriculum tending to promote patriotism and good citizenship received the sanction of the educator.

Although history had been found to some extent in the school curriculum before the Civil War, there had been no general acceptance of it as a required study.[1] Now in the form of United States history it was received with widespread approval. A gradual extension of the requirements grew out of the spirit of the times, and to American history

[1] Cf. Johnson, Henry, Teaching of History in Elementary and Secondary Schools (New York, 1915), ch. v; Russell, W. F., The Early Teaching of History in the Secondary Schools of New York and Massachusetts (Philadelphia, 1915). History was offered in states where there were not statutory requirements. The enumeration of these laws does not, moreover, indicate the amount of history studied.

was added the study of the constitution of the nation and of the state, as well as the study of state history. Twenty-three states, during the four decades following 1860, placed upon their statute books laws requiring the teaching of history in the public schools. Over one-fourth of these commonwealths lay below the Mason and Dixon line, the states of the Middle and Far West becoming the most active after 1880.

In 1862, Vermont, in a law dealing with " the instruction of the young," prescribed history and the constitution of the United States, and special instruction in " the geography, and history, constitution and principles of government of the state of Vermont " as a part of the school curriculum.[2] A later law extended the social studies curriculum, for towns of twenty-five hundred inhabitants, to embrace political economy, general history, and civil government in the high school course.[3] The nearby state of Connecticut included in her law, regarding the branches to be taught in her schools, the subject of " history," later specifying " United States history." [4]

During the early years of the period Southern legislatures were particularly active, both in the border states and in the Confederacy. In each case the legislation was responsive to the nationalistic tendencies of the time; and, in the states of the Confederacy, the study of national history and of the federal constitution were for the first time required

---

[2] *General Statutes* of Vermont, 1862, ch. 22, sec. 19, p. 151.

[3] *Ibid.*, 1894, sec. 700, p. 189. Similar laws had been passed by Massachusetts in 1860. See page 7.

[4] *Laws* of Connecticut, 1883, ch. LXXIV, p. 264. Laws of successive years carried on substantially the same requirements. In 1902 the law appeared with slight modifications, having been accepted in 1868, 1870, 1884, 1888, 1889, 1895, 1897, 1899. *General Statutes* of Connecticut, 1902, ch. 131, par. 2130, p. 561, cites *Revision*, 1888, par. 2118, ch. 6; 1895, ch. 119; 1897, ch. 101; 1899, ch. 54.

by law.[5] Such statutes, sometimes enacted before the restoration of home rule and under the influence of Reconstruction agencies, sought, through the public schools, to overcome the intensified sectionalism of the post-war South. Laws making it a duty of the teacher to inculcate a proper attitude toward " the laws and government of the country " had much the same purpose as those requiring specifically the study of United States history and government. Thus a law of the first legislative assembly of West Virginia, passed December 10, 1863, made it the duty of all public school teachers " to inculcate the duties of piety, morality and respect for the laws and government of their country." All teachers and boards of education were expressly " charged with the duty of providing that moral training for the youth of this state which shall contribute to securing good behavior and virtuous conduct, and to furnishing the state with exemplary citizens." In 1874, a statute designed for the primary schools of the state prescribed the teaching of the common school subjects including geography and history.[6]

Similar enactments were passed by Missouri and Maryland in 1865. In Missouri, it was provided that " all teachers, when employed shall be required to instruct their pupils in the fundamental principles of the Government of the United States and of the State of Missouri, and the duties of loyal citizens thereto." [7] Maryland, in 1865, made it a duty of her teachers to train their pupils in piety and

[5] Virginia in 1849 had prescribed United States history. This state did not enact a law during this period.

[6] *Acts* of West Virginia, 1863, ch. 137, 16, p. 250. Again *Acts,* 1866, ch. 74, 29, p. 62; and *Code,* 1868, ch. 45, 35, p. 300; *Acts,* 1873, ch. 123, 32, p. 403; *Acts,* 1881, p. 185; *Acts,* 1874, ch. 123, 11, p. 388; *ibid.,* p. 173. This law was reënacted in 1881.

[7] *General Statutes* of Missouri, 1864–65, sec. 4, p. 128. Approved February 10, 1865.

justice, loyalty and sacred regard for truth, and in love of country; and to lead them into a clear understanding of the virtues which were the basis upon which was founded a republican constitution; " to preserve the blessings of liberty, promote temporal happiness and advance the greatness of the American Nation." [8]   The study of United States history was likewise required, followed in 1868 by the subject of government, both federal and state. It was not until a few years later that state history was added to the prescribed list.[9]

Among the first of the states of the Confederacy to enact laws requiring the teaching of United States history were Arkansas, South Carolina and Mississippi.[10]   Passed during the period of carpet-bag control, their statutes show plainly the effects of reconstruction influences.   The Arkansas law of 1868 and South Carolina's law of 1870 prescribed not only the study of national history but also required a knowledge of the principles of the federal and state constitutions.   In 1881, North Carolina enacted a statute for the teaching of both national and state history, and Tennessee, in 1873, accorded a place to United States history among the subjects required in her schools.[11]   It was not until later that the Alabama *Code* records similar action by the legislature of that state in prescribing instruction in

[8] *Laws* of Maryland, 1865, ch. 5, sec. 4, p. 284.

[9] *Ibid.*, ch. IV, sec. 2, p. 282; *ibid.*, 1868, ch. VI, sec. 2, p. 754; *ibid.*, 1870, ch. VII, sec. 3, p. 540; *ibid.*, 1872, ch. 7, sec. 3, p. 638; *Revised Code*, 1879, art. XXVII, 39, Vol. I, p. 255.

[10] Virginia had passed such a law in 1849. See page 8. *Laws* of South Carolina, 1870, sec. 24, p. 344; *Revised Statutes*, 1872, ch. XXXVIII, sec. 4, p. 246; *General Statutes*, 1881–1882, sec. 1004, p. 300. *Revised Statutes*, 1893, sec. 1058, Vol. I, p. 368, repeat the law. *Laws* of Arkansas, 1868, sec. 65, p. 184; *Laws*, 1875, sec. 45, p. 68; again in *Acts*, 1913, sec. 62, p. 410. *Laws* of Mississippi, 1873, ch. I, sec. 23, p. 13.

[11] *Laws* of North Carolina, 1881, ch. 200, sec. 38, p. 383. *Laws* of Tennessee, 1873, ch. XXV, sec. 31, p. 46; *Laws*, 1879, ch. 187, sec. 31.

" the Constitution of the United States and the Constitution of the State of Alabama " for " all pupils in all schools and colleges supported, in whole or in part, by public money, or under state control." [12]

Among the border states, Kentucky, as well as West Virginia, called for the teaching of history, to which was added the study of civil government after " July 1, 1889." [13]

Florida reverted to a form of the morality laws for the promotion of citizenship through the public schools. In 1881, she directed and authorized each teacher " to labor faithfully and earnestly for the advancement of pupils in their studies, deportment and morals, and to embrace every opportunity to inculcate by precept and example, the principles of truth, honesty, patriotism, and the practice of every Christian virtue; to require the pupils to observe personal cleanliness, neatness, order, promptness, and gentility of manners, to avoid vulgarity and profanity, and to cultivate in them habits of industry and economy, a regard for the rights and feelings of others, and their own responsibilities and duties as citizens." [14]   In 1889 there was added another duty to the list enumerated above: that of " reading at least once a month the Declaration of Rights as set forth by the constitution of the state of Florida." [15]

[12] *Code* of Alabama, 1897, art. 3, 3456, 4, Vol. 1, p. 998; *ibid.*, 1907, 1685, 4, Vol. 1, p. 741. The *Code* of a decade later repeated the same statute indicating that it was still a law.

[13] *Laws* of Kentucky, 1888, par. 6, Vol. 1, p. 157. *General Statutes*, 1873, p. 212. The latter refers to the law for history. For West Virginia see page 15.

[14] *Digest* of Florida, 1822–1881, sec. 36, p. 910; *Revised Statutes*, 1892, sec. 253, p. 184; *Compiled Laws*, 1914, Vol. I, p. 139.

[15] *Acts* of Florida, 1889, ch. 3872, sec. 31, p. 82. Approved June 8, 1889. A law pertaining to the teaching of citizenship had been passed in Florida on January 24, 1851, and is unique in its period. By this law, two seminaries of learning were established upon the east and west sides of the Suwanee River. The first purpose of these seminaries was to be the instruction of persons in " all the various branches that pertain to a good

The states of the Middle West also desired to inculcate patriotism in the youth of that section and to emphasize the accomplishments of America. In a series of laws, beginning in 1861, Minnesota prescribed the study of the " history of the United States." [16]   In 1878, she sought to carry out the desire for an exemplary citizenry in " An Act to introduce Moral and Social Science in the Public Schools of the State," in which was reëchoed the sentiment of the morality laws of a former time.[17]

By 1876, Wisconsin had allied herself with those endorsing the study of government, by prescribing that " the constitution of the United States and of this state shall be taught in every district school." [18]   By later laws the study of United States history and civil government was required.[19]

common school education; and next to give instruction in the mechanic arts, in husbandry and agricultural chemistry, in the fundamental laws, and in what regards the rights and duties of citizens." *Acts* of Florida, 1850–1861, ch. 337 (no. 26), p. 97; also *Digest*, 1822–1881 inclusive, ch. 178, sec. 1, p. 916; *Revised Statutes*, 1892, ch. V, par. 301, p. 192.

[16] *Laws* of Minnesota, 1861, sec. 22, p. 60; 1862, sec. 29, p. 26; 1864, sec. 29, p. 23; 1873, sec. 64, p. 21. Successive laws do not necessarily mean reënactments, but other subjects have been added with the social studies remaining the same and reappearing in the laws.

[17] *General Statutes* of Minnesota, 1881 (including *Statutes*, 1878), ch. 36, sec. 178, Vol. II; *General Statutes*, 1894, ch. 36 (Title 5), sec. 3889, sec. 3890, sec. 3891, p. 1053. The law provided " that all school officers in the state may introduce, as part of the daily exercises of each school in their jurisdiction, instruction in the elements of social and moral science, including industry, order, economy, punctuality, patience, self-denial, health, purity, temperance, cleanliness, honesty, truth, justice, politeness, peace, fidelity, philanthropy, patriotism, self-respect, hope, perseverance, cheerfulness, courage, self-reliance, gratitude, pity, mercy, kindness, conscience, reflection, and the will." Further provisions suggested the mode for carrying out the law. " That it may be the duty of the teachers to give a short oral lesson every day upon one of the topics mentioned . . . , and to require the pupils to furnish illustrations of the same upon the following morning." If only one lesson were given and only one topic discussed daily by the teacher, a full calendar month would have been spent in the carrying out of this law.

[18] *Revised Statutes* of Wisconsin, 1878, ch. 27, sec. 447, p. 173.

[19] *Laws* of Wisconsin, 1887, ch. 79, p. 77; *ibid.*, 1898, ch. 27, sec. 447, p. 363; *Statutes*, 1913, ch. 27, sec. 447, p. 258.

Among the subjects prescribed in Indiana and Missouri was United States history, the latter state directing that elementary school pupils before entering the high school must have completed the subject.[20] South Dakota, in 1895, made United States history a requirement of her common school curriculum,[21] and North Dakota by a series of laws sanctioned both United States history and civil government.[22] Before statehood had been achieved, the territory of Dakota had prescribed, in 1883, that " the highest standard of morals shall be taught, and industry, truthfulness, integrity, and self-respect inculcated, obedience to law enjoined, and the aims of an upright and useful life cultivated." [23] The same purpose was evident in North Dakota's law of 1890 and that of South Dakota of 1893, which provided for " moral instruction tending to impress upon the minds of pupils the importance of truthfulness, temperance, purity, public spirit, patriotism, and respect for honest labor, obedience to parents and due deference for old age, shall be given by each teacher in the public schools." [24]

The states of the Far West were likewise active. They

---

[20] *Revised Statutes* of Indiana, 1881, 4497, p. 978; *Laws of Missouri,* 1895, p. 267; *Revised Statutes,* 1899, sec. 988, Vol. I, p. 2270; *ibid.,* 1909, sec. 10852; *ibid.,* 1919, sec. 11218. See page 15 for other Missouri laws.

[21] *Laws* of South Dakota, 1895, sec. 13, p. 142.

[22] *Laws* of North Dakota, 1895, ch. 56, p. 79; *ibid.,* 1897, sec. 741, p. 108; 1905, sec. 750, p. 202; 1909, sec. 833, p. 302. Dakota Territory, *Compiled Laws,* 1887, sec. 1770, p. 395. This shows that United States history was required in the common schools, as early as 1883, *Session Laws* of Dakota Territory, 1883, ch. 44, par. 83.

[23] *Revised Code* of Dakota Territory, 1883, sec. 91, p. 585.

[24] *Laws* of North Dakota, 1889–90, sec. 134, p. 211; *Revised Code,* 1895, sec. 754; *ibid.,* 1909, sec. 889, p. 184; *ibid.,* 1913, sec. 1389, Vol. I, p. 333. *Laws* of South Dakota, 1893, sec. 6, p. 126; *ibid.,* 1895, sec. 6, p. 138; *ibid.,* 1901, sec. 6, p. 173; *Compiled Laws,* 1903, sec. 2358, p. 429; *ibid.,* 1913, sec. 143, Vol. I, p. 591.

followed in the wake of the older states by prescribing, in most cases, the teaching of United States history, and in some instances the study of government. In addition, they reverted to the type of law found at an early time in the Eastern states, which required a teacher to instruct in the principles of a free government " to train them [the pupils] up to a true comprehension of the rights, duties, and dignity of American citizenship." Both types of law are found in the legislation of Washington,[25] Montana,[26] California,[27] and Arizona.[28] Nevada and New Mexico allied themselves with

[25] *Code* of Washington, 1881, sec. 3205, p. 558; *General Statutes*, 1890, ch. VIII, sec. 810, Vol. I, p. 300. Similar laws, *Laws*, 1890, sec. 45, p. 372; *Laws*, 1895, sec. 1, p. 8; *Laws*, 1897, sec. 65, p. 384; *Laws*, 1909, sec. 2, p. 262; also *Laws*, 1877, sec. 5, p. 274, for the law prescribing teaching of patriotism. Washington required United States history.

[26] *Revised Statutes* of Montana, 1879, sec. 1119, p. 646, prescribed United States history. *Laws* of Montana, 1871–72, p. 630; *Revised Statutes*, 1879, sec. 1128, p. 648; again on statute books, *Laws*, 1874, sec. 41, p. 132; *Compiled Statutes*, 1887, sec. 1900, p. 1187; *Revised Code*, 1907 (see act of March 11, 1895); *Laws*, 1913, ch. VI, 802, pt. 4, p. 245, for prescribing teaching of patriotism. This law was carried by Montana on her statute books for fifty years. In Washington it passed through a similar experience, being found in the *Code* of 1910. See Remington and Ballinger's *Code*, 1910, sec. 4550, Vol. II, p. 490.

[27] *Statutes* of California, 1863–4, sec. 6, p. 211; *ibid.*, 1865–6, sec. 55, p. 398; *Codes and Statutes of California*, 1885, sec. 1665, Vol. I, p. 290; *ibid.*, 1905, sec. 1874, 2, Vol. I, p. 451. Same law (1885) on statute books in 1905. *Code*, 1905, 1665, Vol. I, p. 391. Civil government was added, 1889. *Laws* of California, 1891, 1665, p. 161; again in *Laws*, 1893, p. 254; *Laws* of California, 1903, 1874, 2, p. 195; *Codes*, 1905, 1665, Vol. I, p. 391; *Laws*, 1907, p. 947. The laws respecting the teaching of patriotism and training for citizenship are found in *Statutes* of California, 1865–86, sec. 70, p. 400; *Codes and Statutes*, 1885, sec. 1702, Vol. I, p. 293; *Codes and Statutes*, 1905, sec. 1701, Vol. I, p. 420.

[28] *Laws* of Arizona, 1883, sec. 59, p. 49; *Laws*, 1885, p. 157; *Revised Statutes*, 1887, p. 284; *Revised Laws of the Territory of Arizona*, 1901, 2214, sec. 85, p. 602. The study of United States history required. *Revised Statutes* of Arizona, 1887, 1566 (sec. 94), p. 285; *Laws*, 1885, p. 160; *Revised Laws of Territory*, 1901, 2243 (sec. 113), p. 608. The law prescribed that a teacher instruct in the principles of " morality, truth, justice, and patriotism . . . to train them [pupils] up to a true comprehension of the rights, duties, and dignity of American citizenship."

the movement to teach United States history in the public schools.[29]

Utah also prescribed United States history as a part of the school curriculum and included in another law an admonition for instruction in patriotism.[30] This statute is a good example of the evolutionary stage through which most states passed in the making of laws, and shows the tendency of the newer states to revert to the old type of laws in the early period of statehood. In Idaho no content subject was prescribed by law, but the teacher was held responsible for inculcating the "principles of morality, truth, justice, and patriotism." [31]

The place of history in the school curriculum was thus thoroughly established by law at the close of the nineteenth century. United States history was required in more statutes than any other field of history, although, in some instances, political economy and general history found a place in the high school program. Frequently added to the requirement of national history, was the study of civil govern-

[29] *Statutes of Nevada,* 1864–5, sec. 42, p. 424. Also *General Statutes,* 1861–1885, 1330, sec. 42, p. 384. This last would indicate the inclusion of the law in the statutes to 1885. *Compiled Laws of Nevada,* 1861–1900, 1346, scc. 4. *Compiled Laws of New Mexico,* 1884, sec. 1101, p. 548; *ibid.,* 1897, sec. 1529, p. 425.

[30] Utah's law regarding the teaching of patriotism came under a statute regarding "Prohibited Doctrines. Moral Instruction." It prescribed that "no atheistic, infidel, sectarian, religious, or denominational doctrine shall be taught in any of the district schools of this state. Moral instruction tending to impress on the minds of the pupils the importance of good manners, truthfulness, temperance, purity, patriotism, and industry, shall be given, . . . and all such schools shall be free from sectarian control." The law prescribing the study of United States history is found in *Laws* of Utah, 1896, p. 486; *ibid.,* 1897, p. 131. *Revised Statutes,* 1898, p. 441; *Compiled Laws,* 1907, sec. 1848, p. 704.

[31] *Laws* of Idaho, 1884, sec. 34, p. 193; *Revised Statutes,* 1887, ch. VII, sec. 687, p. 134; *Laws,* 1899, sec. 48, p. 97; *Political Code,* 1901, ch. XL, sec. 1067, Vol. I, p. 329; *Compiled Statutes,* 1919, sec. 944, p. 269. This last citation would indicate the permanence of the law.

ment, both federal and state, and occasionally local or state history.

During the period one-third of the legislatures enacting social study laws prescribed the teaching of the federal constitution.   A knowledge of the state constitution was required in Maryland, South Carolina, Alabama, Missouri, and Arkansas; and North Carolina and Maryland, besides Vermont, prescribed the teaching of state history.   The emphasis placed upon a knowledge of state institutions was but the reaction from the intense nationalism of the years immediately following the Civil War.   It was especially evident toward the close of the century and during the early years following 1900.   Indeed, from 1880 to 1900 local pride evinced a quickened consciousness in the organization of such groups as the Sons of Veterans in 1881, the United Confederate Veterans and the Sons of the American Revolution in 1889, the Daughters of the American Revolution in 1890, and the Sons of Confederate Veterans in 1896.   In literature, writers like Cable, Eggleston, Harte and Stockton glorified the characteristics peculiar to their localities; and laws relating to the public school curriculum reflected precisely the same temper.[32]

Educational and learned societies likewise bore testimony to the interest in the study of history.   In 1876, a committee of the National Education Association recommended United States history for the elementary school and a study of " universal history and the Constitution of the United States for high schools." [33]   In 1892, the Committee of Ten was created by the same organization to consider " programs of

[32] This is especially evident in the legislation affecting textbooks in history. See page 36 *et seq.* A knowledge of state history was required for teacher certification in Pennsylvania, Mississippi, South Dakota, and Texas.

[33] Johnson, *op. cit.,* p. 133.

the secondary schools in the United States and . . . the requirements for admission to college." [34] Eight years of history were asked by this committee, four for the high school and four for the elementary.[35] In 1896, the Committee of Seven of the American Historical Association was appointed, and in 1899 recommended a four years' course in history.[36] During this time colleges also extended their entrance credits to include more history, which, with the committee reports, aided much in increasing the offerings in the public school curriculum. These activities are an indication of the place that history was coming to hold in the education of the young. They are added proof of the attention which the public was giving to the social studies in a period in which twenty-five states passed laws to include them in a required course of study.[37]

CERTIFICATION OF TEACHERS

During the decade of the 'sixties laws regarding the certification of teachers were passed by New Hampshire, Pennsylvania, Minnesota, Maryland, Wisconsin, Indiana, Missouri, Arkansas, and California. " History " was a requirement of New Hampshire, Minnesota and Maryland,[38]

[34] *Ibid.*, p. 134.

[35] *Ibid.*, pp. 134–135. 1st and 2d years, biography and mythology; 3d year, American history, the elements of civil government; 4th year, Greek and Roman history; 5th year (high school), French history; 6th year, English history; 7th year, American history; 8th year, a special period for intensive study and civil government.

[36] *Ibid.*, p. 143. 1st year, Ancient history to 800 A.D., 814 A.D., or 843 A.D.; 2d year, Medieval and Modern European history; 3d year, English history, and 4th year, American history and civil government.

[37] This includes Massachusetts whose law was discussed in chapter I. See page 7. Florida and Idaho did not name any social studies; hence they are not included in this number.

[38] Connecticut, 1866, and Maine, 1873, still required " history." *General Statutes* of New Hampshire, 1867, ch. LXXXI, sec. 4, p. 169; *Laws of*

and "United States history" received mention in the laws of Pennsylvania, Wisconsin, Indiana, Missouri, Arkansas, and California.[89] To the requirement of United States history, California added that of the "Constitution and Government of the United States," which was further amplified by a requirement for the teaching of the constitution of California, in an amendment of 1874.

From 1870 to 1880 there was little departure from the subjects required in the preceding period, "history" being considered essential in Idaho by a law of 1870, by Arkansas, in 1873 and in 1875, and by West Virginia in 1874 and in 1879 for primary school certificates.[40] In Texas, Washington, Kansas, Colorado, and Delaware, the law specified United States history, and in Oregon, modern history.[41]

Minnesota, 1861, sec. 22, p. 60; *Code of Public Laws* of Maryland, 1903, art. 77, 70, Vol. II, p. 1472. The source of the law is from *Laws,* 1868, title II, ch. 1, sec. 2, p. 757.

[89] *Digest of Laws* of Pennsylvania, 1883, 173, p. 308, in which is source of law from *Public Laws,* 1867, par. II (April 9, 1867). *Laws* of Wisconsin, 1861, ch. 176, sec. 4, p. 100; *Laws* of Indiana, 1865, sec. 34, p. 13. *Statutes* of Missouri, 1870, ch. 123, Vol. II, p. 1260, containing source from *General Statutes,* 1865, sec. 90, p. 273. *Laws* of Arkansas, 1868, sec. 60, p. 181. *Statutes* of California, 1865-6, sec. 87, p. 404, first and second grade certificates. These laws are continued by the following in successive legislation; Minnesota *Laws,* 1862, sec. 29, p. 26; *ibid.,* 1864, sec. 29, p. 23; *ibid.,* 1873, sec. 64, p. 71; *General Laws,* 1881, sec. 66, p. 480; *ibid.,* 1894, sec. 3750, p. 1022; *Laws* of Wisconsin, 1868, ch. 109, sec. 4, p. 110; *Revised Statutes* of Indiana, 1881, 4425, p. 957, *Laws,* 1889, ch. LV, p. 85; *ibid.,* 1899, ch. CCXIV, p. 489; *Revised Statutes* of Missouri, 1879, sec. 7077, Vol. II, p. 1394, which contains amendment of 1874 when civil government was added. These successive laws remained unchanged for the social sciences except where noted. *Digest of Laws* of Pennsylvania, 1894, p. 815; *ibid.,* 1901, p. 859; in 1901, civil government, both state and local, were added. *Acts* of Arkansas, 1873, sec. 62, p. 40. *Codes and Statutes* of California, 1876, sec. 1748, Vol. I, p. 242.

[40] *Laws* of Idaho, 1870-71, sec. 12, p. 10; *Laws* of Arkansas, 1875, sec. 33, p. 65; *Laws* of West Virginia, 1874, ch. 123, sec. 28, p. 399; also *ibid.,* 1879, ch. 74, sec. 28, p. 143.

[41] *Laws* of Texas, 1871-73, sec. 15, Vol. VII, p. 540; *Code* of Washington, 1881, sec. 3240, p. 564, *Laws,* 1871, sec. 6, p. 17, *ibid.,* 1877, sec. 6, p. 424;

Besides history being required in the statute of Arkansas, an applicant for a state certificate was required to have a knowledge of the constitution of the state and nation, an innovation in the required list of subjects.[42] In Wisconsin, the law pertaining to the certification of teachers was revised in 1879 for the express purpose of examining persons in the federal and state constitutions, and was carried over in the statutes of the next thirty years.[43]

In the decade following 1880, New York, Michigan, the Dakotas, Alabama, Arizona, Ohio, and Montana joined the states which had prescribed certification requirements in the previous decade.[44] Upon the statute books of Connecticut, Pennsylvania, Delaware, West Virginia, Wisconsin, Indiana, California, and Washington were continued laws previously enacted.[45] To her requirement of United States

---

Compiled Laws of Kansas, 1879, sec. 6, par. 81 (5181), p. 834; Laws, 1876, ch. 122, art. 6, par. 6; Laws of Colorado, 1870–72, sec. 10, p. 134, ibid., 1876, sec. 15, 2461, p. 811; Laws of Delaware, 1879, p. 52; Laws of Oregon, 1872, par. 25, p. 507.

[42] Laws of Arkansas, 1875, sec. 33, p. 65, also ibid., 1868, sec. 60, p. 181, ibid., 1873, sec. 62, p. 410. Laws of New Hampshire, Minnesota, Missouri, Maryland, Maine, Iowa, Nebraska, Illinois and California were discussed in connection with the passage of earlier laws in the preceding chapter.

[43] Laws of Wisconsin, 1879, ch. 237, p. 346; Laws, 1887, ch. 79, p. 77.

[44] Laws of New York, 1882, ch. 318, p. 382, certificate for prospective teacher; Laws of Ohio, 1882, p. 70. "An act to amend section 4074 of the Revised Statutes of Ohio relating to teachers' certificates, making an examination in United States history essential." General Statutes of Michigan, 1883, par. 5153, Vol. II, p. 1356 (a compilation of laws); Public Acts, 1887, ch. XII, sec. 4, p. 890, left unchanged the social studies by law of 1887, ch. 196, sec. 5153, p. 3539; Laws of Dakota Territory, 1883, ch. 44, par. 16. Revised Code, 1883, par. 16, p. 558, first and second grade certificates; Compiled Laws, 1887, par. 1770, p. 395; for first grade certificate, Dakota added civil government. Acts of Alabama, 1880–81, p. 75, first and second grade certificates, Code of Alabama, 1887, ch. 3, 984, Vol. I, p. 269, same certificates; Laws of Arizona, 1885, p. 140, Revised Statutes, 1887, ch. 2, 1485 (sec. 13), p. 272, first and second grade territorial certificates. Laws of Montana, 1883, sec. 1149, p. 57, for county certificates.

[45] General Statutes of Connecticut, 1888, sec. 2135, p. 466; Digest of

history, Colorado prescribed a knowledge of the federal constitution.[46] Civil government, as well as United States history, was required for licensing in New York, Ohio, Michigan, the Dakotas, Alabama, Montana, and Arizona. In Idaho, by a law of 1884, territorial certificates could be secured only by those showing proficiency not only in United States history, but in general history, political economy, and civil government as well.[47] Oregon also extended her requirements beyond those commonly found, to include modern history.[48]

From 1890 to 1900 only four states passed laws of this character for the first time. All other legislation of the period was enacted by states which had previously prescribed the subjects prerequisite for a teacher's license. In those commonwealths where there had been statutes enacted,

---

Laws of Pennsylvania, 1883, 173, p. 308; required United States history from a law of 1867; *Laws* of Delaware, 1887, sec. 4, p. 120, United States history. *Laws* of West Virginia, 1881, sec. 28, p. 182, "history" required for primary school certificates; see *Laws*, 1874, p. 399; *Revised Statutes* of Indiana, 1881, 4425, p. 957, *Laws* of 1889, ch. LV, p. 85, for common schools, United States history was required; Supplement to *Revised Statutes* of Wisconsin, 1878, required United States history, federal and state constitutions for the first, second, third grade certificates, also *Laws*, 1887, ch. 79, p. 77; *General Statutes* of Kansas, 1889, 5651, par. 90, p. 1831. United States history was required for first, second, and third grade certificates; also *Laws*, 1881, ch. 151, par. 6, amended by *Laws*, 1885, ch. 170, par. 1, p. 274; *Revised Statutes* of Idaho Territory, 1887, ch. VII, sec. 680, county certificates with the requirement of United States history; *Code* of Washington, 1881, sec. 3240, p. 564, United States history was required, from *Laws*, 1871, also *Laws*, 1885, p. 27; *Codes and Statutes* of California, 1885, par. 1772, Vol. I, p. 298, which was the same as in 1876; for county certificates United States history was prescribed.

[46] *General Statutes* of Colorado, 1883, ch. XCVII, 3010, sec. 15, p. 883. This amended *General Laws*, 1879, p. 162, by adding "constitution of the United States"; *Laws*, 1889, sec. 4, p. 381.

[47] *Laws* of Idaho, 1884, sec. 30, p. 192; also *Revised Statutes*, 1887, ch. VII, secs. 682, 683, p. 133. See chapter 1 for requirements in Nebraska, Iowa, Illinois, Connecticut, and Maine.

[48] *Laws* of Oregon, 1885, p. 44, also *Laws*, 1872, sec. 25, p. 507.

the list of required subjects was frequently extended to include political economy.

Florida, Oklahoma, Utah, and Wyoming, in prescribing that their teachers must show a satisfactory knowledge of United States history, followed the usual practice, although acting for the first time. To this requirement was added also that of a knowledge of civil government, a common prerequisite whose popularity had been established in the 'eighties.[49] Florida, however, for the third and second grade certificates did not require a knowledge of civil government, reserving that only for the first grade and state licenses. For the latter, a knowledge of general history was required by the law of 1893.[50] Wyoming required not only United States history and civil government, but for a first grade certificate added political economy.[51]

From 1890 to 1900 Pennsylvania, Delaware, West Virginia, Michigan, Wisconsin, Minnesota, North Dakota, South Dakota, Missouri, Kansas, Mississippi, Texas, Idaho, Washington, Utah, California, and Wyoming required proficiency in United States history and civil government for some grade of teacher's license.[52]

[49] *Statutes* of Oklahoma, 1893 (compilation), ch. 73, art. 5, p. 1094, for first and second grade certificates, also *Laws*, 1897, ch. 34, art. 6, p. 273. *Revised Statutes* of Wyoming, 1899, sec. 627, p. 228; *Laws*, 1899, ch. 70, p. 136, for second and third grade certificates. *Laws* of Florida, 1893, ch. 4192, p. 125, also *Compiled Laws*, 1914, 365, Vol. I, p. 136, for first grade certificates. See footnote, page 86.

[50] *Compiled Laws* of Florida, 1914, 365, Vol. I, p. 136.

[51] *Laws* of Wyoming, 1899, ch. 70, p. 136, also *Revised Statutes*, 1899, sec. 627, p. 228.

[52] *Laws* of Pennsylvania, 1895, 41, p. 155, for high schools demanded general history and civics, but no mention was made of United States history. In *Digest*, 1894, p. 815, United States history was required for certificate from any county, borough, or its superintendent. *Laws* of Delaware, 1893, sec. 5, p. 691, professional certificates; *ibid.*, 1898, sec. 24, p. 198, professional, first, second, and third grade certificates. *Acts* of West Virginia, 1891, ch. 64, p. 169, " history " and civil government for primary certificates; also *Acts*, 1895, ch. 26, 28, p. 81, for first, second and third grade

In 1891, Alabama added to the requirement of United States history for a first grade license, the constitution of the state of Alabama and of the United States, thereby conforming to the popular tendency.[53]   A knowledge of state history was required in Pennsylvania, Mississippi, South Dakota and Texas; and Pennsylvania, West Virginia, Minnesota, Texas, Utah, Washington, and Wyoming required general history for the higher grade of certification.[54] Political economy became a prerequisite for a professional

certificates; adding general history in first grade certificate, see *ibid.*, p. 82, also *Code*, 1899, ch. 45, 28, 29. *Public Acts* of Michigan, 1893, sec. 5, p. 35, also in *Compiled Laws*, 1915 (5881), sec. 5, Vol. II, p. 2213. *Statutes* of Wisconsin, 1898, ch. 27, sec. 447, p. 363, for all grades of licenses. *General Statutes* of Minnesota, 1894, ch. 36, par. 3749, par. 3750, Vol. I, p. 1022, for professional state certificate by law of 1893 approved April 18, 1893. *Laws* of North Dakota, 1895, 52, p. 27, for all certificates, *ibid.*, 1897, par. 741, p. 108. *Laws* of South Dakota, 1891, ch. 56, par. 4, p. 119, *ibid.*, 1893, ch. 78, 105, *ibid.*, 1895, ch. 78, p. 83, in *Compiled Laws*, 1913, par. 55, Vol. I, p. 572. *Revised Statutes* of Missouri, 1899, sec. 9798, Vol. II, p. 2277, any certificates. *General Statutes* of Kansas, 1897, ch. 63, par. 200, p. 671, first grade certificate, but second and third grade required only United States history. *Annotated Code of General Statute Laws* of Mississippi, 1892, 4022, p. 889, first grade license; professional and state in 1896, *Laws*, 1896, p. 111, secs. 6 and 7. *Laws* of Texas, 1822–1897, sec. 65, first, second grades and permanent certificates (23d legislature, 1893); by laws of 1891, state certificate general history and civil government; *Revised Statutes*, 1895, art. 3979, p. 787. *Laws* of Idaho, 1897, sec. 7, p. 75, *ibid.*, 1899, sec. 17, p. 310. *Laws* of Washington, 1891, ch. XCVII, sec. 4, p. 244, *Code*, 1891, par. 773, Vol. I, p. 281, state certificate, *ibid.*, par. 777, p. 285, first grade certificate. *Revised Statutes* of Utah, 1898, 1767, p. 425, state professional certificate, *ibid.*, 1923, p. 455, for primary and grammar certificates, United States history only, but *ibid.*, 1924, high school certificates; both United States history and civics for territorial certificate of first grade in 1890, civics and United States history, *Laws*, 1890, sec. 23, p. 115; *Revised Statutes, op. cit.*, 1767, p. 425, state professional diploma of high school grade, general history, civil government, United States history. *Statutes* of California, 1893, p. 260, primary county certificates. *Revised Statutes* of Wyoming, 1899, sec. 627, p. 228, first, second, and third grade licenses, with political economy required for first grade.

[53] *Acts* of Alabama, 1891, par. 2, p. 250. Approved February 4, 1891; also in *Code*, 1897, art. 6, Vol. I, p. 1007.

[54] See citations in footnote 52.

state certificate in Minnesota by the laws of 1893, in Iowa in 1896, and in Wyoming in 1899 for a first grade license.[55]

United States history only was required in Utah for county certificates of the grammar and primary grades, in Kansas for the second and third grade certificates, in Indiana for common school licenses, and in Arkansas for county certificates.[56]

During the period from 1860 to 1900 thirty-six states enacted laws relating to the certification of teachers. Of this number, only six states had passed laws prior to 1860.[57] In all states a knowledge of United States history was a prerequisite for licensing throughout the period, and, in most cases, civil government was required.[58]

TEACHERS' QUALIFICATIONS: OATHS OF LOYALTY

The fear of an apostasy on the part of the teaching craft led legislatures in this period to impose other than scholastic requirements upon those who would teach in the public schools. These regulations, indicating a distrust of the loyalty of teachers, have required oaths of allegiance from all who would qualify as teachers.

Legislation of this character was originally an outgrowth of the Civil War, the first laws being passed in 1862.[59] And it is not strange that the border state Kentucky was a pioneer in statutes of this character. Here the law was

[55] Citation of reference in footnote 52. Also *Acts* of Iowa, 1896, ch. 39, p. 44, amends 1766 of *Code*.
[56] *Digest of Statutes* of Arkansas, 1894, ch. 139, sec. 7010, p. 1523, Act of April 14, 1893; *Laws* of Indiana, 1899, ch. CCXIV, p. 489; *General Statutes* of Kansas, 1897, ch. 63, par. 201, 202, p. 671; *Revised Statutes* of Utah, 1898, 1796, p. 432.
[57] Maine, Connecticut, Rhode Island, Illinois, Iowa, and Nebraska.
[58] Connecticut, Illinois, Montana, Ohio, Oregon being the states which required only history. Oregon's requirement was modern history.
[59] Kentucky and Oregon passed laws this year.

made to apply to all school commissioners, examiners of
teachers for the common schools, and school trustees and
teachers elected to teach in the common schools, all presidents, professors and teachers in colleges, and high schools
incorporated by legislative enactment. It pledged loyalty
to the Union and denounced the tenets of the Confederacy.

" I do solemnly swear that I will support the Constitution
of the United States, and the Constitution of Kentucky,"
vowed the applicant, " and be true and faithful to the
commonwealth as long as I remain a citizen thereof. That
I recognize the binding obligations of the Constitution of
the United States and the duty of every citizen to submit
thereto as the supreme law of the land. That I will not give
aid to the rebellion against the government of the United
States, nor give aid to the so-called provisional government
of Kentucky, either directly or indirectly, so long as I remain a citizen of or reside in Kentucky, and that this oath
is taken by me without any mental reservation — so help
me God." This oath, given in writing, was kept at the
county court office where the school was located, and a
violation of the oath or false swearing upon conviction, led
to the imposition of a penalty. Evasion of the law, too,
was subject to punishment through a fine of not less than
twenty-five dollars nor more than two hundred dollars.[60]
In 1889 it was made incumbent upon the county superintendent to administer such oaths.

Similar laws appeared on the statute books of West
Virginia and Missouri, where, like Kentucky, these border
states felt a pressing need for a loyal citizenry. On December 10, 1863, the former commonwealth declared that

---

[60] *Laws* of Kentucky, 1862, ch. 636, p. 265. Approved August 30, 1862.
Laws, 1889, Vol. I, p. 169, par. 15. In the law for the qualifications of
teachers, however, the taking of the oath was not mentioned.

no applicant should be admitted to an examination for a teacher's license unless the county superintendent had reasonable evidence that the candidate was not only " of good moral character and temperate habits," but that he was " loyal to the government of the United States and of West Virginia." [61]   To buttress this law it was prescribed that all teachers should take the oath of loyalty required of all state officers.   The latter regulation was operative after November 16, 1863, but no specific mention was made of teachers subscribing to such an oath until 1867.   However, it seems probable that they, as well as state officers, affirmed their loyalty at the earliest period of statehood, since it is recorded that two teachers, J. B. Soloman and C. T. Wilson, in 1869, were exempted from subscribing to the oath prescribed in the act of 1863.

A statute, moreover, directly prescribed for teachers in 1867 the taking of the following oath: " I, A. A. B., do solemnly swear that I will support the constitution of the United States and the constitution of the state of West Virginia, that I have never voluntarily borne arms against the United States, that I have voluntarily given no aid or comfort to persons engaged in armed hostility thereto, by countenancing, counseling or encouraging them in the same, that I have not sought, accepted, nor attempted to exercise the functions of any office whatever under any authority in hostility to the United States; that I have not yielded a voluntary support to any pretended government, authority, power or constitution within the United States, hostile or inimical thereto; and that I take this obligation freely, without any mental reservations or purpose of evasion." [62]

[61] *Acts* of West Virginia, 1863, ch. 137, 35, p. 255; also *Code*, 1868, ch. 45, 31, p. 298; again *Acts*, 1866, ch. 74, 37, p. 65.
[62] *Acts* of West Virginia, 1869, pp. 56, 104.   For the law prescribing the

The cessation of armed hostilities between the North and the South induced Missouri to require an avowal of loyalty on the part of her teachers. On March 29, 1866, there was approved a law by which " all teachers before entering upon the discharge of their duties should take and subscribe to the oath of loyalty prescribed by the constitution." [63]

Regarding the lessons of the War, Arkansas, in 1866, believed there should be no disagreement. Here not only did the applicant for a teacher's certificate swear to support the constitution and laws of the United States and Arkansas, but he also promised that he would encourage all others to do likewise. ". . . I will never countenance or aid in the secession of this state from the United States," the affirmant declared, and added his pledge " to inculcate in the minds of youth sentiments of patriotism and loyalty." [64]

Oregon also required a pledge of her teachers by legislation in 1862. Before the county superintendent of schools, disloyalty to the state and nation must be forsworn by the applicant for a certificate, who promised " without any mental reservation or evasion whatever," that he would " bear true allegiance and fidelity to the same against all enemies, foreign or domestic." [65]

Dissentient opinions received scant courtesy in Rhode Island at the time of the Civil War although no law forbade them. However, a warning from the state commissioner of

---

oath, *Code* of West Virginia, 1868, ch. 45, 32, p. 299; *Acts,* 1863, ch. 106, p. 138. Constitution, *ibid.,* ch. IX, p. 76. On February 7, 1870, this law was reënacted and amended. *Code, op. cit.,* ch. 14, 32, p. 739 of Appendix.

[63] *Laws* of Missouri, 1865–6, par. 89, p. 189.

[64] *Acts* of Arkansas, 1868, sec. 61, p. 182. Again in *Acts,* 1873, sec. 64, p. 412. Repealed by an act of 1875.

[65] *Code* of Oregon, 1862, sec. 9, p. 40.

education to the general assembly at the January session of 1865 undoubtedly evoked the same response as the enactment of a law. Here, too, there was to be no tolerance for a passive loyalty. " The war tocsin has sounded," the report declared, " our country is convulsed in mighty conflict, our friends are in the contesting field, their blood has been made to redden and fertilize the rebel soil. . . . Traitors and rebel sympathizers are *among us*, rendering every available assistance and using every means within their power to further the rebel cause and aid them in the accomplishment of their hellish design. Therefore, let us be on our guard, lest some of them unawares be ushered into our schools as teachers. For if the teacher be a traitor, his actions will correspond therewith, and by example, if not by precept, he will be sowing the seeds of rebellion in the susceptible hearts of our children. Should the pure minds of our little ones be poisoned with the damnable principles of rebellion, or be led astray by the pernicious examples of rebel sympathizers? Shall the hand already stained with the blood of the murdered father, be employed to guide his orphan child? — the hand that applied the lighted torch, and made the orphan a homeless wanderer, shall that be the hand to trace the chart by which his little bark is to be guided to its destined haven? *No, most assuredly, no.* Better by far remain as he is, his untutored mind wrapped up in ignorance, than to be thus guided and piloted by the vile traitor, only to be finally dashed against the rocks and engulfed in the waves of rebellion. But let our teachers be noble, loyal sons and daughters of America — those who, while instructing our little ones in the sciences that pertain to the secular concerns of life, will also teach them their obligations to their country, and at the same time will point them to that *never fading star* by which their frail barks may be safely guided over life's treacherous seas to the port of eternal rest, to gain that blood-washed throng who chant the praises of God and the Lamb from Mount Zion's balmy top." [66]

As a survival of the legislation regarding teachers' qualifications, which had been brought about by the period of Reconstruction, were the statutes of Arizona of 1883 and 1885. By these laws it was made a duty of the superintendent of public instruction and the county superintendents of schools to administer oaths and affirmations of loyalty to teachers. [67]

CITIZENSHIP AS A QUALIFICATION FOR TEACHERS

Beginning in 1899 came legislation eliminating from the teaching profession those who were not American citizens. North Dakota was the pioneer in this movement in a statute prohibiting the issuance of certificates or permits to teach to persons not citizens of the United States, unless they had resided in the United States " for at least one year prior to the time of such applications or permit." [68] The same year Idaho adopted a similar restriction, by forbidding the granting of certificates or the employment of any teacher in the

[66] *Acts and Resolves* of Rhode Island, 1865, pp. 126–127. *The Twentieth Annual Report on the Public Schools in Rhode Island made to the General Assembly at the January Session, A.D. 1865.*

[67] *Laws* of Arizona, 1883, pp. 41 and 157, *ibid.*, 1885, p. 146. The law made it a duty of superintendents of public instruction or county superintendents of schools to administer the following oath, but there was no separate law prescribing that a teacher take such an oath: " I, ——, do solemnly swear that I will support the constitution of the United States and the laws of the territory of Arizona; that I will true faith and allegiance bear to the same, and defend them against all enemies whatsoever, and that I will faithfully and impartially discharge the duties of the office (name of office) according to the best of my ability, so help me God."

[68] *Laws* of North Dakota, 1897, par. 742, p. 109; *ibid.*, 1901, p. 99; *ibid.*, 1905, p. 206. This statute was in the *School Laws* published in 1923. In 1900, North Dakota's total population was 319,146 with a foreign population of 113,091.

public schools, " not a citizen of the United States." [69] A decade later (1907) Nevada attempted to promote patriotism by requiring an oath of all public officials including teachers in schools and university professors. In this was affirmed the dominance of the national over the state government and an abjuration of duelling, a relic of frontier conditions.

" I, ——, do solemnly swear," declared the official, or teacher, " that I will support, protect and defend the Constitution and Government of the United States and the Constitution and Government of the State of Nevada against all enemies, whether domestic or foreign, and that I will bear true faith, allegiance and loyalty to the same, any state convention or legislature to the contrary notwithstanding; and further that I do this, with a full determination, pledge and purpose, without any mental reservation or evasion whatsoever. And I do further solemnly swear (or affirm) that I have not fought a duel, nor sent or accepted a challenge to fight a duel, nor been a second to either party, nor in any manner aided or assisted in such a duel, nor been knowingly the bearer of such challenge or acceptance, since the adoption of the Constitution of the State of Nevada, and that I will not be so engaged or concerned directly or indirectly in or about any such duel, during my continuance in office. . . ." [70]

[69] *Laws* of Idaho, 1897, sec. 17, p. 85, *ibid.*, 1899, p. 310; *Code*, 1901, ch. XL, Vol. I, p. 330. This law is found as late as 1921. Also *Compiled Statutes*, 1919, par. 946, Vol. I, p. 270. In 1900, Idaho's population was 161,772, of which 24,604 were foreigners.

[70] *Laws* of Nevada, 1907, ch. CLXXXII, sec. 30, p. 386; also *Revised Statutes*, 1912, sec. 3277, also *Revised Laws*, 1861–1912, 370, sec. 2, Vol. I, p. 113. Out of a total population, in 1900, of 42,335 Nevada's foreign population was 10,093.

Substantially all legislation regarding history textbooks has developed since the Civil War, only three states passing statutes of this character before 1860.[71] This form of regulation falls, in general, into laws in which certain textbooks are named as suitable for use or are definitely prescribed, laws in which the subjects of the curriculum are enumerated by a statement concerning textbooks, enactments limiting the price of books, statutes by which books of a partisan or political bias are forbidden, and laws prescribing the character of the content for history textbooks, whose source is a sectional or partisan animus.

In 1862, the state of Vermont passed *An Act directing the Board of Education to select a Textbook of the Geography and History of Vermont* which was to be used in all district schools of the state for a period of five years.[72] Ten years later Hall's *Geography and History of Vermont,* which was then in use by sanction of the law, was continued as a textbook until 1878.[73] In Rhode Island, the report of the Superintendent of Public Education, in 1865, named the histories written by Berard and Goodrich as those commonly used in the public schools.[74]   By legislative enactment,

[71] New Hampshire, Virginia and Louisiana.

[72] *General Statutes* of Vermont, 1862, ch. 22, sec. 1, p. 169. The selection of the book was to be made as soon as possible, and was to be binding upon all teachers and boards of education until January, 1867. The law appeared in later statute books. *Revised Laws* of Vermont, 1880, ch. 33, sec. 558, p. 169; *Vermont Statutes,* 1894, sec. 700, p. 189.

[73] *Laws* of Vermont, 1872, no. 14, sec. 1, p. 54. " Hall's *Geography and History of Vermont* now in use by the authority of law, in the schools of Vermont, or such revised editions of the same as may be issued, shall be continued as a textbook for the term of five years from the first day of November, A.D., 1873." Approved November 26, 1872. Legislation of this character is found also in 1888 and in 1890. *Laws,* 1888, no. 9, sec. 171, and 172, *ibid.,* 1890, no. 7, p. 25.

[74] *Acts and Resolves* of Rhode Island, 1865, p. 153. Report of the Superintendent of Public Education.

North Carolina in 1879, designated Moore's *History of North Carolina* for use in her public schools.[75]

Of the textbooks prescribed in West Virginia, Goodrich's *Common School History*, Quackenbos' *History of the United States*, and Holmes' *History of the United States* were named by laws in 1868 and 1873. Later the price of Myers' *General History*, Montgomery's *General History* and Montgomery's *Beginner's American History* were regulated by law.[76] In Virginia "the two works of John Esten Cooke, entitled respectively 'Virginia: A History of Her People,' and 'Stories of the Old Dominion,'" were included in the list of textbooks selected.[77] In Indiana, in 1889, the state board of education was directed to choose a history equal to Thalheimer's *History of the United States*,[78] and two years later it was enacted that the price of the textbook on the history of the United States should not exceed 65 cents a volume.[79]

Minnesota, Kansas, and Montana insisted that their histories be the equal of Barnes' *School Histories*.[80] In

---

[75] *Laws* of North Carolina, 1879, ch. 93, p. 177. Approved March 1, 1879. John W. Moore, author of textbook.

[76] *Code* of West Virginia, 1868, 55, p. 308. For Holmes' *History of the United States, Laws,* 1873, 58, p. 419. For geography, Knote's *Geography of West Virginia*, Mitchell's *New Revised Geographies*, Macy-Howe-Smith's *Lessons on the Globe*, by laws of 1873 and again in 1891. *Laws,* 1891, p. 313. *Laws* of West Virginia, 1895, ch. 37, p. 63. For the *General History* by Myers, contract price $1.10, contract exchange price 82 cents; for the *Leading Facts of American History*, contract price 65 cents, exchange price 50 cents; *Beginner's American History*, contract price 43 cents, exchange price 35 cents. Lewis' *History and Government of West Virginia*, in fixing 80 cents as the contract price, and Dole's *The American Citizen* with 65 cents as the exchange price were likewise named in the law.

[77] *Code* of Virginia, 1887, sec. 1501, p. 404. By a law of 1883–4.

[78] *Laws* of Indiana, 1889, ch. L, sec. 1, p. 75.

[79] *Ibid.,* 1891, ch. LXXX, sec. 1, p. 100.

[80] *General Statutes* of Minnesota, 1881, ch. 36, par. 156, 157, p. 498. Contract for books let to D. D. Merrill, St. Paul. *Laws* of Kansas, 1897, ch. 179, sec. 4, p. 378. *Laws* of Montana, 1889, sec. 4, p. 211.

Kansas the law also made it conditional that the civil government textbook be equal to Thummel's *Government of the United States with the Kansas addendum*,[81] and that among the textbooks selected by the state commission should be included books on general history, history of Kansas and English history.[82]   A Montana law also limited the price to be paid for books: Barnes' *Brief History of the United States*, retail price $1.20; Barnes' *Primary History of the United States*, retail price 70 cents; and Lovell's *Civics for Young People* (also a prescribed textbook), retail price 50 cents.[83]   In South Dakota the maximum price for a textbook on the history of the United States was fixed at 80 cents by a law of 1891.[84]

The duty of choosing textbooks was delegated to various officials in the different states.   Missouri directed, in 1897, that a state commission should select the textbooks in United States history and civil government.[85]   Arkansas delegated the task of choosing a history of the United States to the state superintendent of public instruction,[86] as well as providing, in 1899, that there be included among the textbooks of the schools, the history and civil government of the state and nation.[87]   In Idaho, the county superintendent selected the textbooks in " history," and in California the duty devolved upon the state board of education.[88]

---

[81] *Laws* of Kansas, *op. cit.*

[82] *Laws* of Kansas, 1899, ch. 176, p. 357.   It was required that the general history textbook must equal Myers' *General History* and the English history must equal Montgomery's *English History*.

[83] *Laws* of Montana, *op. cit.*

[84] *Laws* of South Dakota, 1891, par. 11, p. 239.

[85] *Laws* of Missouri, 1897, sec. 5, p. 23.   Approved March 31, 1897.

[86] *Digest of the Statutes* of Arkansas, 1894, ch. 139, sec. 6975, p. 1519. Act of December 7, 1875.   Also in *Digest*, 1904, sec. 7531, p. 1543; *ibid.*, 1916, sec. 9379, p. 2132.

[87] *Laws* of Arkansas, 1899, sec. 5, p. 148.

[88] *Laws* of Idaho, 1884–85, p. 185; *Laws* of California, 1883–84, ch. VIII, sec. 1, p. 6.

Among the branches of study in Texas and Alabama for which law prescribed that there should be a uniform series of books was United States history, and in Alabama was added the history and constitution of the state.[89]

The most common regulation regarding textbooks pertained to the prohibition of books showing partisan, political or sectarian bias.[90] In the South, particularly, were such laws enacted. In February, 1890, a joint resolution " in relation to histories to be taught in the public schools of Mississippi " passed the legislature of that state. It urged " the utmost care in the selection and introduction of school histories," in order to eliminate those considered " biased, prejudiced and unfair," or that suppressed a " full, free and candid presentation of questions upon which the American people " had been " honestly divided," and in the maintenance of which they had acted " according to the promptings of courage and honor." [91]

Precisely the same motive actuated the lawmakers of Alabama later in establishing county school boards to select uniform series of textbooks for the public schools. These boards were instructed to avoid " textbooks containing anything partisan, prejudicial or inimical to the interests of the people of the State " or which would " cast a reflection on their past history." [92]

[89] *Laws* of Texas, 1822–1897, sec. 1, Vol. X, p. 145; *Code* of Alabama, 1897, art. 18, 1810.

[90] Indeed, as early as 1842, New Hampshire had prescribed that " no book shall be directed to be used as a school book which is calculated to favor any particular religious or political sect or tenet." *Revised Statutes* of New Hampshire, 1842, ch. 73, sec. 12, p. 151; *Compiled Statutes*, 1853, sec. 13, p. 178; *General Laws*, 1878, ch. 89, sec. 12, p. 217.

[91] *Laws* of Mississippi, 1890, ch. 74, p. 88. The state superintendent, governor, and attorney-general were made a committee " to examine the various textbooks upon United States history and recommend with their approval such works as accord with their best judgment."

[92] *Acts* of Alabama, 1896–7, p. 204. *County School Book Board* for the county of Winston; *ibid.*, for the county of Limestone; *ibid.*, p. 637, for the counties of Sumter and Madison.

Endorsement of history books favorable to the South was the burden of a resolution of Georgia, in 1866, which commended the Southern University series of school textbooks under the auspices of the University of Virginia from the pens of Captain M. F. Maury, Gilmore Simms, Honorable Charles Gayarre, Judge B. F. Porter, Professors Le Compte, Holmes, Venable, Schele, Devere, because they expressed a "correct sentiment." [93] This particularism became more evident toward the close of the period as Southern legislatures threw off the influence of carpet-bag domination.

Maryland's legislation of 1868 and South Carolina's of 1870 declared that "school books shall contain nothing of a sectarian or partisan character." [94] Virginia as early as 1849 had subscribed to a similar statement,[95] and in 1872 both North Carolina and Georgia forbade the use of books in the public schools which might partake of a "political" or "sectional" bias.[96]

In Georgia, the county boards were not permitted "to introduce into the schools any textbook or miscellaneous book of a sectarian or sectional character." [97] A South Carolina law, pertaining to the general duties of the state superintendent of education, accepted the phraseology

[93] *Acts* of Georgia, 1866, p. 222. The same series were endorsed by Mississippi.

[94] *Laws* of Maryland, 1868, ch. IX, sec. 1, p. 756; *ibid.*, 1870, ch. 10, sec. 1, p. 547; *Laws* of South Carolina, 1870, sec. 10, p. 341.

[95] *Laws* of Virginia, 1849, ch. 113, p. 66.

[96] *Revised Statutes* of North Carolina, 1872–3, sec. 59, p. 583. This provided that "no sectarian or political textbooks or influences shall be used in any public school." In Georgia the law prescribed that "the county board of education shall not be permitted to introduce into the schools any text-book or miscellaneous books of a sectarian or sectional character." *Code* of Georgia, 1882, part 1, title XIII, ch. V, par. 1274, p. 270; also *Acts* of 1872, sec. XXXIII, p. 75; also *Laws*, 1887, sec. XXIII, p. 74.

[97] *Code* of Georgia, 1895, sec. 5, par. 1365, Vol. I, p. 376. Legislation continued from 1872. *Acts*, 1872, sec. XXXIII, p. 75; also *Code*, 1882, part I, title XIII, ch. V, par. 1274, p. 270.

common to many laws regarding textbooks in forbidding
" partisan " books or instruction.[98]

Partisan textbooks were also excluded from the schools
of Alabama, Kansas, Arizona, Washington, and California.[99]
In Idaho and Montana legislation stipulated the rejection
of all books which would propagate " political " doctrines,
and in Texas it provided that nothing of a sectional or
partisan character should be included in the uniform series
of textbooks selected.[100]   In Kentucky the county board of
examiners was given the task of selecting a uniform series
of textbooks for the county providing that the selection did
not include any books of " an immoral, sectional or sectarian
character." [101]   The territory of Dakota legislating regarding school libraries forbade not only books unsuited " to the
cultivation of good character and good morals and manners,"
but all " partisan political pamphlets and books." [102]

The evolution of laws respecting textbooks in this period
indicated the tendency toward a spirit of localism.   The
South seized upon another opportunity in her legislation for

[98] *General Statutes* of South Carolina, 1881–82, sec. 987, p. 294. Also
Laws, 1870, sec. 10, p. 341. *Code*, 1902, sec. 1175, p. 452; *Code*, 1912, sec.
1699, Vol. I, p. 472.

[99] *Code* of Alabama, 1897, art. 18, 1811; *ibid.*, 1907; *Session Laws* of
Kansas, 1897, ch. 179, sec. 4, p. 378; *Revised Statutes* of Arizona, 1887,
1530, sec. 58, p. 281, *Laws*, 1885, p. 153; *Code* of Washington, 1891, par.
791, 10, Vol. I, p. 292; *Laws*, 1883, p. 13; *Codes and Statutes* of California,
1876, sec. 1672, Vol. I, p. 235; *ibid.*, 1905, Vol. I, p. 408.

[100] *Revised Statutes* of Idaho Territory, 1887, ch. IX, sec. 705, p. 135.
Also *Laws*, 1866, p. 27; *Laws*, 1870, sec. 13; *Laws*, 1879, p. 24; *Laws*, 1890,
p. 148; *Laws*, 1893, p. 211; *Code*, 1908, sec. 668, Vol. I, p. 406. This last
forbade "sectarian and partisan instruction." *Compiled Statutes* of Montana, 1885, sec. 1893, p. 1185. The term "partisan" in some states may
have referred to the teaching of religious or political doctrines. *Laws* of
Texas, 1822–1897, sec. 1, Vol. X, p. 145. Passed in 1891.

[101] *Acts* of Kentucky, 1893, art. VI, par. 61, p. 1439. Approved July 13,
1893.

[102] *Compiled Laws* of Dakota Territory, 1887, par. 1798, p. 401; *Revised Code*, 1883, p. 597, *Session Laws*, 1883, ch. 44, par. 130.

textbooks to prohibit the teaching of a Northern viewpoint; nine states of the Confederacy passed laws prohibiting the use of " partisan " histories in their schools. The border state of Kentucky also forbade " sectional " textbooks, whereas the West attempted to exclude " partisan, political books." [103] The laws passed by the North during the period dealt largely with the naming of textbooks to be used in the public schools.

[103] Dakota Territory, Montana, Idaho, Washington excluded from their schools " partisan " textbooks.

CHAPTER III

LAWS FOR THE EXPANSION OF THE HISTORY CURRICULUM
1900–1917

The twentieth century did not usher in unexpected developments in the American educational system, for the school had begun to experience a transformation of purpose in the period following the Civil War. It was not, however, until after 1900 that the forces aroused by the Economic Revolution began to assert themselves to a marked degree and to seek means to equip the individual for the complex responsibilities of his social relationships. The early years of the new century saw a tidal wave of reform sweep into all phases of American life. Agitation for the recall of judicial decisions and the introduction of such measures as the initiative and referendum attested new convictions in the realm of politics. The reform spirit found expression in muck-raking literature, movements for the betterment of dependents on society, legislation to alleviate unfortunate industrial conditions, and schemes of coöperation between employer and employee bore testimony to a new social consciousness and national morality.

The public school also gave evidence of the spirit of the new era through the changed character of its instruction.[1]

[1] This period recognized the importance of vocational training as an important function of the public school, and developed an interest in other " expression subjects." The content subjects were also expanded and liberalized. According to Cubberley, " The modern school aims to train pupils for greater social usefulness and to give them a more intelligent grasp of the social and industrial, as well as the moral and civic structure of our modern democratic life." Cubberley, Ellwood P., *Public Education in the United States* (Boston, 1919), p. 370.

" Preparation for citizenship " became the keynote of the period, perhaps better expressed by John Dewey's definition of education as " The process of remaking experience, giving it a more socialized value through increased individual experience by giving the individual better control over his powers." History and the other social studies gained in popularity as especially adapted to implant the right social attitude.

This wider outlook on life did not confine itself solely to an interest in domestic affairs, for the Spanish-American War had banished the long-cherished theory of national isolation. The international viewpoint was encouraged further by the fact that by 1900 the United States had achieved second place as an exporting nation. As a result, the study of foreign history gained in popularity, and increased offerings in the social studies curriculum evinced the growing favor in which these subjects were held.

In planning the course of study, educational associations showed much activity in committee reports. The report of the Committee of Seven of the American Historical Association doubtless had a pronounced influence in the curriculum making of the greater part of this period. In 1907, it was followed by the report of the Committee of Five, who made slight changes in the list of studies recommended by the Committee of Seven. However, modern European history received greater emphasis than in the first report, a tangible expression of the expanding horizon of the time. In 1909, the Committee of Eight attempted to standardize a course in history for the elementary schools, in which was included not only United States history but a study of European history.[2]

---

[2] Only the outstanding committee reports are mentioned. *Cf.* Johnson, *op. cit.* An N. E. A. committee report appeared in 1916 but played no part

From 1900 to the year of our entrance into the World War, thirty-two states approved laws incorporating history and other social studies in the curriculum of the public schools, approximately twice as many as had legislated from 1860 to 1900.[3] The importance placed upon the study of United States history, federal and local civics and state history in the previous period persisted. The early years of the century were characterized also by laws pertaining to the teaching of patriotism through the celebration of historic events, by statutes to inspire reverence for the flag, and by enactments indicative of sectional interest.[4]

In 1900, Vermont amended her law prescribing the high school course of study, and designated political economy, civil government and general history among the branches to be taught.[5] Other enactments, enumerating the prerequisites for a high school, included thirty-three weeks of history and the natural, political, social, moral and industrial sciences.[6] In 1906, there was provided instruction for elementary pupils in the history and constitution of the United States and the history, constitution and principles of the government of Vermont.[7] In 1915, the teaching of " citizenship " was approved for all rural schools of a six year course, and for elementary schools of eight years.[8]

---

in the social studies curriculum of the period. It expressed, however, the practical and social viewpoint of the time.

[3] Eighteen states.

[4] See chapter VI for a discussion of the activities of the G. A. R. in the North and of pro-Southern groups in the South to direct the content of history textbooks.

[5] *Laws* of Vermont, 1900, no. 25, p. 19. The law of 1912 was substantially the same as that of 1900. *Laws*, 1912, sec. 1016, p. 68.

[6] *Laws* of Vermont, 1902, no. 27, sec. 3, p. 39; *ibid.*, 1904, no. 137, sec. 4, p. 62; *Public Statutes*, 1906, ch. 47, sec. 1016, p. 277.

[7] *Public Statutes* of Vermont, 1906, ch. 46, sec. 1003, p. 275. *Cf. Laws*, 1888, ch. 5, sec. 95, p. 24.

[8] *Public Acts* of Vermont, 1915, sec. 44, p. 131.

The tendency to emphasize a study of the Constitution has no better illustration than in the laws of New Hampshire, where, in 1901, it was made compulsory for every high school to give "reasonable instruction in the constitution of the United States and in the constitution of New Hampshire." [9] Later enactments further stressed the importance of a knowledge of the state and federal constitutions by prescribing that " in all mixed schools and in all grades above the primary, the constitution of the United States and of the state of New Hampshire be read aloud by the scholars at least once during the last year of the course below the high school." [10]   The teaching of citizenship was the purpose of a Connecticut law of 1903 and of 1915, prescribing regular instruction for all pupils above the fourth grade in " the duties of citizenship, including the knowledge of the form of national, state, and local government." [11]

Training in citizenship was the purpose of a Delaware law of 1911, which prescribed that teachers train their pupils in " honesty, kindness, justice, and moral courage . . . for the purpose of lessening crime and raising the standard of good citizenship." Four years later it was followed by an enactment requiring the teaching of United States history and instruction in " the general principles of the constitution of the United States " and of the state.[12]

In 1911 Pennsylvania prescribed for the elementary schools the teaching of United States history, history of the

[9] *Supplement to the Public Statutes of New Hampshire,* 1901–1913, p. 17 (1901, ch. 96, sec. 4, 1903, 31:1; 1903, 118:2; 1905, 19:1).

[10] *Supplement to the Public Statutes of New Hampshire,* 1901–1913, ch. 92, sec. 6, p. 172. (*Laws,* 1903, 31:2; 1909, 49:1; 1911, 136:2.)

[11] *Public Acts* of Connecticut, 1903, ch. 96, p. 65; *General Statutes,* 1918, ch. 45, sec. 852, Vol. I, p. 312.

[12] *Laws* of Delaware, 1911, p. 197; *Revised Statutes,* 1915, ch. 71, 2289, sec. 17, p. 1102; *ibid.,* ch. 71, 2288, sec. 16, p. 1100.

state and civil government.[13] These subjects received the statutory endorsement of Kentucky in 1904, Virginia in 1904 and 1906, North Carolina in 1901, 1905, 1907, 1908 and 1913.[14] South Carolina in several laws from 1892 required for schools under the direction of boards of trustees and of county boards of education, the " history of the United States and of this state, the principles of the constitution of the United States and of this state, morals and good behavior." [15]

Texas gave her sanction to the same subjects in 1905,[16] and Alabama prescribed that in all schools and colleges supported in whole or in part by public money, or under state control, there should be instruction in the constitution of the United States and of the state of Alabama.[17] In Georgia, the law prescribed as part of the curriculum for the common schools that " the elements of civil government shall be included in the branches of study taught in the common or public schools, and shall be studied and taught as thoroughly and in the same manner as other like required branches are studied and taught in said public schools." [18] West Virginia attained some individuality in adding to state

13 *Laws* of Pennsylvania, 1911, sec. 1607, p. 394.

14 *Kentucky Statutes*, 1909, ch. 113, par. 4421a (2), p. 1765; also *Acts*, 1904, p. 11. This law was on the statute books in 1909; also *Acts*, 1916, ch. 24, art. III, par. 24, p. 173. *Code* of Virginia, 1904, ch. 66, sec. 1497, p. 810; *Acts*, 1906, par. 1497, p. 443. *Public Laws* of North Carolina, 1901, ch. 4, sec. 37; 1905, ch. 533, s9; 1907, ch. 641, s853, 957; *Revised Code*, 1908, ch. 89, par. 4060, Vol. II, p. 2049; *ibid.*, 1913, par. 1383, Vol. I, p. 332.

15 *Code* of South Carolina, 1902, sec. 1201, Vol. I, p. 462; *ibid.*, 1912, sec. 1731, Vol. I, p. 480. *Cf.* page 16.

16 *General Laws* of Texas, 1905, sec. 100, p. 289; McEachon's *Annotated Civil Statutes*, 1913, art. 2783, Vol. II, p. 1114. The same subjects are required through 1913.

17 *Code* of Alabama, 1907, 1685 (4), Vol. I, p. 741. See page 17 for the same law in the *Code* of 1897.

18 *Code* of Georgia, 1910, ch. 4, art. 4, sec. 3, par. 1464, Vol. I, p. 376. The law was passed in 1903.

and national history and civil government, "general and West Virginia geography." [19]

In the schools of Florida instruction in "history" was required for the intermediate grades, and in the grammar grades the "history and civil government of Florida and of the United States." [20] Additional emphasis was placed upon the teaching of civics in 1909 when an act provided that the "elements of civil government be taught in the common and public schools of the state, . . . to be studied and taught as thoroughly and in the same manner as any other required subjects." [21]

Louisiana committed herself to the teaching of United States history in every school district as an elementary branch by an act of 1902; [22] and Mississippi, in 1916, prescribed for the "curriculum of the free public schools," civil government with special reference to local and state government, the history of the nation and of the state. [23]

In 1904, Ohio established civil government and the history of the United States as required subjects for an elementary school education. [24] In 1910, it was made obligatory upon each county board of school examiners to examine pupils of township schools in civil government and United States history. [25] In the *Code* of 1910, there were included, in both

[19] *Code* of West Virginia, 1916, ch. 45, par. 78, p. 578; substantially the same in *Acts*, 1872, ch. 123; 1881, ch. 15; 1887, ch. 3; 1891, ch. 63; 1895, ch. 36; 1908, ch. 27; 1915, ch. 56.
[20] *Compiled Laws* of Florida, 1914, 390, art. 4, Vol. I, p. 141; *Laws*, 1905, ch. 5382, sec. 6, p. 34, also *Laws*, 1903, p. 180.
[21] *Laws* of Florida, 1909, ch. 5938, p. 126 (No. 69).
[22] *Constitution and Revised Laws of Louisiana*, 1876 to 1902 (Act 214, 1902), sec. 23, p. 612; again *ibid.*, 1908, p. 45; *Annotated Revision*, 1915, 2532, sec. 16, Vol. I, p. 846. The law was unchanged in the *Revisions* of 1908 and of 1915.
[23] *Laws* of Mississippi, 1916, ch. 187 (4540), p. 277.
[24] *General and Local Acts* of Ohio, 1904, sec. 4007-1, p. 359.
[25] *Ibid.*, 1910, p. 103.

the elementary and high school courses of study, the history of the United States and civil government, and in the high school the history of " other countries " as well.[26]   By an act approved May 18, 1911, but repealed in 1914, teachers in elementary schools were required to qualify in the history of the United States, including civil government, and in the high school in general history, with an election of civil government.[27]   An Illinois law of this period was similar to that of Delaware in phraseology and spirit, and prescribed the teaching of " honesty, kindness, justice and moral courage " to lessen crime and develop a good citizenship.[28]

Wisconsin, as early as 1865, had required as essential for a district school education, United States history and civil government, local history and government, a practice continued through 1917. In schools offering industrial education, citizenship became an obligatory study by the statutes of 1913.[29]   Minnesota made a knowledge of United States history prerequisite for entrance into high schools,[30] and Indiana expanded her list of the required number of studies to include, in all commissioned high schools, civil government, general and state, ancient, medieval or modern his-

[26] *Code* of Ohio, 1910, sec. 7648, sec. 7649, p. 1622.

[27] *General and Local Acts* of Ohio, 1911, sec. 7830, p. 130. Repealed February 17, 1914. *Ibid.*, 1914, p. 109.

[28] *Revised Statutes* of Illinois, 1913, ch. 122, 509, p. 2267. In force July 1, 1909. Again found, *Revised Statutes*, 1917, ch. 122, 509, p. 2736.

[29] *Statutes* of Wisconsin, 1917, 40, 30, p. 375; *ibid.*, 1915, ch. 27s. 447 (1863, c155 s55; 1866, c111 s6; 1869, c50 s1; 1871, c14 s1; R. S. 1878, s447; *Suppl.*, 1906, s447; 1907, c118, 200; 1911, c409). *Statutes* of Wisconsin, 1913, ch. 27 s553 p–5, p. 335; *ibid.*, 1917, s41.17 (1), p. 411. This law was repealed in 1917. The requirement was the same in 1915. *Ibid.*, 1915, c275, s553, p–5, p. 335. In Wisconsin, in normal training courses in the high school, American history was required for at least one semester in the eleventh and twelfth grades.

[30] *Revised Laws* of Minnesota, 1915, ch. 14, 1340, p. 273. *General Statutes*, 1913, 2299, p. 629; *General Laws*, 1895, ch. 17, sec. 2, p. 138. This legislation had been preceded by legislation of 1895, prescribing civil government for county schools.

tory and the history of the United States.[31]   For the curriculum of the common schools, there was required in Indiana the study of United States history, a practice developed from a law first in force in August 1869.[32]

South Dakota,[33] North Dakota,[34] and Kansas[35] also committed themselves to the subjects popular in this period. In Nebraska, " a study of American history for at least one semester in the eleventh and twelfth grades," became a requirement for normal training courses in the high school.[36] Missouri made a knowledge of United States history essential for entrance into the high schools, as well as prescribing that no school could be classed as a high school which did not include a four years' course in history.[37]

Oklahoma, in 1905, illustrated well the social viewpoint characteristic of the time in her law requiring " in each and every public school it should be the duty of each and every teacher to teach morality in the broadest meaning of the word, for the purpose of elevating and refining the character of school children up to the highest plane of life; that they may know how to conduct themselves as social beings in relation to each other, as respects right and wrong and

[31] *Laws* of Indiana, 1907, ch. 192, p. 324. Burns' *Annotated Statutes*, 1914, 6582 (5984), Vol. III, p. 384, and 6584, p. 385.

[32] *Ibid.*

[33] *Compiled Laws* of South Dakota, 1903, 2378, p. 432. The teaching of civil government and United States history in the common schools.

[34] *Revised Code* of North Dakota, 1913, par. 1383, Vol. I, p. 332. The requirement included American history and civil government.

[35] *Laws* of Kansas, 1903, ch. 435, p. 672. History of United States and Kansas history. *Laws*, 1913, ch. 271, p. 454, added civil government. *General Statutes*, 1915, ch. 105, art. 5, par. 8985, p. 1818, for district schools, history of the United States and of Kansas.

[36] *Revised Statutes* of Nebraska, 1913, ch. 71, art. X, 6839, sec. 140, p. 1907.

[37] *Revised Statutes* of Missouri, 1909, par. 10852, and *ibid.*, 1919, par. 11218, and *ibid.*, 1909, par. 10923, Vol. III, p. 3400 respectively. The last law is also in *Session Laws*, 1903, p. 264; *ibid.*, 1909, p. 770.

rectitude of life, and thereby lessen wrong doing and crime." [38] In 1907, another law prescribed " the elements of economics " for all public schools receiving support from the state.[39]

A place of prominence in the normal training curriculum was accorded United States history by Oregon in 1911.[40] In 1913, Wyoming enacted a law requiring of her superintendent of public instruction the preparation of a course of study for the elementary schools in the usual subjects, including United States history and the history and civil government of Wyoming,[41] and by an act of 1917 history and civics were required in the teacher training departments of the high school.[42] California, too, succumbed to the trend of the times, and in 1903 and in succeeding years prescribed the teaching of United States history and civil government for a public school education.[43]

In the revision of her territorial laws in 1901, Arizona again included United States history as a school subject;[44] and by legislation in 1912, New Mexico showed her approval of the social studies in " An Act to Encourage the Instruction in the History and Civics of the State of New Mexico." This law forbade any person to teach in the public schools unless he had passed a satisfactory examination in the his-

[38] *Laws* of Oklahoma, 1905, p. 378; *Compiled Laws*, 1909, sec. 8233, p. 1664.

[39] *Revised Laws* of Oklahoma, 1910, art. III, 7667, Vol. II, p. 2084; *Session Laws*, 1907-8, p. 14.

[40] *Session Laws* of Oregon, 1911, ch. 58, sec. 59, p. 96.

[41] *Session Laws* of Wyoming, 1913, Senate File No. 41, p. 45.

[42] *Ibid.*, 1917, ch. 123, p. 215.

[43] *Statutes* of California, 1903, par. 1874: 2, p. 195; *Codes and Statutes*, 1905, par. 1874: 2, Vol. I, p. 451, *Statutes*, 1907, p. 70; *Consolidated Supplement to Kerr's Cyclopedia*, 1913, par. 1665, p. 194. *Cf.* page 20.

[44] *Revised Laws of the Territory of Arizona*, 1901, 2214 (sec. 85), p. 602. This is the same as *Laws* of 1885, p. 157, also *Revised Statutes*, 1887, 1553, sec. 81, p. 284.

tory and civics of the United States as well as in the history and civics of the state. " It shall be the duty of the teachers in the public schools of the state," the law read, " to give such instruction as is practicable in the history and civics of the United States with special reference to the history and civics of the state of New Mexico; which said instruction may be given orally or by study of textbooks covering the subject and which said textbooks shall have been adopted by the State Board of Education." The statute specified that the textbook in state history and civics must be prepared " by a known historian of the state " and " be sold at a price to be fixed by the State Board of Education not to exceed one dollar per volume." [45]

Of the thirty-two states which had enacted laws during this period for the teaching of the social studies, substantially all required United States history, federal and local civics. State history, which had attained some popularity in the preceding period, received attention in many statutes. Laws requiring the teaching of European history in some form were found in Vermont, Indiana, Ohio and Missouri, and economics was prescribed in the laws of Oklahoma and Vermont.

CERTIFICATION OF TEACHERS

The tendency to enlarge and enrich the social studies curriculum was more evident in the requirements for teachers' certificates than in the courses of study prescribed by law. These requirements, in general, included ancient, medieval and modern history, general history, English history, economics and sociology, besides civil government, state history and history of the United States. Especially

[45] *Laws* of New Mexico, 1911, ch. 41, p. 68. Approved June 8, 1912. Also *Annotated Statutes*, 1915, par. 4958, sec. 152, Vol. II, p. 1429.

was there an increased offering of subjects for high school teachers. In the elementary and county licenses only civics and United States history were required with the greatest frequency. Among those states which passed new laws or reënacted old legislation offering ancient, medieval or modern history were California, Idaho, Oregon, Minnesota, Wisconsin, Ohio, Missouri, and Texas.[46] English history appeared among the subjects in the laws of Idaho, Nevada, Kansas, and Wisconsin;[47] general history was one of the requirements for certification in the laws of West Virginia, Ohio, Arkansas, Louisiana, Texas, Illinois, Minnesota,

---

[46] *Codes* of California, 1905, 1772, Vol. I, p. 426, grammar school certificates; United States history and civil government were also required for this certificate. *Compiled Statutes* of Idaho, 1919, par. 986, Vol. I, p. 276; first grade certificate, with a choice of medieval and modern history or English history added to American history and civics required for other certificates. *Session Laws*, 1911, p. 448; *ibid.*, 1915, p. 333; repealed in session 1921, *Laws*, 1921, p. 473. *General Laws* of Oregon, 1911, ch. 58, sec. 9, p. 89; for state certificate, general history was required. *Revised Laws* of Minnesota, 1905, ch. 14, 1354, p. 275, for professional certificates, ancient, medieval, English, and American history. *General Laws* of Wisconsin, 1919, ch. 601, first grade, modern history and United States history, history of Wisconsin, rural economics. *Laws* of Ohio, 1919, sec. 7831-2, p. 685, modern history, general history, economics, sociology, civics, among sixteen branches from which five were to be chosen for high school certificates. *Laws* of Missouri, 1911, sec. 10939, p. 408, first grade certificate, giving a choice of ancient, medieval or modern or English history for examination. *Laws* of Texas, 1921, ch. 129, sec. 108a, p. 243, high school certificate civil government, ancient and modern history, and for elementary certificate of second class, United States history and Texas history.

[47] *Compiled Statutes of Idaho, op. cit. Statutes* of Nevada, 1912, ch. 114, p. 156, also *Revised Laws*, 1912, sec. 3263, Vol. I, p. 947, general history, United States history, civil government, current events for the first and second grade elementary certificates; sec. 3262, high school certificates; civil government, general history, United States history, with a selection of English history out of a group of subjects. *Laws* of Kansas, 1915, ch. 298, sec. 14, p. 392, first grade certificate, also in *Laws*, 1911, ch. 277, sec. 2, p. 506; *ibid.*, 1913, ch. 268, p. 450. *Statutes* of Wisconsin, 1913, sec. 450-3, first grade certificate required English history, history of United States, civil government, local and national; for the third grade, the latter two were required.

Nebraska, South Dakota, Utah, Nevada, Washington, and Idaho.[48]

Economics, or, as it was more commonly known, political economy, was prescribed in Iowa, Nebraska, and Wyoming.[49] South Dakota permitted for examination either sociology or economics,[50] and Wisconsin and Arkansas insisted upon a knowledge of " rural economics." [51] " Current events " or " current history " were among the requirements of South Dakota in her law of 1919, and of Nevada, in 1907,

[48] *Code* of West Virginia, 1916, ch. 45, par. 87, elementary certificates, *Laws*, 1919, p. 87. *Annotated Revision* of Louisiana, 1915, 2572 (sec. 1, art. 55, 1906, Vol. I, p. 88), state teachers' certificate. *Laws* of Texas, 1905, sec. 118, p. 293, permanent certificate and first grade. *Revised Statutes* of Illinois, 1913, ch. 122, 541, third to first grade elementary certificate, also *ibid.*, 1917, ch. 122, 541, *Laws*, 1919, p. 900. *Revised Laws* of Minnesota, 1905, ch. 14, 1354, p. 275, professional state certificates. *Laws* of Nebraska, 1919, ch. 70, sec. 3, p. 262, professional state and high school certificate; also *Revised Statutes*, 1913, ch. 71, art. XIII, 6859, sec. 158, professional state certificate (*Laws*, 1905, p. 559). *Laws* of South Dakota, 1919, p. 169, repeals provisions of *Revised Code*, 1919, sec. 3; for a life diploma, general history, economics or sociology; also general history, United States history, South Dakota history and civil government in a state certificate; *Laws* of 1905, sec. 2286, p. 136, and *ibid.*, 1911, p. 170. *Compiled Laws* of Utah, 1907, par. 1767, pp. 684–685, and *ibid.*, 1917, par. 4509, p. 914, state professional certificates for grammar grades and high school. *Statutes* of Nevada, 1912, ch. 80, p. 157, first grade elementary school certificate; ch. 114, sec. 24, high school certificates (approved bill March 17, 1913); also *Statutes*, 1912, high school and elementary school certificates; *General Laws*, 1914, sec. 7831, high school certificate general history and a choice in elective history. *Session Laws* of Washington, 1909, sec. 4644, p. 516, first grade elementary certificates and life certificates; *ibid.*, 1911, ch. 16, sec. 4, p. 51, life certificates. *Political Code* of Idaho, 1901, ch. XXXVI, sec. 1028, Vol. I, p. 311, first, second and third grade certificates.

[49] *Supplement to the Code* of Iowa, 1902, sec. 2736, p. 315. *Acts*, 1906, ch. 122, sec. 4, p. 88, first grade certificate had been found as early as 1882. *Laws* of Nebraska, 1903, par. 5542, sec. 5; in 1919, political economy is not mentioned. *Revised Statutes* of Wyoming, 1899, sec. 627, p. 228; also *Laws*, 1901, ch. 57, p. 60.

[50] *Compiled Laws* of South Dakota, 1913, par. 13, Vol. I, p. 565, for life certificates.

[51] *Statutes* of Wisconsin, 1915, ch. 27s. 450–2, p. 272. *Digest of Statutes* of Arkansas, 1921, par. 9022, rural teachers' certificate (Act of March 28, 1917).

and in 1921, for certification of primary, grammar and high school classes.[52]

State history and the study of the state constitution received recognition in the requirements of Pennsylvania, Delaware, West Virginia, Kentucky, Mississippi, Alabama, Oklahoma, Texas, Wisconsin, South Dakota, Illinois, Kansas, and New Mexico.[53] Of all of the social studies required for certification, however, United States history and civil government were the most popular, being prescribed in some law in every state excepting Arizona.[54] In some of the states where there

[52] *Compiled Laws* of South Dakota, 1913, par. 55, Vol. I, p. 572; *ibid.*, 1911, p. 413; *Revised Statutes,* 1919, par. 7392, p. 1847, for first grade certificate; also *Laws,* 1919, p. 170. *Laws* of Nevada, 1907, secs. 15, 16, 17, p. 383, " current news "; *Statutes,* 1921, ch. 208, sec. 25, elementary school certificate, first grade, " current events."

[53] *Statute Law* of Pennsylvania, 1920, 5003, p. 462, professional and provisional certificates. *Laws* of Delaware, 1919, 2326–118, sec. 118, elementary school certificate; *ibid.,* 1920, sec. 170, p. 190. *Code* of West Virginia, 1916 (all statutes in force), ch. 45, par. 87, p. 580, for elementary and first three grades of certificates; again in *Laws,* 1919, p. 87, *ibid.,* 1921, sec. 104, elementary certificate. *Statutes* of Kentucky, 1918, ch. 113, art. XI, par. 4501, p. 941, for all certificates. *Laws* of Mississippi, 1916, ch. 188, 4543, p. 278, first and second grade licenses; also state licenses, *Laws,* 1908, p. 209. *Code* of Alabama, 1907, 1734, Vol. I, p. 757, the first three grades of certificates. *Revised Laws* of Oklahoma, 1910, 7923, Vol. II, p. 2153, the first three grades of licenses. *McEachln's Civil Statutes* of Texas, 1913, articles 2799–2802, Vol. II, p. 1117, permanent certificates (also Sayles' *Civil Statutes,* art. 3974, pp. 1419–20) and first, second, third grade certificates, and *Laws,* 1905, sec. 118, p. 293; *ibid.,* 1921, p. 243. *Laws* of Wisconsin, 1919, ch. 601, 39.18 (1), 39.19 (1), and 39.20 (1), for first, second, and third grade certificates. *Laws* of South Dakota, 1919, p. 169, *Compiled Laws* of South Dakota, 1913, secs. 13 and 14, Vol. I, p. 565, life diploma, state, first, second, third grade certificates, and primary. *Revised Statutes* of Illinois, 1913, ch. 122, p. 2271, county certificates; *ibid.,* 1917, ch. 122; *Laws,* 1919, p. 900, as well as *Laws* of 1903 and 1905. *Laws* of Kansas, 1915, ch. 298, p. 392, for the first, second and third grade certificates; *ibid.,* 1913, ch. 268, p. 450; *ibid.,* 1911, ch. 277, p. 506. *Statutes* of New Mexico, 1915, par. 4957, Vol. II, p. 1429, first and second grade certificates.

[54] Arizona prescribed for first and second grade certificates, civics and " history," which probably meant American history. See *Revised Laws,* 1901, 2142 (sec. 13), p. 584.

was no special enactment prescribing United States history or civics, the examining board may have been given the privilege of naming the subjects for examining the candidates, or, through custom, they may have become a part of the subjects in which examinations were held. It is also true that colleges and normal schools have taken over the preparation of teachers in the subjects which they are to teach, making unnecessary many of the examinations previously held.

FLAG LEGISLATION AND OBSERVANCE DAYS

A means of implanting patriotism in the pupils of the public schools has been legislation pertaining to the display of the American flag, the development of a proper attitude toward it, and the singing of the national anthem. Ten states gave expression to this form of training for patriotism in this period. Similar to such enactments was the legal provision made for the observance of the birthdays of great men and the commemoration of historic events by classroom exercises. In addition, there was a constantly growing number of legal holidays upon which no school was in session.[55]

Laws respecting the flag were, and are, of three general kinds: (1) that each school must possess a flag for display in a conspicuous place, (2) that proper respect for the flag be taught, and (3) that suitable exercises be engaged in at definitely stated intervals. This last type of law often proves the occasion for the reciting in unison of the salute to the flag, the so-called " American Creed," or the preamble

[55] In Florida, for example, June 3 was made a holiday to "perpetuate in the minds of the people the purity of life, the intellectual ability, the heroic fortitude, and the patriotic character of Jefferson Davis." *Laws* of Florida, 1891, ch. 4058, p. 99.

to the Constitution. In the second variety of law a pledge
of allegiance is the keynote of the sentiment expressed, such
as: " I pledge allegiance to my flag and to the Republic for
which it stands; one nation indivisible, with liberty and
justice for all "; or, " We give our hearts and our hands
to God and our Country; one country, one flag, and one
language." [56]

In 1898, New York enacted " flag " legislation which had
the three-fold characteristics of such laws. Within the next
few years this law was followed by statutes of like kind in
Massachusetts, Indiana, Iowa, and Arizona. However, as
later legislation appeared, it took on a more elaborate
phraseology, with a more open avowal of patriotic purpose.[57]
This is well illustrated by an act of 1909 in Indiana, which
ordered that " the state board of education shall require
the singing of the ' Star Spangled Banner ' in its entirety
in the schools of the state of Indiana, upon all patriotic
occasions," with the necessary admonition " that the
said board of education shall arrange to supply the
words in sufficient quantity for the purposes indicated
therein." [58]

" An Act to provide for the display of the United States
flag on the school houses of the state, in connection with the
public schools, and to encourage patriotic exercises in such
schools," became a law in Kansas, March 7, 1907. By
this act the state superintendent was instructed to prepare
a program for the salute to the flag at the opening of each

[56] See *American History and Patriotic Program for all Schools of Oklahoma*, issued by the State Department of Education, 1921, p. 7.

[57] *Laws* of New York, 1898, secs. 1, 2, 3, Vol. III, p. 1191; *Revised
Laws* of Massachusetts, 1902, ch. 42, sec. 50, Vol. I, p. 474; *Laws* of In-
diana, 1907, ch. 253, p. 537; *Acts* of Iowa, 1913, ch. 245, sec. 2, p. 264;
Laws of Arizona, 1903, no. 19, p. 25.

[58] Burns' *Annotated Statutes* of Indiana, 1914, 5852a, Vol. III, p. 385.

day of school, as well as " such other patriotic exercises as may be deemed by him to be expedient." [59]

Relying upon the governor's proclamation, New Jersey, in 1915, set aside the week of September sixth to thirteenth for appropriate exercises to be held, at least one day in the interval named, by schools and churches in commemoration of the one hundredth birthday of the national anthem.[60]

In her *Revised Statutes* which took effect on January 1, 1917, Maine incorporated a flag law evolved from enactments of 1907 and 1915, whereby superintendents of schools were directed to display the flag from public school buildings on suitable occasions. Towns were directed to appropriate annually " a sufficient amount to defray the necessary cost of the display of the flag," and it was made " the duty of instructors to impress upon the youth by suitable references and observances the significance of the flag, to teach them the cost, the object and principles of our government, the great sacrifices of our forefathers, the important part taken by the Union army in the war of eighteen hundred sixty-one to eighteen hundred sixty-five, to teach them to love, honor and respect the flag of our country that cost so much and is so dear to every true American citizen." [61]

Closely akin to the enactments respecting the flag and patriotic exercises were those designating days for special patriotic observance.[62] Laws providing for the establish-

[59] *Laws* of Kansas, 1907, ch. 319, p. 493. The Iowa law, 1913, is much like this law. See *Acts* of Iowa, 1913, p. 264. The Grand Army of the Republic and the Woman's Relief Corps were actively engaged in supplying schools with flags for the purpose of inculcating patriotism throughout this period.

[60] *Acts* of New Jersey, 1915, p. 904.

[61] *Revised Statutes* of Maine, 1916, ch. 16, sec. 52 ; *Laws*, 1907, ch. 182, p. 199 ; *ibid.*, 1915, ch. 176.

[62] No attempt is made to treat legal holidays where the law requires observance by simply specifying the dates of such days. They are discussed only when the enactments indicate patriotic exercises to be held within the

ment of Memorial Day are of such a character. In general, Memorial Day legislation was sectional in character and acclaimed the results of the Civil War from the Northerner's standpoint. In 1886, the Kansas legislature, moved by patriotic feeling, had resolved to observe the day in fitting manner, inasmuch as " during the past ten or twelve years the loyal people of the United States, inspired by a sentiment of reverent respect for the memory of our heroic dead, have by spontaneous consent, dedicated the thirtieth day of May of each year to ceremonies in honor of the soldiers who cheerfully sacrificed their own lives to save the life of the republic. ' They need no praise whose deeds are eulogy,' and nothing that we can now say or do will add to the glory or brighten the fame of the gallant host who, a quarter of a century ago, came thronging from farms, workshops, offices and schools, to fight, to suffer and die for the Union and freedom. But the story of their sublime self-sacrifice, and their dauntless courage, should be kept forever fresh and fair in the hearts and minds of the young, until the end of recorded time. So long as men and women teach their children to revere the memory of patriot heroes, so long as the peaceful present honors and emulates the example of the war-worn past, there need be no fear that the dead have died in vain, or that ' a government of the people, by the people, for the people,' will perish from the earth. The steadily growing popularity of Memorial Day, and the universal interest taken in its beautiful ceremonies, is one of the most hopeful developments of American sentiments." [63]

---

public schools, or where the purpose of teaching history through the observance of such days is stated.

[63] *Laws* of Kansas, 1886, ch. CXXV, p. 167. Approved February 18, 1886. Especially active in their desire for a proper observance of Memorial Day were the G. A. R., who in annual encampments frequently expressed a faith in it as a means for promoting patriotism as well as for memorializing the deeds of their comrades.

Conceding the importance of a proper recognition of Memorial Day, Vermont in 1894 appointed the last half day's session before May the thirtieth for exercises " commemorative of the history of the nation during the war of the Rebellion, and to patriotic instruction in the principles of liberty and the equal rights of man." The popularity of this law is attested by its continuance on the Vermont statute books in her *Compilation* of 1917.[64]

In 1890, Massachusetts, and in 1897, New Hampshire established in these commonwealths the custom of observing May the thirtieth by exercises of a patriotic nature in the schools.[65] New York, in 1898, Arizona in 1903, and Kansas in 1907, also subscribed to the sentiment which dictated that Memorial Day be given special recognition.[66]

The birthdays of Lincoln and Washington were also given recognition by New York in 1898, Arizona in 1903, and Kansas in 1907.[67] The year 1909 witnessed an expression of patriotic enthusiasm over Lincoln's contribution to the American nation, awakened, no doubt, by the centenary of his birth. During this year California, Maine, and New Mexico prescribed special observance of February the twelfth. Rhode Island followed in 1910, West Virginia in 1911, with Vermont in 1912 and in 1917.

" February 12, the birthday of Abraham Lincoln is hereby declared a legal holiday," stated the law of California,

---

[64] *Statutes* of Vermont, 1894, no. 25, par. 685, p. 21; *Public Statutes,* 1906, ch. 46, sec. 1005, p. 275; *General Laws,* 1917, ch. 57, sec. 1240.

[65] *Acts and Resolves* of Massachusetts, 1890, ch. III, sec. 1, p. 94; *Laws* of New Hampshire, 1897, ch. 14, p. 16; also *Laws,* 1921, ch. 85, sec. 23, p. 127. The latter date in New Hampshire might indicate a reënactment. South Dakota, in 1921, specially designated Memorial Day as " Citizenship Day." See page 98.

[66] *Laws* of New York, 1898, ch. 481, Vol. II, p. 1191. *Laws* of Arizona, 1903, no. 19, p. 25. *Laws* of Kansas, 1907, ch. 319, p. 493.

[67] *Laws* of New York, *op. cit. Laws* of Arizona, *op. cit. Laws* of Kansas, *op. cit.*

which is typical of others of this group, " *provided, however,* that all public schools throughout the state shall hold sessions in the forenoon of that day in order to allow the customary exercises in memory of Lincoln; and *provided further,* that when February 12 falls on Sunday, then the Monday following, shall be a legal holiday and shall be so observed; and *provided still further,* that when February 12 falls on Saturday such exercises in the public schools shall take place on the Friday afternoon preceding." [68] In Rhode Island, the day was called " Grand Army Flag Day," and was, in 1914, still one of those days upon which special exercises were held.[69]

Michigan prescribed the reading of the Declaration of Independence to all pupils in the public schools above the fifth grade upon the twelfth and twenty-second of February, and upon the twelfth of October, with an obviously patriotic intent, in her legislation of 1911.[70] Washington's birthday occasioned legislation in Maryland in 1904 and in Maine in 1913, as a day suitable for the propagation of patriotism.[71]

In the latter state Columbus Day, October 12, was included in those observance days upon which exercises should " aim to impress on the minds of the youth the important

[68] *Statutes* of California, 1909, ch. 527, p. 861, approved April 13, 1909. *Acts and Resolves* of Maine, 1909, ch. 190, sec. 1, p. 190. *Acts* of New Mexico, 1909, ch. 121, sec. 7, p. 342. *Acts* of West Virginia, 1911, ch. 40, p. 117. Also in West Virginia *Code,* 1916, ch. 15, par. 1, p. 246. *General Laws* of Vermont, 1917, ch. 57, sec. 1241, p. 295.

[69] *Acts and Resolves* of Rhode Island, 1914, ch. 1071, sec. 2, p. 110; also *Acts,* 1901, ch. 818, p. 55.

[70] This law was passed in 1911. *Compiled Laws* of Michigan, 1915, ch. 108 (5823), sec. 1, Vol. II, p. 2198. Non-compliance might cause the revocation of the teacher's certificate by the county commissioner of schools or by the superintendent of public instruction.

[71] *Laws* of Maryland, 1904, sec. 47, p. 991. *Acts and Resolves* of Maine, 1913, ch. 195, sec. 88, p. 240.

lessons of character and good citizenship to be learned from the lives of American leaders and heroes and from a contemplation of their own duties and obligations to the community, state, and nation of which they constituted a part." [72]   Columbus Day received the recognition of several other state legislatures, Michigan, West Virginia, Louisiana, and Oregon especially setting it aside for patriotic purposes. [73]

Flag Day, likewise, was deemed worthy of observance. New York in her legislation of 1898, Arizona in 1903, and Kansas in 1907 included it among those days set aside for special exercises in the schools. [74]   Connecticut decreed, in 1905, that the governor, annually in the spring, should designate by official proclamation the fourteenth day of June as Flag Day, upon which " suitable exercises, having reference to the adoption of the national flag be held in the public schools." [75]

In 1906, a proclamation of the governor of New Jersey, couched in grandiloquent phraseology, recommended that suitable exercises be held in the public schools for commemorating the birthday of the American flag. It urged a more extended knowledge of the flag's history. " The history of our flag is the history of the growth of our nation," he proclaimed, " and the celebration of the anniversary of its birth is not only a patriotic duty but an educational privilege. On the day of its inception it stood as an emblem

[72] *Ibid.*

[73] *Compiled Laws* of Michigan, 1915, *op. cit. General Laws* of Oregon, 1921, ch. 41, p. 62. This law, although coming in 1921, possesses the characteristics of those of the earlier period. See page 93. *Annotated Revision of Statutes of Louisiana,* 1915, 2659, 2660, secs. 1, 2, Vol. I, p. 893. (Act 56, 1919, p. 92.) West Virginia in 1911, also, set aside October 12 for celebration in the common and graded schools. *Laws,* 1911, ch. 40, p. 117.

[74] *Laws* of New York, *op. cit. Laws* of Arizona, *op. cit. Laws* of Kansas, *op. cit.*

[75] *Public Acts* of Connecticut, 1905, ch. 146, p. 355. Approved June 16, 1905. This amended 2140 of the *General Statutes.*

of the unity of a few modest little colonies. To-day it is the symbol of a mighty nation. It has floated over many a battlefield, inspiring the sons of patriotism with a courage and strength that made possible the triumph of the right and the preservation of the Union. It has been carried to far distant lands and has aroused the enthusiasm of thousands to whom its advent meant emancipation from cruelty and oppression." [76]

Reminiscent of the local history movement of the decades following the Civil War was legislation prescribing the celebration of days of interest peculiar to different states. In 1897, Massachusetts passed a resolution recommending to the governor that he issue a proclamation to public school teachers suggesting commemorative exercises for the centennial of the inauguration of " John Adams of Massachusetts," in order " to impress upon their pupils the significance of the inauguration of the president of the United States and the importance of the part sustained by the commonwealth in American history." [77]

" Rhode Island Independence Day " was acclaimed in 1909, for May the fourth. At this time, so the statute read, the celebration of the " first official act of its kind by any of the thirteen American colonies " in a declaration of sovereignty and independence took place. From the date of the passage of the law, every fourth of May in the future, it was determined, should become the occasion for the salute of thirteen guns by detachments of the state artillery, at all places in the state where artillery was stationed, besides a display of state and national flags, as well as patriotic exercises in the public schools. [78]

[76] Proclamation of the Governor of New Jersey (E. C. Stokes). *Laws*, 1906, p. 787.

[77] *Acts and Resolves* of Massachusetts, 1897, p. 628. This bill passed the Senate February 3, 1897, and the House on February 8, 1897.

[78] *General Laws* of Rhode Island, 1909, title X, ch. 64, sec. 8, p. 267.

March the eighteenth assumed a distinctive place in the school calendar of South Carolina by a law enacted in 1906, being known as " South Carolina Day." The selection of this date sprang from a desire to honor John C. Calhoun, and from the hope that an observance of this day would " conduce to a more general knowledge and appreciation of the history, resources and possibilities of the State." [79] In like spirit Georgia, in 1909, endeavored to awaken local pride in the pupils of the public schools by a celebration of " Georgia Day " on February twelfth, " as the landing of the first colonists in Georgia under Oglethorpe." [80] Confederate heroes received special tribute by patriotic exercises on January nineteenth, the birthday of Robert E. Lee, through a law of Arkansas. The program of exercises, the law prescribed, should deal with events connected with the life of General Lee and " other distinguished Southern men " with attention to those men of renown in civil and military life.[81]   In Maryland, the state board of education, by a law of 1904, was given the privilege of naming a time suitable for the observance of " Maryland Day." [82]

" The geography, history, industries and resources " of Minnesota, through a law of 1911, received especial attention in the public schools on " Minnesota Day." [83]   Montana, through a celebration of " Pioneer Day " endeavored to instruct in the pioneer history of the region.[84]   Missouri

[79] *Code* of South Carolina, 1912, par. 1810, Vol. I, p. 496. *Laws,* 1906, XXIII, 22; approved February 17, 1906.

[80] *Code* of Georgia, 1910, art. 7, par. 1528, Vol. I, p. 395. See page 96 for North Carolina's law setting aside October twelfth for commemoration. The next chapter continues the discussion for laws passed after 1917.

[81] *Digest* of Arkansas Statutes, 1916, sec. 9654, p. 2166.

[82] *Laws* of Maryland, 1904, sec. 47, p. 991.

[83] *Laws* of Minnesota, 1911, ch. 81, sec. 1, p. 97. The day known as Minnesota Day was designated by the superintendent of public instruction by proclamation, the governor concurring.

[84] *Laws* of Montana, 1913, ch. XIV, 1400, p. 263. In this year the first

paid homage to her state history in a law of 1915 through observance by teachers and pupils on the first Monday in October. At this time, the law prescribed the " methodical consideration of the products of the mine, field and forest of the state " and the " consideration of the achievements of the sons and daughters of Missouri in commerce, literature, statesmanship and art, and in other departments of activity in which the state has rendered service to mankind." [85] The American Indians, through a law of 1919, in Illinois, were likewise deemed worthy of commemorative exercises. [86]

The persisting desire of the lawmaker to instil patriotism, either local or national, in pupils in the public schools has been the incentive for laws respecting the flag and observance days. Local pride is evident in the Northern laws for the observance of Memorial Day and the birthday of Lincoln; whereas in the South a sectional interest is shown in days memorializing the heroes of their section. The Middle and Far West have also attempted to inculcate local pride. There is a dearth of legislation in the Southern states for the commemoration of Flag Day by special exercises, but Washington and Columbus have been accorded homage by both the North and the South.

TEXTBOOK LEGISLATION

Textbook legislation from 1900 to 1917 followed the trend of other legislation of the time. As the curriculum of the

Monday in November was named. A previous law, 1903, provided for an observance on the last Friday in May. (*Laws,* 1903, ch. LXXXVIII, p. 161.)

[85] *Laws* of Missouri, 1915, p. 301.

[86] *Laws* of Illinois, 1919, Sen. Bill, no. 238, p. 894. In a case such as this the law has been discussed here rather than in the following chapter. The chronological limits of the chapters have not always been strictly adhered to.

social studies expanded, laws dealing with textbooks were made to include more subjects for which there was to be a uniform series selected. State history and civil government, both local and national, as well as foreign history and other social studies, were found more frequently among the subjects enumerated. The reaction which had set in against the enforced nationalism of the Reconstruction period in the South continued to express itself in those states in which there had hitherto been no open remonstrance.

In 1904, the Mississippi legislature instructed the textbook commission to select a uniform series of textbooks in United States history, civil government, state history and other subjects, and took occasion to prescribe that " no history in relation to the late civil war between the states shall be used in the schools in this state unless it be fair and impartial, ..." [87]

Presumably of like character was the action of North Carolina in 1905. In " An Act to Promote the Production and Publication of School Books relating to the History, Literature or Government of North Carolina for use in the Public Schools," there was appropriated $5,000 for the years of 1905 and 1906 for the state board of education " to encourage, stimulate and promote the production and to procure the control and publication of such books as in the judgment of the board properly relate to the history, literature and government of North Carolina." [88]

Florida's sectionalism was openly avowed in her " Act for Providing a Method of Securing a Correct History of the United States, Including a True and Correct History of

[87] Approved March 11, 1904. The law also prohibited " partisan " books. *Laws* of Mississippi, 1904, ch. 86 (S. B. no. 51), p. 116. Also *Code*, 1906, ch. 125, 4595, p. 1246. *Cf.* chapter VI for the activities of pro-Southern groups in this period.

[88] Ratified March 4, 1905, *Laws* of North Carolina, 1905, ch. 707, p. 863.

the Confederacy, and Making an Appropriation for such Purpose." The act declared: " Whereas, no book called History, which does not tell the truth or withholds it, is worthy of the name or should be taught in public schools; and,

" Whereas, the South is rich in historical facts that are either ignored or never mentioned in the so-called histories taught in our schools; and,

" Whereas, the Southern States have been derelict in their duty to posterity in not having provided for past and future generations a history that is fair, just and impartial to all sections "; therefore it was enacted that Florida appropriate $1500 as her share toward a fund of $16,500 to be offered as a prize to the person writing the " best history of the United States in which the truth about the participation of the eleven states " be told.[89]

In the creation of a textbook board in 1907, Texas regarded it essential that a uniform series of books be selected among which there should be textbooks on the history of Texas, civil government and United States history, in which " the construction placed on the federal constitution by the Fathers of the Confederacy shall be fairly presented." [90]

A uniform series of textbooks not of a partisan character were prescribed by laws in Georgia, Alabama, Mississippi, and Kansas, and included the subjects of United States history, state history, and civil government.[91] Louisiana,

[89] *Laws* of Florida, 1915, ch. 6939 (no. 133), Vol. I, p. 311. Approved June 3, 1915. The appropriation was not available until each of eleven ex-Confederate states, or a majority of them, did likewise. The governor of Florida was appointed to communicate with other Southern governors about carrying out the act.

[90] *Laws* of Texas, 1907, ch. IX, p. 449. Approved May 14, 1907. The law of 1911 added general history to the list of books. *Laws,* 1911, ch. 11, sec. 4, p. 90.

[91] *Code* of Georgia, 1910, art. 1, sec. 2, par. ꞓ139, Vol. I, p. 367. Also

Indiana, and Kansas added ancient, medieval and modern history textbooks to others previously prescribed.[92]   In 1901 Nevada included the history of the United States among the textbooks to be prescribed by the state board of education,[93] and Idaho, in 1907, imposed the choice of a civil government textbook and one in United States history upon her State Board of Textbook Commissioners and the superintendent of public instruction.[94]   In 1913, California directed her state board of education to revise the state series of textbooks which included United States history.[95]

Three states, Ohio, New Mexico, and West Virginia placed laws upon their statute books regarding state history, Ohio accepting Howe's *Historical Collections of Ohio* as a reference book,[96] and New Mexico limiting to one dollar a volume the price of a state history which was to be prepared by a " known historian of the state." [97]   Davies' *Facts in Civil*

Laws, 1903, sec. 2, p. 54. *Laws* of Alabama, 1903, sec. 1, p. 167. *Code* of Mississippi, 1906, ch. 125, 4595, p. 1246. *Laws* of Kansas, 1915, ch. 297, p. 383.

[92] *Annotated Revision of the Statutes* of Louisiana, 1915, 2519, Vol. I, p. 841 (sec. 3, act 214, 1912, p. 465). The books were to remain unchanged for a period of six years. *Laws* of Indiana, 1913, ch. 58, p. 115. *Laws* of Kansas, 1915, ch. 297, p. 383. In Indiana, the price of the history of the United States to be used in the common schools, could not exceed 65 cents. Burns' *Annotated Statutes* of Indiana, 1914, 6338 (5867), Vol. III, p. 253.

[93] *Laws* of Nevada, 1901, p. 50. Approved March 8, 1901.

[94] *Revised Code* of Idaho, 1908, sec. 574, Vol. I, p. 370; *Laws* of 1907, sec. 3, p. 477. (Sen. Bill no. 84. Approved March 14, 1907.)   There was also found on the statute books Idaho's previous stipulation prohibiting political documents in the schools. *Compiled Statutes*, 1919, Vol. I, p. 297.

[95] *General Laws* of California, 1913, ch. 482, art. 4542, p. 1713.

[96] *Laws* of Ohio, 1892, p. 241; also *Code*, 1910, sec. 7719, p. 1635.

[97] *Statutes* of New Mexico, 1915, par. 4959, sec. 153, Vol. II, p. 1429. Act of June 8, 1912. Legislation in West Virginia, Oklahoma, and Wisconsin included the stereotyped restriction regarding " matter of a partisan character." See *Laws* of West Virginia, 1909, ch. 23, sec. 4, p. 346; *General Statutes* of Oklahoma, 1908, sec. 6324, p. 1313, *Laws* of 1907, ch. 77, p. 681; *Statutes* of Wisconsin, 1913, ch. 27, sec. 553m-12, p. 319, *ibid.*, 1915, ch. 27 s 553m-12, p. 330.

Government, by an act of 1901 of West Virginia was again endorsed and the price fixed at 55 cents.[98]

Four states, during the period, in addition to three commonwealths which named " partisan " textbooks, enacted laws to exclude histories held to be sectional in spirit. Legislation in all other cases dealt with provisions for a uniform series of textbooks. The statutes of Louisiana, Indiana, and Kansas showed the expansion of the social study curriculum in providing for textbooks in ancient, medieval and modern history. Georgia, Alabama, Mississippi and Kansas regulated the purchase of textbooks in state and national history and in civics. In California, Ohio, New Mexico and West Virginia provisions were made relative to state history textbooks, and Idaho and Nevada in their laws recognized a need for textbooks in civil government or United States history.

[98] *Code* of West Virginia, 1916, ch. 45, par. 165a, p. 599 (Acts of 1901, ch. 141).

CHAPTER IV

THE EFFECT OF THE WORLD WAR ON LAWS FOR TEACHING HISTORY

THE CURRICULUM

When the Fathers of New England adopted the famous laws of 1642 and 1647, they acted on the belief that by the school the character of the nation can be moulded. Throughout nearly three centuries of development the confidence of the American people in the regenerating power of the public school has grown. They have come to hold high faith in education as an effective tool for the conservation and promotion of national well-being. In each epoch, the school has attempted to accommodate its offerings to the demands of the time, thereby reflecting the needs of a people whose point of view is constantly changing. First conceived as a force in the religious life of the people, the school soon became an instrument for the development of " morality, virtue and good behavior." The latter eighteenth century captured the vision of a people fired with patriotism and service to the state, and then by a citizenry trained to " preserve and perfect a republican constitution." The occasion of a diverse and scattered electorate caused by the democratic awakening of the Jacksonian era compelled acceptance of the theory that it was a duty of the state to provide education for all. After the Civil War, a renewed faith in nationality and a realization of the economic and social demands of the time left their imprint upon the public school curriculum.

The opening of the twentieth century witnessed the expansion of the "citizenship aim" to include training for efficient participation in a complex social and industrial life. Since then, many traditional subjects of the previous period have been superseded by those tending to give point to the new aims in education; and of the traditional subjects retained many have been refashioned to fit a new and present-day point of view.

This wider horizon has tended to encourage to a greater degree than hitherto the introduction of many social studies, including economics, sociology and foreign history. Although encumbered with survivals, the history curriculum of the twentieth century has sought independence of purely political and military events and has striven for a scientific presentation of historical truths which should fit for " complete living." This new viewpoint was well exemplified in the report of a committee of the National Education Association in 1916, which proposed a six year course in the social studies from the seventh to the twelfth grades, stressing the teaching of practical and present-day problems.[1]

Shortly thereafter the United States entered the World War. America at once faced not only the necessity of mobilizing the economic and military resources of a country unprepared for war, but also that still more difficult problem — the consolidation of public opinion. Various agencies were created for the express purpose of coördinating the spiritual resources of the country. Such was the design of the Committee on Public Information. Speakers and writers gave freely of their talents, and " hyphenism " and pacifism were driven to cover. The Espionage Law betrayed the

---

[1] *Report of the Committee on Social Studies of the Commission on the Reorganization of Secondary Education of the National Education Association,* " The Social Studies in Secondary Education," Bulletin, 1916, No. 28, Department of the Interior (Washington, 1916).

apprehension of the federal government regarding unbridled speech and writing, and sedition laws in different commonwealths served to arrest an open opposition to the War.

Following the War the fear of radicalism and disloyalty to the established institutions of the country continued to express itself in drastic legislation. In the public schools, the desire to develop an unalloyed patriotism proved the motive for the passage of statutes to promote a dynamic loyalty. In general, these laws relate to the teaching of patriotism through instruction in the history and government of the United States, open affirmations of loyalty by the teaching personnel, the exclusion of alien teachers from the public schools, flag legislation and observance days, enactments regarding textbooks, and the Americanization of foreigners. Practically all legislation since 1917 dealing with the curriculum contains provisions pertaining to the social studies, and the greater amount reflects the wartime glow of patriotic enthusiasm.[2]

In 1917 three states passed regulatory provisions respecting the curriculum. Vermont's legislation dealt with four-year high schools and required the teaching of the political and social sciences.[3] On February 17, Montana approved a law which called for instruction in United States history, the history of Montana, and state and federal civics among other required subjects for the elementary school, and three days later Arkansas approved a similar law.[4] New Hampshire, Connecticut, Pennsylvania, Kentucky and Texas continued laws enacted at a previous time,[5] and Delaware,

---

[2] According to a statement in *The New York Times*, March 30, 1924, the National Security League has been partly responsible for many enactments requiring the teaching of the federal constitution.

[3] *General Laws* of Vermont, 1917, ch. 60, sec. 1277, p. 301.

[4] *Laws* of Montana, 1917, ch. 128, par. 601, p. 309; *Digest of the Statutes of Arkansas*, 1919, ch. 158, par. 9066, p. 547. Accepted February 20, 1917.

[5] In 1921, New Hampshire included in her curriculum the study of

through legislation in 1919 gained the unique distinction of
prescribing " community civics " besides the history of the
nation and of the state.[6] Alabama and Georgia under laws
designed primarily to prescribe a uniform series of textbooks
included in the list of studies for which textbooks were
mentioned, the history of the state embracing the constitution of the state, and the history of the United States with
the constitution.[7] In Tennessee, to the requirement of
United States history for the elementary schools, was added
in 1917 the study of the federal constitution in the secondary
school curriculum.[8] Texas placed distinct emphasis upon
the teaching of state history through a regulation insisting
that this " history be taught in the history course in all
public schools " and " in this course only." [9] The popularity
of civil government, state history, and United States history
is further proved by South Dakota's prescription in 1919.[10]

Laws for dynamic patriotism were initiated by a statute

history and civil government in a law to reinstate foreign languages as a
study in the public schools. In 1919 history and civics were required for
all schools. *Laws* of New Hampshire, 1921, ch. 85, sec. 10(3), p. 125;
ibid., 1919, ch. 106, sec. 13(1). In 1918, Connecticut carried over a law
from the *Revision* of 1902 prescribing United States history, *General Statutes* of Connecticut, 1918, ch. 44, sec. 835, Vol. I, p. 308. Pennsylvania
incorporated a law of 1911 prescribing instruction in general history and
civil government in her *Statute Law* of 1920, *Digest of the Statute Law* of
Pennsylvania, 1920, par. 5102, p. 470. In Kentucky, United States history,
state history and civil government were required in 1918, carried over from
a law of 1893. *Statutes* of Kentucky, 1918, art. III, par. 4383, Vol. III, p.
866; *Laws*, 1916, ch. 24, art. III, sec. 24, p. 162. In Texas in the *Compiled
Statutes* of 1920, was again included a law requiring the teaching of civil
government and state and national history. *Statutes* of Texas, 1920, art.
2783, p. 467.

[6] *Laws* of Delaware, 1919, 2283, sec. 11, p. 356. This is found also in
Laws, Special Session, 1920, 97th Assembly, sec. 12, Vol. XXXI, p. 113.

[7] *General Laws* of Alabama, 1919, art. 3, p. 571; *Acts* of Georgia, 1919,
sec. 18, p. 295.

[8] *Compilation of the Statutes of Tennessee*, 1917, art. XV, 1453, Vol. I,
p. 983, *ibid.*, 1454.

[9] *Statutes* of Texas, *op. cit.*

[10] *Laws* of South Dakota, 1919, sec. 7511, p. 154.

of California in 1917. One of the mildest of the laws of this type, its chief purpose was training in the duties of citizenship through the study of United States history, with special reference to the history of the Constitution and the reasons for the adoption of each constitutional provision. Instruction in local civil government was provided for as well, with a specific statement regarding instruction in the duties of citizenship.[11]

In 1918, South Dakota, Texas and New York placed upon their statute books laws that were likewise a direct outgrowth of the war spirit. In the first two states, patriotism, the laws declared, should spring from lessons of "intelligent patriotism" inculcated by special exercises. The South Dakota law specified an hour a week in the aggregate, to be devoted in both public and private institutions " to the teaching of patriotism, the singing of patriotic songs, the reading of patriotic addresses and a study of the lives and history of American patriots." Should an instructor, school officer or superintendent fail to enforce obedience to the law the statute provided for a fine of not less than five dollars nor more than one hundred dollars, or imprisonment in the county jail from five to thirty days, or both. In the case of the malfeasance of a teacher, the superintendent of public instruction had the power to revoke his certificate.[12]

In Texas, the law declared that " the daily program of every public school should be so formulated that it includes at least ten minutes for the teaching of lessons of intelligent

[11] *Laws* of California, 1917, ch. 549, p. 728. Approved May 18, 1917. It was the same for the social studies for the elementary schools in 1921. *Statutes*, 1921, ch. 486, p. 739. A law of Illinois in which instruction was to be devoted to " raising the standard of good citizenship " was passed in 1909, and was still on the statute books in 1917. *Revised Statutes*, 1917, p. 273.

[12] *Revised Code* of South Dakota, 1919, par. 7660, p. 1917. Source 1918, ch. 39.

patriotism, including the needs of the State and Federal Governments, the duty of the citizens to the State, and the obligation of the State to the citizen." [13] The statute concluded with this statement: " The fact that this nation is now at war with a foreign foe, and that the strength of a government of the people, by the people, and for the people must necessarily come of its citizenship, creates an emergency and an imperative public necessity that the constitutional rule requiring bills to be read on three several days be suspended and that this act shall be in force from and after its passage, and it is so enacted." [14]

New York's statute, known as the Lusk Law, is the most conspicuous of all of the laws of this period because of its drastic character and its later applications. This law became effective September 1, 1918. The phase of the law relating to instruction had two parts: one prescribing courses of instruction in patriotism and citizenship, the other specifying rules for inspection, supervision, and enforcement of the law.

" In order to promote a spirit of patriotic and civic service and obligation and to foster in the children of the state moral and intellectual qualities which are essential in preparing to meet the obligations of citizenship in peace or in war," the law declared, " the regents of the university of the state of New York shall prescribe courses of instruction in patriotism and citizenship to be maintained and followed in the schools of the state. The boards of education and trustees of the several cities and school districts of the state shall require instruction to be given in such courses, by the teachers employed in the schools therein. All pupils

[13] *Statutes* of Texas, 1920, art. 2904, aa, p. 492. *Acts*, 1918, ch. 17, sec. 1, p. 29.
[14] *Ibid.*, approved March 20, 1918.

attending such schools, over the age of eight years, shall attend upon such instruction."

The statute further prescribed similar courses of instruction for private schools, and was required of all pupils over eight years of age. In case such courses were not maintained in the private school, attendance upon instruction in such school was not deemed equivalent to instruction given to pupils of like age in the public schools.

The law empowered the regents of the University of the State of New York to determine the subjects to be included in courses in patriotism and citizenship, and to arrange such other matters as were required for carrying into effect the objects and purposes of the law. The commissioner of education was made responsible for its enforcement, and to him fell the supervision and inspection of instruction. He was given authority at his discretion to withhold, from a school district or city, school money, if the authorities neglected such courses or failed to compel attendance upon such instruction.[15]

In 1918, Massachusetts subscribed to training in the duties of citizenship, including United States history, civil government, and thrift in her public schools; and two years later, in a statute relating to all elementary and secondary schools, she prescribed " courses in American history and civics for the purpose of promoting civic service and a greater knowledge of American history and of fitting the pupils, morally and intellectually, for the duties of citizenship." [16]

[15] *Laws* of New York, 1918, ch. 241, art. XXVI-C, secs. 705, 706, pp. 886–887. See the discussion under Oaths of Allegiance as Teacher Requirements for a statement regarding the repeal of the Lusk Law.

[16] *General Acts* of Massachusetts, 1918, pp. 294–295; *Acts,* 1920, ch. 411, p. 418. *General Statutes* of Connecticut, 1918, ch. 45, sec. 852, Vol. I, p. 312. In 1903, Connecticut was a pioneer in this form of law, which was slightly changed in 1915. At this time it was prescribed that normal schools

In 1919, New Jersey, Pennsylvania, Ohio, Iowa, Kansas and Washington passed laws of like character. Although each embodies certain distinctive features, yet all assert a belief in the study of American history and government as a preparation for a patriotic citizenship.

The New Jersey law contains concrete requirements. In each high school, courses of study in " Community Civics " and in " Problems in American Democracy " were prescribed through the agency of the Commissioner of Education, with the approval of the State Board of Education. The law required that " Community Civics " be completed not later than the end of the second year, and the course in " Problems of American Democracy " be commenced not later than the beginning of the third year. Sixty full periods of not less than forty minutes each were specified for the teaching of these subjects. For the elementary grades, the geography, history and civics of New Jersey were prescribed. These courses of study, the law provided, " shall be given together with instruction as to the privileges and responsibilities of citizenship as they relate to community and national welfare with the object of producing the highest type of patriotic citizenship." [17]

In Pennsylvania, too, it has become a duty of the state superintendent of public instruction to prescribe " a course of study conducive to the spirit of loyalty and devotion to the state and national governments," and for all elementary public schools instruction in the history of the state and nation, including the elements of civil government. [18] For

and teacher training schools should give instruction concerning methods of teaching citizenship, including the knowledge of the form of the national and local governments. Connecticut left her law of 1915 unchanged in her *General Statutes* of 1918.

[17] *Acts* of New Jersey, 1919, ch. 125, p. 304.

[18] *Laws* of Pennsylvania, 1919, sec. 1607, pp. 544–545. Amends an act of May 18, 1911. In 1921 the law relating to courses of instruction for

the seventh and eighth grades Ohio prescribed civil government and United States history; and Iowa, as a prerequisite to graduation from any high school, required a course in United States history and civil government for one year, as well as the offering of a semester of social problems and economics in a four-year high school. In Kansas, where the course in civil government and United States history was designed for the elementary grades, provision was made, in the case of noncompliance with the law, for the closing of the school by the action of the county attorney or the attorney-general. It was in a like spirit with other commonwealths that Washington declared the " study of American history and American government " to be " indispensable to good citizenship and an accurate appreciation of national ideals." [19] A similar provision, with the aim of promoting " Americanism " and in training in the " ideals and principles underlying the government of the United States," met defeat in Maryland in 1920 by the veto of the governor.[20]

The year 1921 was particularly prolific in legislation of a wartime character. A variety of expression but a unity of purpose continued to be in evidence. Laws were enacted in Maine, New Hampshire, Wisconsin, Michigan, Illinois,

---

public and private elementary schools was amended but carried with it the requirement of United States history, history of Pennsylvania, and civics including " loyalty to the state and national government." Commonwealth of Pennsylvania, Department of Public Instruction, *The School Law* . . . 1921, sec. 1607, p. 116.

[19] *Laws* of Ohio, 1919, secs. 7645 and 7762, p. 542. Approved June 6, 1919. *Acts* of Iowa, 1919, ch. 406, p. 535. Approved April 25, 1919. Private as well as public schools were included. *Laws* of Kansas, 1919, ch. 257, secs. 2 and 3, p. 352; *Session Laws* of Washington, 1919, p. 50. Alabama in 1919 added community civics to her elementary school curriculum but merely enumerated her subjects. *General Laws* of Alabama, 1919, art. 3, sec. 7, p. 571.

[20] *Laws* of Maryland, 1920, ch. 656, p. 1248.

Iowa, Nebraska, Oklahoma, Colorado, Utah, Arizona, Nevada, New Mexico, and California.

The Maine statute prescribed the teaching of American history and civil government in all elementary and high school grades, both private and public, and made these subjects a requirement for graduation from all grammar schools.[21] The law of her neighbor, New Hampshire, required the reading of the constitution of the United States and of New Hampshire " at least once a year in the last grade below the high school." [22]

In line with the other states Michigan declared, by a statute of May 17, 1921, that the study of the state and federal constitutions should begin not later than the eighth grade and continue throughout the high school course to an extent to be decided upon by the state superintendent of public instruction.[23] In Wisconsin, provision was made for instruction in the history and civil government of the United States and of Wisconsin, and in citizenship,[24] and Illinois, on June 21, 1921, passed " An Act to make the teaching of representative government in the public schools and other educational institutions in the State of Illinois compulsory." [25] This law endorsed the teaching of patriotism through a knowledge of " the principles of representative government, as enumerated in the Declaration of Independence and the Constitution of the United States and the Constitution of the State of Illinois," and was required in all schools maintained in whole or in part by state funds. The law provided, also, for one hour of such instruction

[21] *Resolves* of Maine, 1921, ch. 25, p. 27.
[22] *Laws* of New Hampshire, 1921, ch. 85, sec. 5(3), p. 114.
[23] *Acts* of Michigan, 1921, no. 209, secs. 1, 2. *Cf.* Iowa's law of 1921, page 80.
[24] *Wisconsin Session Laws*, 1921, ch. 81, p. 152. Amends sec. 40. 30.
[25] *Laws* of Illinois, 1921 (House Bill, no. 483), pp. 820–821.

each week in the seventh and eighth grades, with an equal amount of time in the high school.

On March 31, 1921, Iowa added to her requirements a provision that all public and private schools should give regular courses of instruction in the constitution of the state and nation, beginning not later than the eighth grade and continuing in the high school to an extent to be determined by the superintendent of public instruction. A Nebraska statute of that year established for all schools courses in American history and civil government to give "a thorough knowledge of the history of our country and its institutions and of our form of government." [26]

In Oklahoma, instruction in American history must commence in the primary grades of all schools, both public and private, beginning with the lowest and continuing through all primary years, with the privilege of substituting state history in one of the grades. For this instruction, there should be allotted at least one hour each week. It was specifically stated that the purpose of the statute was to instil in the hearts of the pupils "an understanding of the United States and of a love of country and devotion to the principles of American government," and that "such instruction . . . shall avoid, as far as possible, being a mere recital of dates and events." For the high school, at least one full year's work in American history and civics was required, and no college, normal school, university or chartered institution of learning in the state was allowed to confer a degree until a student had passed a course in American history and civil government. [27]

---

[26] *Acts* of Iowa, 1921 (S. F. 770), pp. 81–82; *Laws* of Nebraska, 1921, ch. 53, sec. 6924, p. 230.

[27] *Acts* of Oklahoma, 1921, ch. 112, secs. 1, 2, 3, 4. The state superintendent of instruction had power of enforcement. In case of a violation a fine of not less than $100 and not more than $500 or imprisonment in

The social study requirement of Colorado for her public schools consisted of the history and civil government of the state,[28] and Arizona in her law specified that not less than two years' instruction in civics, economics, and American political history and government be provided for all common schools, high schools, normal schools and universities.[29] Nevada, in her enactment of February 24, compelled all schools including colleges, save exclusively scientific schools, to teach American history, history of the state, and American civil government.[30] Included as a part of this law was a provision for patriotic exercises for at least an hour in each school week. New Mexico, declaring that the passage of a law prescribing the teaching of national and state history and government was " necessary for the public peace and safety," made the statute effective immediately,[31] and California again essayed an endorsement of the history of the state and nation with emphasis upon the adoption of the Constitution.[32]

In 1922 the commonwealth of Virginia enacted a law similar to those passed the previous year in fourteen other states. By this statute, pupils enrolled in the public free schools are taught civil government, history of the United States and the history of Virginia. The 1922 session of the Rhode Island legislature adopted much the same kind of a provision for all public and private schools by making oblig-

---

the county jail for not less than thirty days nor more than six months, or both, may be the penalty. A teacher is subject to discharge or removal in case of malfeasance and a college (corporation) is liable to a revocation of its charter.

[28] *Laws* of Colorado, 1921, ch. 216, p. 728. Approved April 5, 1921.

[29] *Acts* of Arizona, 1921, ch. 140, sec. 1, p. 312.

[30] *Statutes* of Nevada, 1921, p. 28 (Senate Bill No. 43).

[31] *Laws* of New Mexico, 1921, ch. 172, p. 364. See law of 1912, page 52.

[32] *Statutes* of California, 1921, ch. 486, p. 739. See page 43.

atory the teaching of the principles of popular and representative government and the history of Rhode Island.[33]

An adherence to the early method of endorsing the teaching of patriotism characterized enactments in Idaho, Nevada, and Utah. In the last state, instruction " tending to impress upon the minds of the pupils the importance and necessity of good manners, truthfulness, temperance, purity, patriotism, and industry," was prescribed in connection with the regular school work.[34] Nevada, four years before the passage of Utah's law, provided for civic training in her high schools, whose purpose was to " inculcate a love of country and a disposition to serve the country effectively and loyally," both in times of peace and of war.[35]

Idaho, through the office of the teacher, continued the practice of prescribing the teaching of patriotism as a duty of the teacher through that intangible method of impressing upon the minds of the pupils "the principles of truth, justice, morality, and patriotism." [36] Wisconsin, also, sanctioned moral instruction through training by the teacher.[37]

Since 1923, nineteen states have passed laws affecting the social study curriculum. In general, their purpose is to

[33] *Acts* of Virginia, 1922, p. 69 (amending section 702 of the *Code*). *Virginia School Laws*, 1923, p. 41; *Public Laws* of Rhode Island, 1922, ch. 2195, sec. 17.

[34] *Laws* of Utah, 1921, ch. 95, p. 284. Approved March 5, 1921.

[35] *Laws* of Nevada, 1917, ch. 146, p. 245. Approved March 21, 1917. This was less than one month before the United States entered the World War, and the avowal of service in peace or in war, therefore, acquires a peculiar significance. See page 81 for Nevada's law of 1921.

[36] *Compiled Statutes* of Idaho, 1919, p. 269, par. 944. From the *Political Code*, 1901, sec. 1067, Vol. I, p. 329. See page 21 for the first discussion of the law.

[37] " In all public schools of this state it shall be the duty of each and every teacher to teach morality, for the purpose of elevating and refining the character of school children up to the highest plane of life; that they may know how to conduct themselves as social beings in relation to each other, as respects right and wrong and rectitude of life, . . ." *Statutes* of Wisconsin, 1917, 40. 30 (5), p. 376.

instil " into the hearts of the various pupils . . . an understanding of the United States, . . . a love of country, and . . . a devotion to the principles of the American Government." [38]

Through statutes passed in 1923, Arkansas, Mississippi, Ohio, Tennessee and West Virginia require the teaching of United States history and the Constitution; and Kansas adopted the same requirement in 1925.[39] Instruction in the federal constitution is prescribed in Alabama, Idaho, New Jersey, Oregon and Utah by enactments in 1923, and in New York by a law of 1924. Statutes in Delaware and North Carolina[40] require the study of the constitutions of the nation and the state, and Texas adds to that regulation a recommendation that special emphasis be placed on " the guarantees contained in the Bill of Rights." [41] The Minnesota law prescribes for all schools " regular courses in the Declaration of Independence and the Constitution of the

[38] Statement of the Arkansas law. *Cf.* Oklahoma law passed in 1921, page 80.

[39] *Digest of School Laws . . . of Arkansas . . . 1923*, p. 166. Approved March 23, 1923, this law provides that no person can graduate from high school without at least one full year's work in American history and civics. *School Laws of Mississippi*, 1924, ch. 283, p. 3; *School Laws of Ohio*, 1923, p. 41; *Public School Laws of Tennessee* . . . 1923, p. 35; *Acts of West Virginia*, 1923, ch. 10, sec. 92, p. 40; State of Kansas, Senate Bill No. 13, repealing Sec. 72-1103 of the *Revised Statutes* of Kansas, 1923.

[40] *Laws* of Alabama, 1923, p. 87, approved July 27, 1923; *School Laws of the State of Idaho* (1923), p. 57; *Acts* of New Jersey, 1923, ch. 17, p. 17; *Laws* of Oregon, 1923, ch. 7, sec. 102; *Laws* of Utah, 1923, ch. 4, approved January 27, 1923; *Laws* of New York, 1924, ch. 64, article 26-d, sec. 707, approved March 24, 1924. *School Laws of Delaware*, 1923, pp. 62-63. *The Public School Law of North Carolina Codification* of 1923, p. 120.

[41] *School Legislation of the Thirty-Eighth Legislature* (of Texas), pp. 36-37. The Texas requirement comes through a resolution of the Senate of the state with the House of Representatives concurring, because " the American Bar Association, the Texas Bar Association, the bar associations of various other states, as well as other patriotic societies, are advocating the teaching of the Constitutions of the United States and of the several states in the public schools."

United States, to an extent to be determined by the State Commissioner of Education." [42]   In New Mexico a similar enactment requires an understanding of the Declaration of Independence, as well as a knowledge of state and national history and government.[43]

For her schools California establishes " regular courses of instruction in the constitution of the United States, including the study of American institutions and ideals," and Georgia adopts a similar requirement adding the study of state government.   In both states it is provided that no pupil shall receive a certificate of graduation who has not passed satisfactorily examinations in the required subjects.[44]

Substantially all these enactments provide that instruction in the required subjects shall begin in the elementary grades, continue in the high school and in courses in state colleges, universities and educational departments of state and municipal institutions to an extent to be determined by the superintendent of public instruction or by the state board of education.[45]

Endorsement of the study of the Constitution was given by Congress in March, 1925, when the Senate passed a

[42] *Laws* of Minnesota, 1923, ch. 291, p. 388.   Approved April 17, 1923.

[43] *Laws* of New Mexico, 1923, ch. 148, sec. 1417, p. 325; also *New Mexico School Code*, 1923, p. 34.

[44] *Statutes* of California, 1923, ch. 176, secs. 1 and 2.   *Georgia School Code* . . . 1923, p. 70, approved August 20, 1923.

[45] The following provide that the course start not later than the eighth grade: *Statutes* of California, 1923, ch. 176; *Laws* of Alabama, 1923, p. 87, law approved July 27, 1923; *School Laws of Delaware*, 1923, pp. 62–63, approved March 14, 1923; *School Laws of the State of Idaho* (1923), p. 57; *Laws* of Minnesota, 1923, ch. 291, p. 388, approved April 17, 1923; *Oregon School Laws*, 1923, p. 39, *Laws*, 1923, ch. 7, sec. 102; *Public School Laws* of Tennessee, 1923, p. 35, *Laws* of Tennessee, 1923, ch. 17, sec. 1, pp. 61–62.   In New Jersey, the seventh grade is prescribed for the beginning of the study. *Acts* of New Jersey, 1923, ch. 17, p. 17.   In Arkansas, it is required that " such teaching shall commence in the lowest primary grade," but Arkansas history may be substituted for American history in one of the grades. *Digest of School Laws of Arkansas, op. cit.*

House resolution expressing "the earnest hope and desire that every educational institution, whether public or private, will provide and maintain as a part of the required curriculum, a course for the study of the Constitution of the United States. . . ."

The many laws enacted during the years following the World War are indicative of the high value placed upon the social studies as an essential part of education. Besides laws requiring the teaching of these subjects purely for their content, many enactments express a high faith that the social studies will serve to inculcate patriotism and to train for citizenship. Forty-three commonwealths have engaged in legislation of this character since 1917, and all states have at some time endorsed history as a required subject in the public schools.[46]

OATHS OF ALLEGIANCE AND CITIZENSHIP FOR TEACHERS

Few laws requiring American citizenship and oaths of allegiance, in the case of teachers, appeared on the statute books prior to 1914. The World War precipitated the movement for enactments which insist upon an openly avowed loyalty, as well as upon a teaching personnel consisting of citizens only.[47]

[46] *Congressional Record*, 68th Cong., 2d Sess., Vol. LXVI, No. 77, pp. 5396–5398. The five states not enacting social study laws for the curriculum (1917 to 1924) are Florida, Maryland, Missouri, North Dakota, and South Carolina.

[47] Few states during this period have enacted new laws requiring the examination of teachers in the social studies. Nevada, by a law of 1921, has required United States history, civics and current events for elementary school certificates. *Laws* of Nevada, 1921, ch. 208, sec. 25, p. 302. In 1923, Tennessee prescribed that all persons applying for a certificate to become teachers or superintendents in the public schools must pass a satisfactory examination upon the provisions and the principles of the Constitution of the United States. *Laws* of Tennessee, 1923, ch. 17, sec. 2. Washington, likewise, by an enactment of 1923, has prescribed United

In 1915, three states enacted anti-alien laws for teaching. A Michigan statute required a teacher, if twenty-one years of age, to be a citizen of the United States.[48] Nevada directed the superintendent of public instruction, the regents of the state university and school trustees to dismiss " any teacher, . . . , professor or president employed by the educational department of this state who is not a citizen of the United States; or who has not declared his or her intention to become a citizen." The law forbade any state controller or county auditor to issue salary warrants to the persons mentioned, in case of non-citizenship.[49]

In California a law of 1915 prescribed that " no person except a native-born or naturalized citizen of the United States, should be employed in any department of the state, county, city and county or city-government of this state." An exception, however, was made in favor of teachers who had declared their intention to become naturalized and of any native-born wife of a foreigner.[50]

In 1917, the one hundred and fortieth session of the New

States history for a standard elementary certificate. *Laws* of Washington, 1923, p. 579. Florida, in 1923, enacted legislation requiring United States history, including the Constitution of the United States for primary and third grade certificates, civics for second grade, and general history, in addition to the other social studies for a first grade license. *Compilation of School Laws of Florida*, 1923, *Supplement*, pp. 4–5. Maryland, in 1922, required United States and Maryland history and community civics for elementary school certificates. *Maryland Public School Laws*, 1922, p. 40. See pages 52–56. Iowa, in 1924, made mandatory a knowledge of " the fundamental principles of a republican form of government and the Constitution of the United States and of the State of Iowa." *Code* of Iowa, 1924, ch. 193, sec. 3862. Kansas, in 1925, prescribed United States history and civil government for certification. See Senate Bill No. 13, 1925.

    [48] *Public Acts* of Michigan, 1915, p. 13.
    [49] *Statutes of Nevada*, 1915, ch. 274, secs. 1, 2, 3, 4. Approved March 26, 1915.
    [50] *Statutes* of California, 1915, approved May 20, 1915. *School Laws* of California, 1921, p. 203. This law does not forbid aliens to teach in colleges and universities.

York legislature gave its assent to a bill which has become known as one of the Lusk laws. This law reflects precisely the same sort of apprehension which moved some of the legislators of the Civil War period. It became the precursor of three others of a like nature, one in 1918, one in 1919, and one in 1921. The law of 1917 related to treasonable or seditious utterances by teachers, the second and third to the granting of teachers' licenses to citizens only, and the fourth to the employment of teachers who have criticized the government of the United States.

The law of 1917 relating to freedom of speech prescribed that "a person employed as superintendent of schools, teacher or employee in the public schools, . . . shall be removed from such position for the utterance of any treasonable or seditious act, or acts, while holding such position." [51] The laws of 1918 and 1919 made citizenship an essential qualification for becoming a teacher. Any person employed as a teacher on April 4, 1918, however, who was not naturalized, was given permission to remain in his position provided he, within a year, should make application for citizenship. The law of 1919 exempted from the foregoing requirement teachers who were citizens of the Allied Powers in the World War, and who had been employed as teachers in the New York schools on or prior to April 4, 1918, provided that "such teacher make application to become a citizen before the first day of September, 1920, and within the time thereafter prescribed by law shall become such citizen." [52]

The third link in the chain of constraint was an enactment which declared that an applicant, even though a citizen, must be "a person of good moral character" and must

[51] See page 76. *Laws* of New York, 1917, ch. 416, par. 568, Vol. II, p. 1280.

[52] *Ibid.*, 1919, ch. 120, 3, p. 218. Law, March 31, 1919. *Ibid.*, 1918, ch. 158, par. 550, p. 749. Approved April 4, 1918.

be "loyal and obedient to the government of this state and of the United States," in order to obtain a license to teach. For "no such certificate shall be issued to any person who, while a citizen of the United States, has advocated either by word of mouth or in writing, a change in the form of government of the United States or of this state, by force, violence or any unlawful means." The statute provided that the discovery that a teacher were guilty of any of the prohibitions mentioned, made him liable to a revocation of his certificate through the commissioner of education.[53] The sum of $15,000 was appropriated to carry the act into effect.[54]

Much discussion and agitation attended the Lusk laws after their passage and in the attempts at their enforcement, for many believed that the right of free speech was endangered by such measures. In 1923, under considerable pressure, the legislature revoked the statute, and Governor Alfred E. Smith affixed his signature to the repeal.

Laws similar to the statutes passed by New York are found in Ohio, Michigan, West Virginia, Tennessee, Oklahoma, Nebraska, South Dakota, Nevada, Idaho, Montana, and Washington. In 1919, Michigan, Nebraska, Tennessee, Montana, and Washington enacted statutes requiring that all teachers of the public schools must be citizens of the United States, and Idaho retained upon her statute books a law of 1897 which had the same intent. The same action was taken by North Dakota in 1921. In addition to those engaged as instructors in the public schools, Nebraska included teachers in private and parochial institutions. In Washington, California and Michigan the privilege of a license was granted to those aliens who declared their intention of becoming citizens, and in Washington, there were

---

[53] *Ibid.*, 1921, par. 555a, Vol. III, p. 2048.   [54] *Ibid.*

added to the proscribed group, those teachers whose certificates or diplomas had been revoked on account of a failure to impress upon the minds of the pupils " the principles of patriotism or to train them up to a true comprehension of the rights, duty, and dignity of American citizenship." [55]

An open declaration of loyalty and of an intention to inculcate patriotism in their pupils was required of all teachers by Ohio in a law of 1919, by Colorado, Nevada, Oklahoma, Oregon, and South Dakota in 1921. Ohio, Colorado, Oklahoma, Arizona, and South Dakota made it incumbent upon teachers not only in the public schools, but in private and parochial schools, to take an oath to support the constitution of the state and of the United States and to obey their laws. Ohio insisted upon an " undivided allegiance to the government of one country, the United States of America," and Colorado and Oregon sanctioned the same form.[56] Nevada required of teachers the oath in her constitution, prescribed for all public officers.[57] In Oklahoma, any teacher violating the law, or any person or officer paying out any school funds

[55] *Laws* of Washington, 1919, sec. 1, p. 82; *Laws* of Nebraska, 1919, ch. 250, sec. 1, p. 1020; *Acts* of Michigan, 1919 (no. 220), sec. 1, p. 392; *Laws* of Tennessee, 1919, ch. 91, p. 223; *Compiled Statutes* of Idaho, 1919, par. 946, Vol. 1, p. 270. Idaho, in her *Laws* of 1921, has another enactment, but it has the same purpose; *Laws* of 1921, sec. 77, p. 464. *Laws* of Montana, 1919, ch. 196, sec. 18, p. 429, amending law of 1905, by which any teacher holding a certificate and not a citizen was given time (six months) to declare his intention. *Political Code*, ch. 77, sec. 1912, p. 167. For California's law see *School Law of California*, 1921, p. 203. North Dakota's previous citizenship requirement is discussed on page 34. See *Laws* of North Dakota, 1921, ch. 111, p. 90. According to letters received from the state superintendents of Mississippi and Maryland, aliens are not permitted to teach in those states.

[56] *Laws* of Ohio, 1919, supplements 7852 of *General Code*, sec. 7852–1, p. 514. *Laws* of Colorado, 1921, ch. 213, sec. 1, p. 719. *Laws* of Oregon, 1921, ch. 115, p. 226, approved February 18, 1921.

[57] *Statutes* of Nevada, 1921, sec. 38, p. 303. Approved March 22, 1921. This was required of all teachers paid by the state, even those in the University.

to a person teaching without subscribing to the oath, was deemed guilty of a misdemeanor. Upon conviction such a person was penalized by a fine of not less than one hundred or more than five hundred dollars, or imprisonment in the county jail from sixty days to six months, or both.[58] Oregon, upon conviction, prescribed a maximum fine of one hundred dollars for non-enforcement of the law.

In West Virginia, a law of 1923 has enjoined upon all teachers, at the time of signing a yearly contract, an oath to support the constitution of the United States and West Virginia.[59]

In addition to the regulations imposing an oath of allegiance on teachers, South Dakota, like Washington, in her law included a prohibition of treasonable utterances. " Any teacher," the law declared, " who shall have publicly reviled, ridiculed or otherwise spoken or acted with disrespect and contumacy towards the flag of the United States or its official uniforms or insignia, or towards the system of government of the United States, and its Constitution, or shall refuse to take and subscribe to the oath of allegiance hereinbefore required, shall thereafter forever be disqualified to teach in any public or private school within this state, and the certificate of any such teacher shall be revoked by the superintendent of public instruction upon satisfactory proof of the commission of any such offense." [60]

An Oklahoma statute has excluded from all public and

[58] *Acts* of Oklahoma, 1921, ch. 15, p. 141. Approved March 24, 1921.
[59] *The School Law of West Virginia*, 1923, p. 44. According to the superintendents of public instruction in Rhode Island and Kansas a pledge to support the national and state constitutions is a requirement in those states for all teachers. See *Teachers' Pledge of Loyalty*, Rhode Island Public Education Service, and *Teachers Contract*, State of Kansas.
[60] *Laws* of South Dakota, 1921, ch. 210, p. 317. Approved February 1, 1921. This law became effective at once, because it was " necessary for the immediate preservation of the public safety and for the support of the state government and its existing public institutions."

private schools of that state persons " guilty of teaching or inculcating disloyalty to the United States or of publicly reviling the flag, or the system of government of the United States." Yet the statute prescribed that " criticism of any public official shall not be construed as within the purview " of this regulation.   California, in a bill relating to American histories and other textbooks which passed the Assembly in 1923, would have leashed her teachers in much the same way.   But the bill failed of passage in the Senate.[61]

The appropriation bill passed by the Sixty-Eighth Congress for the District of Columbia, in 1925, provided that no money should be available " for the payment of the salary of any superintendent, assistant superintendent, director of intermediate instruction, or supervising principal who permits the teaching of partisan politics, disrespect for the Holy Bible or that ours is an inferior form of government." A similar provision relates to teachers.[62]

[61] *Oklahoma School Laws,* 1923, p. 18; *Acts* of Oklahoma, 1921, ch. 15, sec. 2, p. 141.   California *Assembly Bill,* No. 1329, 1923, sec. 6.   " Any teacher or official of any educational institution in California who shall teach or speak before his or her pupils or public gatherings of an educational nature, or publicly, slightingly or contemptuously of the Constitution of the United States, or of the framers thereof, or of the men who founded this republic, or helped preserve and defend it, or its heroes and patriots, or shall teach un-American principles, or fail to carry out and support the spirit of this act according to its true intent and meaning, shall be deemed to have voluntarily violated his or her contract or oath of office and shall be automatically removed if the charges are proven. . . ." See page 102 for the section of the bill relating to textbooks.

[62] 68th Congress, Public — No. 595 — *H. R.* 12033.   An act making appropriations for the government of the District of Columbia and other activities chargeable in whole or in part against the revenues of such District for the fiscal year ending June 30, 1926, and for other purposes. According to *The World Tomorrow,* " Missouri attached a rider to its last appropriation bill forbidding State colleges and schools to employ any person ' who teaches, or advocates in public and private that the citizens of this State should not protect the government of the United States from aggression by other nations.' " *The World Tomorrow,* Vol. VIII (June, 1925), p. 186.

Two states, on the other hand, have passed laws emphasizing a faith in the integrity and patriotism of their teachers. Although their action preceded the legislation of the World War, yet it is significant that there have been no restrictive laws since then in these commonwealths. In 1911, Pennsylvania sanctioned a policy of freedom of thought for her teachers by declaring that " no religious or political test or qualification " should be required of " any director, visitor, superintendent, teacher, or other official, appointee, or employee, in the public schools of this commonwealth." [63] In 1913, the General Court of Massachusetts forbade any school committee, by rule, regulation or other means to restrain or penalize any teacher for " exercising his right of suffrage, the signing of nomination papers, and the petitioning or appearing before committees of the legislature "; but it permitted school committees to forbid a teacher to exercise any of the aforesaid rights, suffrage excepted, on school premises during school hours or where the exercise interfered with the performance of school duties.[64] Of great significance was the Massachusetts law of March 17, 1917, which expressly prohibited inquiries relative to the religious or political belief of applicants for positions in the public schools and forbade the rejection or selection of the applicant on such grounds.[65]

Many commonwealths, however, like New Jersey, have enacted laws pertinent to teachers as citizens, but not openly and avowedly " teacher " legislation. Such a law was ap-

[63] *Statute Law* of Pennsylvania, 1920, art. XXVIII, par. 5393, p. 494. *Public Laws*, 1911, art. XXVIII, par. 2801, p. 309, May 18. This is quite the opposite of Arkansas' law which prescribed that all teachers must believe in a " Supreme Being."

[64] *General Acts* of Massachusetts, 1913, ch. 628, p. 556. Approved May 8, 1913.

[65] *Ibid.*, 1917, ch. 84, p. 76. A fine of no more than fifty dollars could be imposed for violation of this law.

proved February 13, 1918, by the governor of New Jersey. It provided that " any person who shall advocate, in public or private, by speech, writing, printing, or by any other means, the subversion or destruction by force of the government of the United States, or of the State of New Jersey, or attempt by speech, writing, printing, or in any other way whatsoever to incite or abet, promote or encourage hostility or opposition to the government of the United States, or of the State of New Jersey, shall be guilty of a high misdemeanor, and on conviction shall be punished by imprisonment for a term not exceeding ten years, or by a fine not exceeding two thousand dollars, or by both fine and imprisonment, in the discretion of the court." [66]

Of all legislation dealing with the teaching craft, that which has attempted to control and direct the speech of the teacher has provoked the greatest protest. Our political development has been such that an interference with the free expression of opinion creates the impression that a jealously guarded right has been invaded. It is this feeling which has led to an agitation against such laws, although the fear that a teacher may be an instrument for corrupting his pupils is not a product of recent times either in this country or in world history.[67]

FLAG LEGISLATION AND OBSERVANCE DAYS

Legislation concerning the flag and special observance days takes on the characteristics of other laws passed since 1917. One of the first " flag laws " was passed in 1918 by

---

[66] *Laws* of New Jersey, 1918, ch. 44, sec. 2, p. 131. Laws have been passed in California, Connecticut, Indiana, Iowa, Kansas, Louisiana, Michigan, Minnesota, Nebraska, New Hampshire, New York, Ohio, Oregon, Pennsylvania, Rhode Island, South Dakota, Mississippi, and West Virginia.

[67] Socrates is an example of one who, in ancient times, was penalized for holding doctrines then unacceptable.

Maryland. This law declared as the purpose of its enactment that " the love of liberty and democracy, signified in
the devotion of all true and patriotic Americans to their flag
and to their country, shall be instilled in the hearts and
minds of the youth of America." [68]   Two years later, when
the tide of legislation for encouraging patriotism was at full
flood, a law embracing all schools through institutions of
higher learning passed the legislature. By this statute all
public and private schools, with the exception of professional
schools, were required to open their exercises " on at least
one day of each school week, whether morning, afternoon,
or evening, with the singing of the ' Star Spangled Banner.' " [69]

Reverence and respect for the flag was the purpose of
Oklahoma's statute in 1921. To insure obedience to the
law, which was applicable to all public, private, parochial
and denominational schools, the penalty of imprisonment or
a fine could be imposed upon an offender. " Any teacher,"
affirmed the law, " neglecting to display said flag or carry
out said ceremonial, or any person forbidding or hindering
the display of said flag or the carrying out of said ceremonial
shall be subject to discharge or removal and shall also be
punished by a fine of not less than one hundred dollars or
more than five hundred dollars, or by imprisonment in the
county jail for not less than sixty days and not more than six
months, or both." [70]

Minnesota, in passing " An act to provide for the teach-

[68] *Laws* of Maryland, 1918, ch. 75, sec. 1, 176a, p. 121. Approved
April 10, 1918.

[69] *Ibid.*, 1920, ch. 381, sec. 1, p. 665. Approved April 16, 1920. In
Michigan all applicants for an eighth grade diploma have been required
to pass an examination on " the first verse of the Star Spangled Banner
and the words of America." *General School Laws of Michigan*, 1923, p.
107, am. 1919, act 72 (275), par. 5824, sec. 2.

[70] *Acts* of Oklahoma, 1921, ch. 111, p. 137. Approved March 24, 1921.

ing in all the common, graded, and high schools of this state of exercises tending to promote and inculcate patriotism," was actuated by a like motive in 1917. Here a half hour daily must be devoted to patriotic exercises in all public schools, and every teacher should, by special exercises and by the teaching of subjects especially suitable, encourage and inculcate the spirit of patriotism. Such exercises were to consist of the singing of patriotic songs, readings from American history and from the biographies of American statesmen and patriots.[71]

Of slightly different character was the agency for propagating patriotism devised by the Alabama legislature in 1919, by which was established the "Alabama Patriotic Society." This organization, non-political and non-sectarian, essayed as its objects "to stimulate patriotism among the people; to teach the fundamental principles of American institutions, or free government; to develop in the hearts and minds of Alabamans a deeper love of country and reverence for the American flag; to expound the underlying principle of self-determination; to immortalize the heroes who have brought fame and renown to Alabama by reason of their courage and leadership in all the great wars, in which Alabamans have engaged; to teach the people to love their State, to respect her laws and to support the Constitution of both the State and Federal Government; to bring the people together to the end that unity of purpose and solidarity may be promoted; to hold discussions of patriotic and political questions affecting the general welfare of the whole people, and to issue educational pamphlets and matter to aid in carrying the purpose of the society fully into effect." [72]

[71] *Laws* of Minnesota, 1917, ch. 108, sec. 1, p. 135. Approved March 26, 1917.

[72] *General Laws* of Alabama, 1919, no. 733, p. 1083. See page 62 for a law of Oregon passed in 1921.

In North Carolina, October twelfth has been set aside for appropriate exercises in the public schools " to the consideration of some topic or topics " of state history.[73] In Oklahoma, November sixteenth has been designated for a like purpose in order to teach " loyalty and patriotism." to state and Union.[74]

Since 1918, the date November eleventh has become the occasion for a commemoration of the general rejoicing which was caused by the signing of the Armistice. In the state of Washington, the law has ordained that it shall be " the duty of each teacher in the public schools . . . , or principal in charge of the school building, to . . . present a program of exercises of at least sixty minutes in length, setting forth the part taken by the United States and the state of Washington in the world war for the years 1917–1918, and the principles for which the allied nations fought, and the heroic deeds of American soldiers and sailors, the leading events in the history of our state and of Washington Territory, the character and struggles of the pioneers, and other topics tending to instill a loyalty and devotion to the institutions and laws of our state." West Virginia also has recognized Armistice Day as a time fitting for " appropriate ceremonies." [75]

A joint resolution of the legislature of Maryland in 1920 memorialized the President of the United States to designate November eleventh of each year as a day for national thanksgiving. This day, the General Assembly believed, had been " made sacred to the hearts of the American people,

[73] *Public School Law of North Carolina*, pt. XIII, art. 38, sec. 367.
[74] *School Laws of Oklahoma*, 1923, p. 69; *Session Laws*, 1921, sec. 342.
[75] *Laws* of Washington, 1921, ch. 56, p. 171. " Victory and Admission Day." California added Armistice Day to her legal holidays in 1921, likewise including " Admission Day " on September ninth. *Statutes* of California, 1921, ch. 350, p. 481. *School Law* of West Virginia, 1923, p. 32.

in that it was the day on which the world's greatest tragedy was arrested and the awful pull at the people's heart strings relaxed," and on which "there terminated that war which overthrew the inhuman monster who laid blood-hands upon nearly every home of a peace-blest earth." The world was further assured on this day, the lawmakers declared, that "the struggle of democratic nations for liberty and for righteousness had triumphed over the kultur and the crime of the scientific barbarians, and that autocracy and diabolical tyranny lay defeated and crushed behind the long rows of white crosses which stretch across Europe. . . ." The legislators desired that the day should be the occasion for "strengthening of those noble sentiments of patriotism common to the American people, and to the love for the cause for which the sons of Maryland fought and gave their lives in the World War," and it was recommended that the schools observe the day in a "fitting and impressive manner." [76]

An act amending the law relating to holidays in Wisconsin, in 1923 set aside Lincoln's and Washington's birthdays for commemorative exercises in the public schools of that state.[77] North Dakota took similar action, adding October twelfth and November eleventh for observance except in communities where special exercises were held.[78] In Michigan, in addition to observance days previously prescribed, Roosevelt's birthday, October twenty-seventh, and "Liberty Day," November eleventh, have been designated for "proper and appropriate commemorative ceremonies." [79]

[76] *Laws* of Maryland, 1920, pp. 1448–1449.
[77] *Laws* of Wisconsin, 1923, ch. 337, amending section 40.28 of the statutes.
[78] *Educational Laws* of North Dakota, 1923, ch. 282, p. 45. See page 62 for Oregon's law of 1921 setting aside Columbus Day for observance.
[79] *General School Laws of Michigan*, 1923, p. 107.

South Dakota, in 1921, declared that Memorial Day should also be known as " Citizenship Day " in that state, at which time each citizen who had become twenty-one years of age during the year, or who had been admitted into full citizenship of the United States during that period, should receive a " citizenship certificate signed by the Governor, attested by the Secretary of State, and countersigned by the Chairman of the Board of County Commissioners of the County in which such citizen resides." The certificate included the name, age, and residence of the citizen, who also received a " manual of citizenship " containing " the Mayflower Compact, the Declaration of Independence, the Constitution of the United States and of South Dakota," and " non-political axioms and discussions of the principles of popular citizenship." [80]

Such laws were but the outpouring of a dynamic and enthusiastic patriotism, and were considered by the legislator another means of awakening and encouraging a love of country.

TEXTBOOK LEGISLATION

Few states since 1917 have passed laws requiring a uniform series of textbooks: North Carolina, Georgia, Florida, Alabama, Arkansas, Tennessee, and West Virginia. In all of these states, except North Carolina, textbooks in local history and in local and national civics were added to the

---

[80] *Laws* of South Dakota, 1921, ch. 144, secs. 1, 2, pp. 235–236. The certificates were to be presented with proper ceremony at some place where there were patriotic addresses and music. Approved March 8, 1921. In South Dakota an observance of " Frances Willard Day," besides the recognition of the benefits of prohibition, had the additional duty of stimulating " patriotism and civic improvements." *Revised Code*, 1919, par. 7662. Washington set aside January sixteenth as " Temperance and Good Citizenship Day " for studying the biographies of great leaders in " temperance and good citizenship." *Session Laws* of Washington, 1923, ch. 76, p. 236.

uniform series in United States history.[81]   In North Carolina the state textbook commission was empowered to select histories for the elementary grades.

The only other legislation of this period, except that designed to censor the content of history textbooks, was the resolution of the Georgia legislature of 1918.   This resolution endorsed the preparation of a suitable textbook in civil government.   It came from the State Board of Education, who, in 1913, had condemned the textbook then in use and had suggested the readoption of Peterman's *Civil Government,* temporarily, until one which would be satisfactory could be prepared.   From the action of the legislature in 1918, it is evident that no book had been written which met the approval of the State School Book Commission.   The restatement of the resolve of 1913 merely sought to call attention to the need for such a book.[82]

The outstanding legislation of the period, which deals with history textbooks, results from opening the flood-gates of apprehension regarding the content of school histories.   It is the same misgiving which prompted restrictive legislation regarding the speech of the teacher and required an open avowal of allegiance to the government of the United States. Here, again, the vital thing in the mind of the lawmaker is

[81] *Acts* of Georgia, 1919, sec. 18, p. 295; *Laws* of Florida, 1917, ch. 7374 (no. 116), p. 230, added to United States history, history of the state and civil government, *Laws* of 1911–12, for high schools American history and civil government, English history, and general history; *General Laws* of Alabama, 1919, art. 23, p. 634; *Digest of the Statutes* of Arkansas, 1921, par. 9066, p. 2330, also *Laws,* 1921, act 285, p. 328 for regular grade work; *Compilation of Laws* of Tennessee, 1917, art. XVII, 1461a 24, Vol. I, p. 993, also *Laws,* 1919, ch. 142, sec. 3, p. 525, Sen. Bill no. 506; *Code* of West Virginia, 1916, ch. 45, par. 155a, p. 594.   General history was also included.   *Public School Law of North Carolina,* 1923, p. 87, art. 30, sec. 322.

[82] *Laws* of Georgia, 1918, p. 919 (no. 60).   This is probably an outgrowth of the movement found in the previous period to teach history and government from a pro-Southern viewpoint.

to repress any statements considered by him as likely to undermine American patriotism.

In 1918, New York approved another Lusk law prohibiting the use of any textbook which contained statements seditious in character, disloyal to the United States or favorable to the cause of any enemy country. The law created a commission composed of the commissioner of education and two persons designated by the Regents of the University of the State of New York. To this body any person might present written complaints against textbooks in " civics, economics, English, history, language and literature," which were then to be examined " for the purpose of determining whether such textbooks contain any matter or statements of any kind which are seditious in character, disloyal to the United States or favorable to the cause of any foreign country with which the United States is now at war." [83]   In case the commission disapproved of the book after examination, the law prescribed that the reasons be forwarded to all boards of education, who then must abandon the use of the book. It was further provided that any person in authority continuing to use a condemned book would be considered guilty of a misdemeanor.

Less drastic legislation than the New York law was passed in New Hampshire in 1921, declaring that " no book shall be introduced into the public schools calculated to favor any particular religious sect or political party." [84]   Other legislation which can be considered in the same category was passed in Alabama, Georgia, Tennessee and California, in their prohibition of " partisan and sectarian " books.[85]

---

[83] *Laws* of New York, 1918, 674, p. 892, approved April 17, 1918.
[84] *Laws* of New Hampshire, 1921, ch. 85, sec. 13, p. 125.
[85] *Acts* of Georgia, 1919, p. 295; *General Laws* of Alabama, 1919, p. 634; *Compilation of Laws* of Tennessee, 1917, 1461a 24, Vol. I, p. 993; *Statutes and Amendments* Code of California, 1917, ch. 552, 1607, p. 736.

During the years of 1922 and 1923, systematic efforts were made by private organizations to control the content of history textbooks. In general, the criticisms against the histories then in use were directed by patriotic and racial organizations seeking to revive the traditional treatment of relations with Great Britain, particularly during the American Revolution and the War of 1812.[86]

An outgrowth of this agitation against school histories was the law of Wisconsin approved April 5, 1923. This statute has prescribed that " no history or other textbook shall be adopted for use or be used in any district school, city school, vocational school or high school, which falsifies the facts regarding the war of independence, or the war of 1812 or which defames our nation's founders or misrepresents the ideals and causes for which they struggled and sacrificed, or which contains propaganda favorable to any foreign government." The law has also provided that a complaint against any textbook filed by any five citizens with the superintendent of public instruction, must be heard within thirty days at the county seat of the county in which the complainants reside. The statute has made it the duty of the superintendent to pass upon the case ten days following the hearing and to exclude from the schools any book found to contain statements prohibited by the enactment. In 1925, a bill embodying substantially the same spirit and phraseology was presented to the Massachusetts House by Mr. Garrity of Boston, but was not enacted into law.[87]

[86] For a full discussion see chapter VII.

[87] " . . . , the state superintendent shall fix a time for a public hearing upon such a complaint, which shall not be more than thirty days from the date of filing said complaint, and shall be conducted by the state superintendent or the assistant state superintendent, or by one of the state inspectors of schools, to be designated by the superintendent, and which hearing shall be held at the county seat of the county where the complainants reside. Notice of such hearing shall be given at least ten days prior to the date

Oregon has a similar law. The use of any textbook has been prohibited which "speaks slightingly of the founders of the republic, or of the men who preserved the Union, or which belittles or undervalues their work." [88]

In the spring of 1923, the Assembly of the state of California passed a bill excluding from the schools of the state any history or other textbook "which falsifies the facts regarding the war of independence, the war of 1812, or any other war of this country, or which defames our nation's founders, defenders, heroes or patriots, or misrepresents the ideals and causes for which they struggled and sacrificed, or misleads by stating but partial facts, or which contains propaganda that is unfavorable to this country and government, and favorable to any other government or other type of government." The bill met defeat in the Senate.[89]

In the spring of 1923 a bill of like nature passed the Senate of New York but failed in the Lower House. By this proposal, known as the Higgins Bill, any American history was prohibited in the primary or secondary schools of the state, "which falsifies, distorts or denies the acts of oppression recited in the Declaration of Independence, or which, if a textbook dealing with the period immediately preceding the Declaration of Independence, fails to refer, . . . to the principal acts of oppression as set forth in the Declaration of Independence." It further forbade the use of any history which "belittles, ridicules, doubts or denies the services and sacrifices of American patriots," or which "emphasizes and enlarges upon the possible human failings

---

thereof through the public press and by registered mail to the complainants, the school board interested and to the publishers of such textbooks." *Laws of Wisconsin*, 1923, ch. 21, sec. 40.30. Massachusetts House Bill No. 718. "An Act relative to Certain Textbooks in the Public Schools."

[88] *Oregon School Laws*, 1923, ch. III, sec. 571, p. 169.

[89] Assembly Bill (California) No. 1329, introduced by Mr. Ball.

or shortcomings of such patriots without giving at least equal prominence to their virtues or merits." The bill prescribed for primary schools the presentation of episodes calculated " to arouse in children a justifiable pride " in the winning of " our national independence." It further placed under ban any textbook which " misrepresents " or " fails to mention . . . the compelling causes of the respective wars waged . . . against foreign interference, aggression or encroachment, or which . . . fails to emphasize . . . the final victory of the United States in any war it prosecuted to a successful conclusion," or which " belittles or ridicules . . . American soldiers, sailors or marines in our wars against foreign nations . . . as to leave . . . a contempt " for them or " an unwarranted skepticism regarding their successes under arms." [90]

A bill of like import was introduced in the New York Senate in 1924. It included a provision for the training of teachers in the best methods of teaching American history, as well as the requirement that American history textbooks include the Declaration of Independence " in its entirety," if dealing with the American Revolution.[91] Senator Higgins was also responsible for a resolution instructing the Commissioner of Education to investigate the history textbooks used in the schools of New York to ascertain whether any contained matter misrepresenting events of the Revolution or ridiculing the Revolutionary patriots.[92]

In January, 1924, a bill relating to the selection of American histories as textbooks and reference books in the public schools was introduced into the Assembly of New Jersey.

[90] State of New York, 3d Rdg. 652, Nos. 602, 1781, 1997, Int. 581. In Senate, February 7, 1923.
[91] State of New York: No. 1186, Int. 1086. In Senate, March 5, 1924. Introduced by Mr. Higgins.
[92] *The New York Times,* March 19, 1924.

It was designed to exclude any history which " belittles, falsifies, misrepresents, distorts, doubts or denies the events leading up to the Declaration of American Independence or any other war in which this country has been engaged, or which belittles, falsifies, misrepresents, distorts, doubts or denies the deeds and accomplishments of noted American patriots, or which questions the worthiness of their motives or casts aspersions upon their lives." [93]

A spirited protest against the bill as introduced in the New Jersey Assembly came from the faculty of Princeton University who resolved that " such legislation is in direct contravention of the fundamental principles of freedom of speech and of the press, and calculated to impair the integrity of education in both the public and private institutions in the State of New Jersey." [94]

The New York Times also objected to the censorship proposed in that state, declaring that it was not conceivable that " any honest man would wish to write textbooks in history for children under such statutory prescription," and *The Freeman,* in an article regarding the Wisconsin law, pointed out that " historians sometimes find it a difficult matter to get at the truth in regard to the past, but for the superintendent of schools in the state of Wisconsin it is no job at all. . . ." [95]

[93] *Assembly, No. 14 (with Amendments), State of New Jersey.* Introduced January 8, 1924, by Mr. Williams. (For the Speaker.) The bill provided also that any forty citizens of a school district could file complaints against histories and a public hearing should be held within thirty days.

[94] *The New York Times,* February 12, 1924. The endorsement given this bill by patriotic and fraternal groups is treated on pages 275-276.

[95] *Ibid.,* April 19, 1923. *The Freeman,* Vol. VII (May 2, 1923), p. 170. The Oklahoma legislature of 1923 forbade the use of textbooks teaching the "' Materialistic Conception of History ' (*i.e.*) The Darwinian Theory of Creation vs. the Bible Account of Creation." Approved March 24, 1923. House Bill No. 197. The use of the term " materialistic conception of history " is interesting in this connection.

AMERICANIZATION OF FOREIGNERS

The desire to instil a knowledge of American institutions has led to much legislation for the education of the foreign element in our population. Some states have attempted to eliminate illiteracy by evening classes for adults, by continuation schools and like means. In all cases, the teaching of the English language has been a primary purpose, as well as training in a knowledge of American institutions. However, not all Americanization laws have definitely stated the purpose of training in citizenship, and therefore do not come properly into this discussion.

Since 1917 more than one-third of the states have enacted legislation for the purpose of developing a love for this country in the foreign born.[96] In that year, California inaugurated the policy of "home teachers" to visit the homes of pupils instructing both children and adults in matters pertaining to "school attendance, sanitation, the English language, and in the fundamental principles of the American system of government and the rights and duties of citizenship."[97] Two years later, this enactment was followed by another law for the teaching of civic and vocational subjects in evening classes, in which instruction was provided in the " duties and responsibilities of citizenship " for those unable

[96] Among the states which have Americanization laws that have no specific statement prescribing the teaching of American citizenship are Alabama, Connecticut, Iowa, Missouri, Nevada, New Mexico, North Dakota, Oregon, South Dakota, Virginia and West Virginia. Most of these laws were enacted in 1919, some prescribing the establishment of classes for uneducated adults, others specifying Americanization courses. In North Carolina, there is a law to remove illiteracy, and in New Mexico the schools are to give "nocturnal courses of instruction." These laws are not discussed because they do not provide for the teaching of citizenship. One of the earliest evening schools was in Massachusetts, 1886, where United States history was one of the prescribed subjects. *Supplement to Public Statutes of Massachusetts*, 1882–1888, ch. 174, p. 117, "An Act for the Establishment and Maintenance of Evening Schools."

[97] *Statutes* of California, 1917, ch. 552, p. 742.

to speak or read the English language to the proficiency of the sixth grade." [98] In 1921, California continued her Americanization program by approving a law to provide for the establishment of classes for training in citizenship for applicants who had filed their declaration of intention to become citizens of the United States and for other persons desiring such instruction. The course of study includes the teaching of United States history, state and community civics, the " constitution of the United States with special reference to those sections in the constitution which relate directly to the duties, privileges and rights of the individuals, and such allied subjects . . . as shall properly prepare such applicants to understand and assume the responsibilities of citizenship." [99]

In 1918, New York passed a law necessitating the attendance of all non-English speaking and illiterate minors at school or at classes established by employers in shops, stores, factories, or plants in which were taught English and civics.[100] In 1921, it became a duty of the commissioner of education to see that schools for the education of these illiterate groups be established, in which should be taught " English, history, civics, and other subjects tending to promote good citizenship and increase vocational efficiency. . . ." [101]

In Massachusetts, power has been granted to the director of the division of immigration and Americanization, with the approval of an advisory board, to employ methods which will develop in the foreign born " an understanding of American government, institutions and ideals." [102]

[98] *Ibid.*, 1919, ch. 605, sec. 4, p. 1049.
[99] *Ibid.*, 1921, ch. 489, p. 742. Approved May 27, 1921.
[100] *Laws* of New York, 1918, ch. 415, pp. 1257–1258.
[101] *Ibid.*, 1921, ch. 327, Vol. II, p. 1037.
[102] *General Laws Relating to Education, Massachusetts*, 1923, p. 18. " Education and Protection of Aliens," 1917, 321, par. 2; 1919, 350, par. 59; 1920, 72.

Arizona's law of 1918 permitted the establishment of night schools in school districts for those over sixteen who were unable to read or write the English language, in which there was to be instruction in "American ideals" and an "understanding of American institutions." [103]

The year 1919 saw the adoption of Americanization programs by the legislatures of Maine, New Hampshire, Rhode Island, Pennsylvania, Delaware, Minnesota, Oklahoma, Utah, Montana and California in which the purpose of teaching American ideals and institutions received express mention.

Maine's statute, designed for those persons "of normal mentality over eighteen years of age who are unable to read, to write, and to speak the English language to a reasonable degree of efficiency," prescribed the teaching of "the duties of citizens in a democracy" and of "such other subjects as will increase their civic intelligence." [104]   In her legislation, New Hampshire called for "the abolition of illiteracy and the instruction of illiterates over sixteen years of age in the common school branches and in the privileges, duties and responsibilities of citizenship." Immigrants over sixteen years of age were to be taught "to appreciate and respect the civic and social institutions of the United States," and to be instructed "in the duties of citizenship," which are "an essential part of public school education." [105]   In Rhode Island, people between the ages of sixteen and twenty-one years of age, unable to read and write English or to speak it with reasonable facility, have been given the privilege of a continuation school held for the purpose of teach-

---

[103] *Acts* of Arizona, 1918, ch. 10, sec. 1, p. 29 (Sen. Bill No. 19). In 1921 a bill for the education of foreigners in the public schools was passed.

[104] *Laws* of Maine, 1919, ch. 148, p. 148. Revision of ch. 116, sec. 137. Approved April 1, 1919.

[105] *Laws* of New Hampshire, 1919, ch. 106, secs. 5 and 30, pp. 157, 165. Also *Laws*, 1921, ch. 85, sec. 5, p. 113.

ing the English language and American citizenship.[106] Pennsylvania's attempt to cope with the problem has led to the passage of an act " to provide instruction in citizenship and the principles of the government of the United States of America and of this commonwealth to foreign-born residents of the state of Pennsylvania, in the several counties thereof, who are not required to attend the public schools of this commonwealth." [107]

The Delaware law was designed for the foreign-born over sixteen years of age not able to speak English, but who, through evening classes, might be instructed in that language and " in the institutions and forms of government of the United States and the State of Delaware." [108]

An appropriation of the Minnesota legislature of 1919, to carry out a provision of an Americanization law of 1917, became available for work providing for instruction in English for those whose knowledge is too limited to carry on business or to read intelligently periodicals and newspapers, and in the essential and vital facts of American history, American government and ideals, and the duties and obligations of citizenship.[109]

By a joint resolution of 1919 the Oklahoma legislature created a committee on Americanization and made it incumbent upon public school officials to organize classes in English and in citizenship instruction wherever a petition signed by ten residents of foreign birth over sixteen years of age was presented to them.[110]   A minimum of two hundred

[106] *Acts and Resolves* of Rhode Island, 1919, ch. 1802, sec. 2, p. 212.
[107] *Laws* of Pennsylvania, 1919, no. 311.
[108] *Laws* of Delaware, 1919, ch. 158, sec. 1, p. 452; also by a similar law approved April 7, 1921, *Laws*, 1921, ch. 165, p. 550. For California, see page 106.
[109] *General Laws* of Minnesota, 1919, for ch. 356 of *General Laws*, 1917.
[110] *Session Laws* of Oklahoma, 1919, ch. 135, p. 467. Approved March 10, 1919.

hours of instruction during the school year aided Utah in her Americanization program which included classes in the " fundamental principles of the Constitution of the United States, American history, and such other subjects as bear on Americanization." [111] Montana's legislation, designed for those over sixteen years of age who were not familiar with the English language, provided for instruction in " American history and the Principles of Citizenship and any other school subjects which the school trustees deem necessary for the Americanization of the students enrolled." [112]

The Americanization movement was further aided by a law approved April 19, 1920, in which New Jersey provided instruction for the foreign born residents of her state, over fourteen years of age, in English and " in the form of government and the laws of this State and of the United States." [113] American history, the Constitution of the United States, with an exposition of the privileges and the duties of American citizenship tending to produce a spirit of loyalty, were phases of the Americanization programs of Ohio, Idaho, Wyoming, and Oregon in 1921. [114] In the last state, " home teachers," whose duty it is to instruct in the fundamental principles of the American system of government and the rights and duties of citizenship, were named as an aid in carrying on the work of Americanization. [115] In Michigan, the superintendent of public instruction has been given power to provide for the education of aliens and of native illiterates over

---

[111] *Laws* of Utah, 1919, ch. 93, sec. 4, p. 285.   Approved March 20, 1919.   This law was added to in 1921 with a provision for fees.

[112] *Laws* of Montana, 1919, ch. 38, sec. 1, p. 91.   Approved February 21, 1919.

[113] *Acts* of New Jersey, 1920, ch. 197, p. 387.

[114] *General Laws* of Ohio, 1921, sec. 7761–3, p. 101; *General Laws* of Idaho, 1921, p. 418; *Session Laws* of Wyoming, ch. 127, sec. 1, p. 188; *General Laws* of Oregon, 1921, ch. 87, sec. 1, p. 139 (S. B. 171).

[115] *Ibid.* New York and Arizona also have laws in 1921. See page 106.

eighteen years of age who are unable "to read, write and speak the English language and who are unlearned in the principles of government" of Michigan and of the United States.[116]

In general, the most popular means for educating the alien population is by attendance at a night school, where, through evening classes, teachers regularly employed in the public schools seek to instruct in the English language and in an appreciation of and respect for "the civic and social institutions of the United States." New York has tried the employers' school to effect the same purpose, whereas "home teachers" are endorsed by California and Oregon. In the four years preceding the outbreak of the World War, 5,174,701 immigrants came to the United States, of whom 22.1 were unable to read and write any language. In 1920, nearly one and a half million, or 11 per cent, of the foreign-born whites in this country could not speak English. For this group, even more than for the native element, has it seemed wise to encourage education, because it has become a common belief that a lack of education endangers the well-being of the state.

[116] State of Michigan, Department of Public Instruction, *Explanation of School Laws of Michigan*, Supplement to Bulletin No. 13. Published 1921, p. 7.

CHAPTER V

DISLOYALTY CHARGES AGAINST TEACHERS SINCE 1917

Great events occasion diverse opinions, and it is not strange that the World War and its aftermath often tempted public school teachers to enter the area of controversial issues. Thus the question of whether the teacher should be permitted free and open expression of opinion became a point of contention between the upholders and opponents of unrestricted speech. It became a matter of considerable concern whether the teacher be allowed to sow the seed of an idea alien to that held by the child's parents, or, perhaps, in disagreement with that of the school's administrators. It was not a new question nor unexpected.

The great mass of public school teachers were conscious of the censorious eye fixed upon them and realized that " the wise man foreseeth the evil and hideth himself, but the foolish pass on and are punished." Diligent search in public records and through personal inquiry reveals few occasions where actual charges of disloyalty were lodged against teachers in the public schools. Indeed, the superintendents of public instruction in thirty-two states report that from 1917 to 1924 no accusations involving the loyalty of teachers were brought to the attention of their offices.[1] One is disposed to concur in a statement made by the Lusk Committee of New York investigating seditious activities that

---

[1] Personal letters to the author under the date of December, 1923, and January, 1924. All states but Ohio and Illinois responded to the inquiry of the author. The Superintendent of Public Instruction in Washington (Mrs. Josephine C. Preston) refused to furnish information for that state.

"on the whole, it may safely be said that our public school system is comparatively free from the taint of revolutionary teaching."[2] Yet some teachers faced accusations impugning loyalty. Doubtless there were others whose utterances were considered disloyal or ill-advised, but who escaped with little or no publicity attending their dismissal from service.

In the city of New York, the trials of teachers for disloyalty were most numerous, for it was here that legislation to restrain the speech of the teacher was most rigorously applied. Under the Lusk Law persons failing to secure a certificate of loyalty were forbidden to teach in the schools of New York, the Commissioner of Education having the sole right to refuse such a certificate.[3]

In general, charges of disloyalty were preferred against six groups of teachers: those objecting to sign the pledge of loyalty, those whose sympathies in the War were pro-German, the pacifists, those whose speech was considered disloyal, those who opposed and obstructed the draft, and those who held membership in a political party which advocated a change in the established form of government.[4]

[2] *Revolutionary Radicalism,* Vol. I, p. 1118.

[3] At the suggestion of the Teachers' Council, an advisory committee to sift charges was appointed who reported cases to the Commissioner of Education should they need his attention. The investigations of this committee aroused much criticism, especially from the Teachers' Union, whose members were frequently the principals in the trials conducted. The advisory committee was composed of Condé Pallen, editor of the *Catholic Encyclopedia,* Olivia Leventritt, a former member of the Board of Education, Hugh Frayne, New York representative of the American Federation of Labor, Archibald Stevenson, counsel of the Lusk Committee, and Finley J. Shepard as chairman. *The New York Times,* May 17, 1922; *ibid.,* May 25, 1922; *ibid.,* June 4, 1922.

[4] Instances of local friction tending to obscure the issues alleged to be involved frequently entered into the evidence presented in some of the trials. This was true in the trials of Schmalhausen, Schneer, and Mufson (see pages 116–120), where opposition to the so-called Whalen resolution for longer school hours was alleged by the defense to be a cause for their dismissal.

In the eyes of the school administrators an unwillingness to sign pledges of loyalty without qualification was but the evidence of a hybrid patriotism. In no other light did they believe could be considered the objection to a pledge which declared an "unqualified allegiance to the Government of the United States," and which promised by "word and example" to "teach and impress" upon "the pupils the duty of loyal obedience and patriotic service as the highest ideal of American citizenship."[5]

Opposition to signing the pledges under compulsion was led by the Teachers' Union, and their protest against an implication of disloyalty was endorsed by eighty-seven teachers.[6]   Among those refusing at first to sign a pledge were Miss Isabel Davenport of the New York Training School for Teachers and Harrison C. Thomas of the De Witt Clinton High School. The examination started to determine their fitness to teach was discontinued when they agreed to sign the pledge.[7]

In March, 1918, the charge of pro-Germanism was lodged against Miss Gertrude A. M. Pignol, a teacher in the Manual Training High School in Brooklyn, and her suspension was asked by the Board of Superintendents. Miss Pignol, a native of Berlin, had been a resident of the United States since 1905. In 1911 she had taken out citizenship papers.[8]   When questioned by secret service

[5] The pledge of the Board of Education. Other pledges, including that of Mayor John Puroy Mitchell, also were presented for signing. See *Toward the New Education: The Case Against Autocracy in Our Public Schools* (The Teachers' Union of the City of New York), p. 23.

[6] *Ibid.* The Teachers' Union charged that the loyalty pledges were introduced for political purposes into a controversy between the Board of Education and the teaching staff. The Teachers' Union wrote President Wilson asking him to frame a pledge which teachers could sign "without violating their consciences." *The New York Times*, December 2, 1917.

[7] See page 122 for a further discussion of the loyalty of Mr. Thomas.

[8] *The New York Times*, May 18, 1918.

agents, it developed that, although her sympathies were with Germany, she had in no way been connected with German activities in this country. In the hope that her views might undergo a change Miss Pignol was given a leave of absence for three months. In May, 1918, however, Associate Superintendent Tildsley preferred the following charges against her before a committee of the Board of Education: that she did not believe in war, that she was under the impression that it was not necessary for the United States to be engaged in the War, that she would not pledge her coöperation in every way in her power to the United States government in its measures for the prosecution of the War against Germany.[9]

In Miss Pignol's trial, statements from fellow-teachers were cited as proof of her pro-German bias. A remark, alleged to have been made eleven years prior, that she would be ashamed to be an American citizen, was adduced as evidence. Further proof was found in a statement that she doubted the accuracy of the accounts regarding German outrages; that she had attempted to dissuade a German woman from returning to Germany because she would eat food needed by the Germans; that she objected to the posting of a food card by the school librarian; and that she was deeply touched by the slaughter of the War. The possession of a locket, engraved by her father and carrying the picture of the Kaiser's grandfather on one side and the cornflower on the other, was put in evidence as additional proof of her hostility to the cause of the United States.[10] Although she asserted her desire for an American victory, the confession that she did not want her native

[9] "More Educational Inquisition," *The New Republic*, Vol. XVII (January 11, 1919), pp. 305–307.
[10] *Ibid.*

land crushed militated against her.[11]   On June 26, she was dismissed from service by the Board of Education.[12]

On October 24, 1918, Fritz A. E. Leuchs was suspended from duty in the schools, charged with "conduct unbecoming a teacher." His suspension was confirmed on October 30 by the Board of Education. According to his own testimony, he had tried for four years to enlist in the German army, but on October 25 had entered upon military service in this country. Under the circumstances the Board of Education resorted to suspension in order that he could not claim the difference in pay as a teacher and a soldier.[13]

Similar treatment was accorded pacifists serving in the schools. In this group was Miss Mary McDowell, a Quakeress, employed in the schools of Brooklyn, who was suspended from duty on March 12, 1918. She based her defense in the unrestricted exercise of religious faith as a birthright, her previous contributions to relief for American sufferers to the Red Cross and other charitable projects, as well as the distribution of thrift stamp circulars in the schools. Miss McDowell's retention as a public school teacher was opposed on the ground that her pacifist views were ill-advised at a time when patriotism should be taught in act as well as in speech.[14]   On June 19, 1918, she was dismissed from service by the Board of Education.[15] Following the close of the War Miss McDowell's case was reopened, which resulted in her reinstatement on July 11, 1923. On reviewing the causes for Miss McDowell's dismissal, Commissioner Bowe declared: "After full consideration of the case, the committee has decided

---

[11] *The New York Times, loc. cit.*
[12] *Ibid.,* June 27, 1919.
[13] *Ibid.,* October 31, 1918.

[14] *Ibid.,* May 16, 1918.
[15] *Ibid.,* June 20, 1918.

that the punishment meted out to Miss McDowell was too severe. She was tried at a time of great public excitement. Since then public feeling has undergone considerable modification. For thirteen years she had done excellent work as a teacher. . . ." [16]

An unwillingness to engage in active service resulted likewise in the suspension of Louis H. Blumenthal, a teacher of history and civics in Public School 148, Brooklyn, on June 19, 1918.

Nor were all teachers willing to obey a law precluding criticism of the government. To secure permanency of tenure through silent assent was to some but a bribe against their convictions. And not all were agreed that it was wise to refrain from teaching what they held true because others saw in the same belief the germs of disloyalty.

Such a disagreement as to how freely a teacher could express opinions led to investigations of the loyalty of Florence Levine, Samuel D. Schmalhausen, Thomas Mufson, and A. Henry Schneer. In the case of Miss Levine, a teacher in Public School 168, Brooklyn, the Teachers' Council, to whom the case had been referred, recommended that she be admonished by the Acting Superintendent of Schools so that thereafter she be careful in her public utterances, but no charges were preferred against her. [17]

It was quite different in the cases of Mr. Schmalhausen, Mr. Mufson, and Mr. Schneer. On November 13, 1917, they were suspended from the faculty of the De Witt Clinton High School for holding views considered not only subversive to discipline in the schools but injurious to good citizenship. [18] Their trials took place before a committee

[16] *Ibid.*, July 12, 1923.
[17] *Ibid.*, March 16, 1918.
[18] *Ibid.*, November 14, 1917.

of the Board of Education on December third, at which they were represented by counsel. The charges against Mr. Schmalhausen involved the writing of essays by his students, in which, it was said, an unpatriotic attitude was permitted to pass unchallenged by the teacher. According to the testimony, the pupils were directed to write " An open letter to the President " commenting frankly within the limits of their knowledge upon his conduct of the War against the German Government.[19]   Mr. Schmalhausen was also accused of asserting that he did not consider it his duty " to develop in the students under his control instinctive respect for the President of the United States as such, for the Governor of the State of New York as such, and other Federal, State and Municipal officers as such." [20]

One of the themes, upon which attention at the trial was focused, had been written by Hyman Herman, a Jewish student sixteen years of age. It was addressed " to the Defender of Humanity and Champion of Democracy, Woodrow Wilson." In his testimony Mr. Schmalhausen asserted complete ignorance of this essay until it was called to his attention in an interview with Associate Superintendent Tildsley two weeks after it had been written.[21]

In the theme the writer propounded such questions as the following: " But how is it that the United States, a country far from democratic (and daily proving itself to be such) and England, the imperial and selfish (and we exclude all

---

[19] *The Trial of the Three Suspended Teachers of the De Witt Clinton High School* (New York), p. 26.

[20] *Ibid.*, p. 64; *The New York Times*, December 4, 1917.

[21] The theme (in the form of a letter) had been collected by Miss Ellen Garrigues, head of the English Department, in a visit to Mr. Schmalhausen's class. During her visit, Miss Garrigues became angry at the "lack of spirit of love of country among the boys who had read themes," and asked that the themes be handed to her. *The Trial of the Three Suspended Teachers of the De Witt Clinton High School*, p. 22.

minor participants) undertake to slam democracy upon a nation whether it likes it or not? What unparalleled audacity to attempt to force 70,000,000 people to adopt a certain kind of government. If we mean their benefit, then the Germans surely know what they want and need us not. . . .

" . . . Finally if our aim be the annihilation of Prussianism, then why in the name of Heaven have you refused the offer made by Germany, which included the evacuation of Belgium, disarmament of nations and freedom of the seas? Surely then your purpose is to get supreme domination and to crush Germany for no reason it seems, except a mad desire for murder, meanwhile making us the goats." [22]

Mr. Schmalhausen had annotated the theme, after it had been placed in his hands by Dr. Tildsley, with such statements as " irrelevant," " not accurately presented," and " for a thoughtful student this statement sounds irrational." [23] The defense contended that such annotations were sufficient to prove Mr. Schmalhausen's disapproval of the sentiments expressed, but the prosecution argued that his failure to denounce them openly indicated his lack of loyalty.

As a witness for Mr. Schmalhausen, Herman, the author of the theme, testified that he had not received his impressions of this country's attitude toward war questions in any sense from Mr. Schmalhausen, although since the time of writing the theme he had changed his attitude due to a study of his history textbook [24] and the attitude of his history teacher.[25]

In turn, Mr. Schmalhausen, defending his own patriotism,

[22] *The Trial*, pp. 42–43; Dotey, Aaron I., *The Exploitation of the Public School System of New York* (Teachers' Council, New York), LXXXV.

[23] *The Trial*, pp. 46–47.

[24] Robinson and Beard's history. See *Toward the New Education*, p. 72.   [25] *The Trial*, pp. 135, 141.

declared that President Wilson's " interpretation, his attitude, his points of view in relation to the war for democracy " met with his "complete intellectual approval," and that, although he had opposed the policy of conscription instead of a volunteer system, when adopted, he had complied with the request of the Government, as did others within the proper ages.[26]

The second instructor in the De Witt Clinton High School who was arraigned before the Board of Education on December third was Thomas Mufson, charged with thinking it proper to be neutral while his class debated such subjects as the purchase of Liberty Bonds, the active support of the Government in various measures for carrying on the War, the wisdom of an early peace, and the relative merits of anarchism and the form of the government of the United States.[27]

Mr. Mufson defended himself against these charges on the ground that he was not justified in imposing personal views upon his classes on controversial subjects. Furthermore, he said that he would not permit a discussion of anarchism in his classroom, a topic he held far too difficult for immature minds.[28]

The specific charges brought against Mr. Schneer arose from statements it was alleged he had made regarding patriotism and the wearing of the uniform of the United States army. It was held that he was opposed to discussing patriotism in the schoolroom and that he objected to persons wearing the uniform when speaking before the school, because it tended to encourage militarism.[29] All of the charges Mr. Schneer denied, protesting his loyalty to school

[26] *Ibid.*, pp. 119–120.
[27] *Ibid.*, p. 158. Mr. Mufson was a teacher of English.
[28] *Ibid.*, pp. 174–175.
[29] *The New York Times*, November 20, 1917. *The Trial*, p. 200. In

and national authorities, and citing as proof, among other things, the signing of the loyalty pledge of the Board of Education.

Considerable discussion by the public and by teachers attended these trials. Among those commending the Board of Education for their vigilance were the Schoolmasters' Association of New York and Vicinity, who adopted a resolution expressing the hope that efforts to suppress disloyal influences in the schools would be energetically sustained.[30] On the other hand, the Teachers' Union voted to give the teachers on trial their " legal, moral and financial support," [31] and eleven college teachers requested that the decision against them be delayed for further investigation.[32] Professor John Dewey was reported to have likened the trial to "the Inquisition," [33] and the New York *Evening Post* editorially declared that " the case not only was prejudiced from the beginning, but was disingenuous in inception, unfair in method and un-American in spirit." [34] On December 19, 1917, these teachers were dismissed by the Board of Education.[35] Later their appeal for reinstatement was denied by the Commissioner of Education.[36]

addition to these charges a bibliography on recent literature compiled by Mr. Schneer was introduced as evidence of his unfitness to teach. The " characterizations " of books in the bibliography, read at the trial, in general pertained to the relations of the sexes. See *ibid.*, pp. 203–204.

[30] *Ibid.*, November 17, 1917; also " New York's Disloyal School Teachers," *Literary Digest*, Vol. LV (December 8, 1917), pp. 32–33.

[31] *The New York Times*, *loc. cit.*

[32] *Ibid.*, December 20, 1917. Among these were John Dewey, James Harvey Robinson, David Snedden, Carlton J. H. Hayes, H. A. Overstreet, W. P. Montague, Thomas Reed Powell, M. R. Cohen, A. J. Goldfort, N. P. Mead, and J. P. Turner.

[33] " Charges against New York City Teachers," *School and Society*, Vol. VI (December 22, 1917), p. 733.

[34] The New York *Evening Post* quoted in *School and Society*, *loc. cit.*

[35] *The New York Times*, December 20, 1917.

[36] *Ibid.*, November 5, 1918. In reviewing their cases, *Toward the New*

In November, 1917, six other teachers of the De Witt Clinton High School were transferred to other schools because lacking a positive loyalty. Friends of the teachers ascribed their transfer to their " independence " and not to a lack of loyalty.[37] The absence of academic freedom and democracy in school organization, an indefiniteness in the charges preferred against them, were all advanced by the teachers themselves in extenuation of their acts.[38] According to a statement of *The New York Times,* in the inquiry to determine their fitness to teach, the teachers declared they had been asked such questions as the following: " Should not a teacher inculcate instinctive obedience to supervisors, no matter what the acts of the superior officers may be? What is your opinion of the Bolsheviki? Do you believe in revolution? Are teachers qualified to criticise superiors? Do you believe in internationalism? Do you think a teacher ought to impose his views on pupils? Is there not a presumption that whatever is, is right? Would you rather have Hillquit or Roosevelt for mayor? What would you do if a boy called President Wilson a murderer? Do you accept Hillquit's treasonable utterances? Does not the critical attitude in children need suppression? Would you be willing for the boys in your class to discuss Liberty Bonds pro and con? In the matter of the longer day should the teach-

Education, a publication of the Teachers' Union, ascribed the dismissal of these teachers not to disloyalty, but to their opposition to the " autocracy " of superior officials and to an anti-Semitic bias of these officials. All three teachers were Russian Jews.

[37] *Ibid.,* December 1, 1917. Dotey, *op. cit.,* LXXXVI; *The New York Times,* November 15, 1917.

[38] The Central Federated Union, November 17, 1917, resolved " in the interest of justice and of the schools that the charges made against the teachers be definitely formulated by a committee of responsible officials, and that a copy of the charges be given to each of the teachers transferred or suspended and that the charges be heard in public." *Ibid.*

ers have been consulted?"[39]　That the teachers were asked these questions was stoutly denied by Superintendent William L. Ettinger.[40]

Closely allied with charges of disloyal speech were those growing out of attempts to obstruct the government in its prosecution of the War. Of such a nature was the charge brought against Miss Fannie Ross, a teacher in Public School 88, Brooklyn, who, while acting as a registrar in the state census, was reported to have expressed opposition to the draft, to have given advice outside her line of duty, and to have gone so far as to influence a man to claim exemption.[41]　On December 26, 1917, Miss Ross was suspended from service for six months because of "conduct unbecoming a teacher," due "to tactless remarks."[42]

The apprehension of the school authorities of New York City was further reflected in the trial of teachers who were suspected of radical views. This anxiety expressed itself in the withholding of certificates of loyalty and morality at least during the investigation. Following the War, membership in the Socialist Party, advocacy of Communism, and a sympathetic attitude toward the Bolshevist program of Russia were the chief charges preferred in the trials.

Among the first teachers summoned before the high school committee of the Board of Education because of radical views was Harrison C. Thomas, a teacher in the De Witt Clinton High School. Mr. Thomas was an advocate of internationalism and of socialism, a conscientious objector who had been excused from the draft, and avowedly not enthusiastic over wartime enterprises like Liberty Bonds. When questioned regarding his attitude in the classroom, he

[39] *Ibid.*, November 15, 1917.
[40] *Ibid.*, November 16, 1917.
[41] *Ibid.*, November 29, 1917; *ibid.*, December 25, 1917.
[42] *Ibid.*, December 27, 1917.

confessed that he would not conceal the fact that he was an objector; that he believed resistance to aggressiveness by force wrong; and that if Germany wanted to rule this country submission would be better than forceful resistance. Yet he declared that he had tried to get into reconstruction work in France and that he would do anything except fight. As a result, his certificate of morality and loyalty was withheld.[43] Similar action was taken in the case of Bernard M. Parelhoff, of the George Washington High School, who maintained that a nation which " teaches patriotism in its schools is merely driving nails into its own coffin," and because he believed there should be no reverence for the uniform as such.[44]

Licenses were likewise withheld from other teachers, among whom were Eugene Jackson, Austin M. Works, Garibaldi Lapolla, Abraham Lefkowitz, Edward Delaney, and Wilmer T. Stone of the De Witt Clinton High School; Ruth G. Hardy of the Girls' Commercial High School; John J. Donohue, Louis A. Goldman, Felix Sper and John J. Shipley of the Stuyvesant High School; Max Rosenhaus of the Bushwick High School; Alexander Fichlander of Public School 165, Brooklyn; and Henrietta Rodman, Benjamin Gruenberg, and Benjamin Mandel of the Julia Richman High School.[45]

[43] Dotey, op. cit., LXXVIII, XCVII.   Mr. Thomas was called in November, 1917.

[44] Ibid., LXXVIII.   Mr. Parelhoff was questioned regarding his opinions in November, 1917.

[45] According to Dr. Henry Linville of the Teachers' Union. The New York Times of January 24, 1918, reported that twenty-four teachers in School 62 of New York had been questioned about their war views. Although assurances had been given the teachers that no charges against them were contemplated, the Teachers' Union called it a " fishing expedition " to obtain evidence against Philip Perlstein, a teacher who had been suspended two weeks before. In November, 1919, sixteen " radical " teachers were reported to have been called by Deputy Attorney-General Samuel A.

The action of the authorities in withholding certificates of loyalty from some of these teachers called forth a protest from Dr. Henry Linville of the Teachers' Union, of which many of the accused were members. Dr. Linville assailed the methods employed in the investigations and the reasons for which certificates were being withheld. He asserted that during the War these teachers had been unmolested by the federal government and had not been summoned to face charges of disloyalty by the school authorities. Although non-conformists in relation " to static views of society and politics," he declared that " most of them actively supported all war enterprises, a minority only being pacifist in belief and action." [46] Moreover, in denial of the charge that teachers of alleged radical views were indoctrinating their pupils with minority and undesirable opinions, he declared that none of these teachers had ever maintained the right of a teacher to press upon the pupils the political views that he himself held.[47]

But the authorities throughout were insistent in their desire to rid the schools of all teachers holding a political belief which to them was anathema. To this end in November, 1919, a permanent license was denied Miss Sonia Ginsberg, of Public School 170, because she admitted membership in the Communist Party; [48] for the same reason action was taken against Miss Rachel (Ray) Ragozin, in February,

---

Berger, because of their connection with radical propaganda. *The New York Times*, November 20, 1919.

[46] *The New York Times*, October 23, 1922. The teachers whom Dr. Linville was reported to have mentioned were Austin M. Works, Eugene Jackson, Wilmer T. Stone, John F. Donohue, Louis Goldman, Joseph J. Shipley, Felix Sper, Ruth Hardy, Henrietta Rodman, Jessie Hughan, Abraham Lefkowitz, and Max Rosenhaus.

[47] *Ibid.*

[48] Dotey, *op. cit.*, LXXXVIII; also *The New York Times*, November 18, 1919.

1921; [49] and in February, 1922, resolutions were adopted by the Board of Education directing the Superintendent of Schools to reprimand Miss Sarah Hyams for signing the membership card of the Left Wing of the Socialist Party.[50] For advocating the reading of an article on Bolshevism, in November, 1919, Associate Superintendent Tildsley recommended that a permanent license be refused Benjamin Horwitz, a teacher of English in the De Witt Clinton High School.[51]

The suspicion that Benjamin Glassberg, a teacher of history in the Brooklyn Commercial High School, was preaching the doctrines of Bolshevism led to his suspension from service in January, 1919. Among the objections raised against Mr. Glassberg as a teacher were statements alleged to have been made by him to the effect that a teacher in the public schools was not allowed to tell the truth, that the State Department did not permit true reports to be given about conditions in Russia, and that Red Cross workers were forbidden to express true opinions regarding that country.[52]

At his trial before the Board of Education on May 9, 1919, Mr. Glassberg confessed that he had quoted from several noted Bolshevists in reply to a question whether Lenine and Trotsky were German spies. He declared that the statements with which he was charged were in answer to questions asked by his class and not as " a lecture laudatory of the Bolsheviki and severely critical of the Government of the United States." In regard to the remark about

---

[49] Dotey, *op. cit.*
[50] *Ibid.*
[51] *Ibid.*, CXII. Mr. Horwitz resigned his position in 1920.
[52] " Freedom of Teaching in the New York City Schools," *School and Society*, Vol. IX (February 1, 1919), pp. 142–143; also Dotey, *op. cit.*, LXXXVII.

freedom of speech in the public schools he asserted complete innocence.[53]   On May 29, 1919, Mr. Glassberg was dismissed from service.[54]

Considerable discussion attended the trials of the New York City teachers. To some there was no substantial foundation upon which to base charges of disloyalty, and the question resolved itself into whether a teacher need forfeit his rights to a political faith in which he believed. The answer of the school authorities came in the statement of Dr. John L. Tildsley, Associate Superintendent of Schools: " No person who adheres to the Marxian program, the program of the Left Wing of the Socialist Party in this country, should be allowed to become a teacher in the public school system, and if discovered to be a teacher, should be compelled to sever his connection with the school system, for it is impossible for such a person to carry out the purpose of the public schools . . . [the purpose] that the public schools of any country should be the expression of the country's ideals, the purpose of its institutions, and the philosophy of its life and government." [55]

But even in the eyes of the New York City school authorities the great mass of public school teachers were loyal, for out of approximately twenty-five thousand employed in the

[53] *The New York Times*, January 19, 1919. Also Department of Education of the City of New York, *In the Matter of the Trial of Charges of Conduct Unbecoming a teacher and to the prejudice of good order, efficiency and discipline preferred against Benjamin Glassberg. . . . Brief and Argument of Gilbert E. Roe in Behalf of Benjamin Glassberg, Teacher* (New York), pp. 7–8.

[54] *Ibid.* Mr. Gilbert E. Roe, counsel for Mr. Glassberg, intimated that the boys who had been selected to testify against Mr. Glassberg had been chosen " according to race and religion," that Mr. Glassberg, a Socialist and a Jew, had " guided his classes along the road of true Americanism " during the War and had received from his superiors " the highest ratings possible for his work." See also Dotey, *op. cit.*, LXXXVII.

[55] Trachtenberg, Alexander, ed., *The American Labor Year Book 1919–1920* (New York, 1920), Vol. III, p. 89.

system less than half a hundred were called to account for the views they held.[56]

Outside of the city of New York other cases of alleged infringement of the Lusk Law occurred. Among these was that of P. Hiram Mattingly, of Poughkeepsie, dismissed from the schools because at a Socialist meeting he characterized the Espionage Law as a measure of despotism, and declared that it was time that the republic be restored to this country, a first step toward which would be the acceptance of a Socialist administration in that city.[57]

Membership in the Communist Party cost Miss Julia D. Pratt her position as a music teacher in Buffalo in 1921. In passing upon her case, Frank B. Gilbert, deputy commissioner and counsel of the State Department of Education, set forth the opinion of those with whom final judgment rested when he declared: " A teacher in the public schools is a member of a state system and a servant of the people of the state. A teacher cannot properly perform the duties of her position and give expression, either verbally or by affiliation with any political or other organization, to her belief that our present government should be overthrown by revolution or by force and violence through direct action by any group or class. . . ."[58]

Teachers beyond the confines of New York suffered similar penalties, although the hand of the law did not press so heavily upon them. They, too, found it necessary to guard their speech and to abstain from proscribed political tenets, or else pay the price of reprimand or dismissal. Precisely this kind of a condition was brought forcibly upon the teachers of Washington, D. C., in the spring of 1919,

[56] *The New York Times,* May 25, 1922. According to a statement of Superintendent William L. Ettinger.
[57] Trachtenberg, *op. cit.,* p. 88.
[58] *The New York Times,* January 19, 1921.

when one of their members — Miss Alice Wood — was suspended for a week without a hearing, charged with discussing "Bolshevism and other heresies" in her classroom. Among the topics which Miss Wood later found forbidden was that of the League of Nations.[59]

The suggestion made by a supervisor of primary education in Des Moines, Iowa, that a blind patriotism might be fostered through the selection of songs and poems narrowly patriotic led to an investigation of her Americanism by the commander of the Sons of Veterans.[60]

Since 1917, however, in only twelve states besides New York cases involving disloyalty charges have been brought before the office of the state department of education. In Delaware, Louisiana, Minnesota, Montana, Nevada, North Carolina and South Dakota the charges resulted in the dismissal of teachers. In California, Maine, Minnesota, Nevada, New Hampshire, North Dakota and South Dakota, although charges were preferred against teachers the cases were dismissed for insufficient evidence.[61]

In Montana, school authorities in some cases failed to reappoint teachers at the end of the year because of alleged

[59] Trachtenberg, *op. cit.*, p. 88; also "Other Heresies," *The New Republic*, Vol. XVIII (April 12, 1919), pp. 330–331; also McAndrew, William, "American Liberty More or Less," *The World's Work*, Vol. XLVII (December, 1923), p. 180. Miss Wood declared that she gave definitions only, and referred to current magazine literature when questions were raised by a pupil concerning Bolshevism and anarchism. She also asserted that she had not discussed the Russian situation, nor had she defended Bolshevism.

[60] "The War is Over in Iowa," *The Survey*, Vol. XLVIII (September 15, 1922), p. 712; also *The Des Moines Register*, April 6, 1922. The name of the teacher was Miss Kate Kelly. She was completely exonerated of "anti-Americanism."

[61] Personal letters from the Superintendents of Public Instruction: Delaware, under date of January 30, 1924; Louisiana, December 6, 1923; Minnesota, December 1, 1923; Montana, December 3, 1923; Nevada, December 3, 1923; North Carolina, December 3, 1923; South Dakota, December 5, 1923; California, December 8, 1923; Maine, December 1, 1923; New Hampshire, December 5, 1923; North Dakota, December 20, 1923.

objectionable " utterances," although " no proof of disloyalty was ever made positive." The Department of Public Instruction of Indiana reported "a few instances " in
that state where positions were lost because of disloyalty
charges.[62]

In Louisiana, the State Superintendent of Public Instruction reported the revocation of a man's certificate because
" he capitalized the patriotism which ran high in his community, to lend money to a number of small farmers in
the community for use in purchasing War Savings Stamps
and Liberty Bonds, and for the use of which he charged an
exorbitant rate of interest." The teacher was said to have
bought " no stamps or Liberty Bonds," and boasted that he
could make more money by lending to " the suckers in the
community than by buying the low-interest paying Federal
obligations." This state also revoked the certificate of a
woman whose religious scruples forbade her endorsement of
the War and whose zeal led her to advise against the purchase of Liberty Bonds.[63]

North Carolina's case of dismissal was that of a county
superintendent charged with pro-Germanism shortly after
the entrance of the United States into the War. Although
most of the pro-German utterances of this man had been
made prior to the declaration of war by the United States,
the County Board of Education held that his influence and
usefulness had been lessened and therefore asked his resig-
nation.[64]

In Rhode Island " disclosures of thoroughly organized
preparation to cultivate in the United States a public opinion

[62] Letter from the Department of Public Instruction, December 7, 1923.
[63] Letters from the Department of Education, November 30, 1923, and
December 6, 1923.
[64] Letter from State Superintendent of Public Instruction, December 11,
1923.

favorable to Pan-Germanic aspirations for world empire led, during the War, to several investigations for the purpose of determining to what extent and through what agencies propaganda either hostile to America and to American ideals, or tending insidiously to undermine democratic institutions, had been conducted." [65]   At the request of the Governor, the Commissioner of the Public Schools undertook an investigation of the loyalty of public and private school teachers.   Questionnaires containing the following questions were dispatched to the proper authorities:

" To what extent, if any, have teachers under your observation, in the classroom or out of it, been

(a) Active in promoting German propaganda?

(b) Active in promoting anti-American propaganda?

(c) Disloyal in word, deed, or manner to nation or state?

(d) Disrespectful of law and public authority?

(e) Passive or indifferent with reference to patriotism?

(f) Cynical in their discussion of democracy, or in their discussions of history, or in their general attitude toward American public probity?

(g) Teaching that democracy and democratic institutions are crude and inefficient? "

In turn, the Commissioner of the Public Schools pointed out that " while a few teachers have not fully recognized their civic obligations in giving instruction, or have failed to realize the relation of public education to loyal citizenship, or have been remiss in upholding American ideals, the ardent patriotism of the many and their larger activities as noted by the committee of inquiry attest the civic loyalty of our teachers in our schools."   He assured the public that " no disloyal teacher " would " be suffered to teach." [66]

[65] *Forty-Ninth Annual Report of the State Board of Education . . . of Rhode Island,* January, 1919, p. 75.   [66] *Ibid.,* pp. 78-79.

This insistence upon conformity among teachers bounded on all sides their freedom of speech. It was readily and unquestioningly accepted by the great majority. It sprang from the belief that the teacher as an employee of the government should always agree with the government. The advocate of repression and control held that the public school should never be a haven where personal opinions could leaven the book-lore which was prescribed by authority. Others agreed with Zechariah Chafee that there was not only an individual but a social interest in free speech, that between that individual interest and the social interest, the former should always give way, that freedom of speech meant liberty, not license; but that freedom of speech in itself was a social interest, and that one of the purposes for the existence of society was the discovery and spread of truth, a purpose which could be accomplished only by permitting teachers to think for themselves.[67]

[67] See Chafee, Zechariah, " Freedom and Initiative in the Schools," *The Public and the Schools* (New York, 1919).

PART II

THE ACTIVITIES OF PROPAGANDIST AGENCIES

" . . . for it is the business and duty of historians to be exact, truthful, and wholly free from passion, and neither interest nor fear, hatred nor love, should make them swerve from the path of truth, whose mother is history, rival of time, storehouse of deeds, witness for the past, example and counsel for the present, and warning for the future."

CERVANTES, *Don Quixote.*

PART II

THE ACTIVITIES OF PROPAGANDIST AGENCIES

CHAPTER VI

ATTEMPTS TO CONTROL TEXTBOOKS

The public school deals with that period of life in which strong impressions find easy lodgment in the child's memory. Altruism, glorification of national achievements, hero worship, and other emotions are excited by contacts with teachers and books. It is the age in which the child's ideals can be fired by the sayings of famous men and in which the story of valorous deeds stirs a responsive enthusiasm. Indeed, it is a common belief that the influences of these early associations and impressions persist far into maturity, for " as the twig is bent, so the tree is inclined." With a keen appreciation of the possibilities of this plastic period of child life, authors of textbooks in history and the other social studies, obedient to the spirit of their times, have exalted and condemned as the prevailing temper has dictated.

History for the sake of propaganda is not a unique possession of any one country. It has been employed in the name of " patriotism " by many nations. Livy extolled Rome, Green exalted England, Bancroft eulogized the exploits of the founders of America, and Treitschke and Nietzsche pictured the glories of an imperialist régime in Germany. As a result, there has developed an overweening pride in national and racial attributes and achievements. From such a source has sprung much of the hereditary enmity between

France and Germany. Indeed, it has been said that an analogous situation exists in the United States, and a well-known writer recently declared that, through the study of American history, "Americans are taught to hate Britishers, . . . and not only descendants of the men who made the Revolution, but every newly arrived immigrant child imbibes the hatred of Great Britain of today from the patriotic ceremonies of the public schools." [1]

Propagandist history, however, is not merely an instrument of the ultra-nationalist. By the pacifist it may be employed to depict with a vivid gruesomeness the horrors of war; by it the militarist may demonstrate the advantages of preparedness; the racially conscious may narrate, in their history, achievements of their heroes to the exclusion or derogation of those of other groups; the religious enthusiasts may commend the contributions of their sect to the neglect of others; and economic and social organizations may seek to serve their particular purposes. Demands for revised history textbooks, such as emanated during the World War, to teach the point of view then current, are but a recent instance of a practice as old as the teaching of history.

HISTORY TEXTBOOKS IN THE SOUTH

In the United States, as well as elsewhere, propagandist influences have played their part in shaping the content of history textbooks. The South, in particular, has shown such tendencies, attempting in the *ante-bellum* days to propagate a history favorable to the slave-holding interests, and since that time endeavoring to justify the past in the eyes of posterity. The desire to depict events from a sectional point of view was especially apparent in the decade preced-

[1] Stephens, H. Morse, "Nationality and History," *The American Historical Review*, Vol. XXI (January, 1916), pp. 225-237.

ing the Civil War when a concerted effort to prescribe the content of history textbooks expressed itself in frequent agitations against the use of Northern textbooks. By the Southerner was raised the same query which has been raised in our own time — whether the author of a textbook has a right " to step aside from his proper course to drag in his own private views on vexed questions of national import " about which a writer should " maintain an impartial stand." [2] Such criticisms were directed against Northern textbook writers; for Southerners were agreed that an author would not be guilty of a heinous offense if he should " step aside . . . to drag in " views favorable to the institution of slavery. Indeed, a sectional presentation of history was deemed a necessity; and a movement for " home education " to combat the teachings of the " abolitionist North " attained considerable vigor in the 'fifties. To the Southerner, " home education " meant Southern trained teachers and textbooks filled with the convictions of the slave-holding South. Through such agencies it was hoped to expel from their midst " the wandering incendiary Yankee school-master " with " his incendiary school books " [3] parading under " the black piratical ensign of abolitionism." [4]

Even prior to the 'fifties, the South had realized the value of a propagandist literature, for Duff Green, a relative of John C. Calhoun, had secured a charter from South Carolina for a Southern Literary Company for the purpose of publishing school books adapted to his section.[5] Green's

---

[2] " Our School Books," *De Bow's Review*, Vol. XXVIII (1860), p. 435 et seq.   [3] *Ibid.*, p. 439.   [4] *Ibid.*, p. 437.

[5] *The United States Telegraph*, October 5, 1836, in which appeared Duff Green's prospectus for the American Literary Company, which was to have a capital of $500,000 to print the *Telegraph*, manufacture paper, publish books, prepare a new series of elementary school textbooks, elevate the general standing of literature, and " render the South independent of Northern fanatics."

efforts must have proved unsuccessful, for it was followed by much newspaper discussion of the situation, which gained in asperity as the South became more belligerent in the assertion of her rights.

Writing in *De Bow's Review* of 1855, one alarmist declared: " Our text-books are abolition works. They are so to the extent of their capacity, and though the poison of anti-slavery dogmas has not found its way into arithmetic and mixed mathematics, yet we should not be surprised to find that some work is now in progress in which the young learner will find his sums stated in abolition phrases, and perhaps be required to tell how many more sinners might have gone to Heaven if Abraham, the ' father of the faithful and the friend of God ' had not been a slave holder and a dealer in human chattels; . . . and so long as we use such work as Wayland's *Moral Science* and the abolition geographies, readers and histories, overrunning as they do, with all sorts of slanders, caricatures and blood-thirsty sentiments . . . [they will] array our children by false ideas, against the established ordinances of God, ..." [6]

Another writer could not condone the indifference of his section to the existence of such conditions. "When the public mind of our section was divided as to the justice and propriety of this institution [slavery] . . . ," he remarked, " it was not then to be wondered at that we should remain indifferent to the views presented to our youth on the subject, and that we should carelessly allow them to peruse, even in their tender years, works in which slavery was denounced as an unmitigated evil, and the universal race of Ham's descendants were blazoned forth as a set of dusky angels and martyrs. Such a course may have been defensible at that period, but tell me, what show of propriety is

[6] *De Bow's Review,* Vol. XVIII (1855), pp. 660–661.

there in its continuance at the present day? We have become awake to the rightfulness and justice of our stand; we have come to know that we are more sinned against than sinning; and we have witnessed the complete failure of many quixotic attempts to transform negroes into prosperous and thriving freemen. Why then should we wish that the rising generation, who are to frame and control public opinion, after we have passed from being, should be on this question of vital importance taught doctrines which are in direct conflict with what we now believe? " [7]

Because " southern life, habits, thoughts, and aims " were " so essentially different from those of the North," another protagonist of " home education " maintained that a different character of books and training was required to " bring up the boy to manhood with his faculties fully developed." [8] Nor could this " true man " be developed if he must sit " at the feet of some abolition Gamaliel of the North," but he must have " books and teachers of history from the South who should point out the destiny of the South." [9]

As a result of the agitation of the press, the commercial conventions, which met during the years from 1853 to 1860, committed themselves with one accord, to the Southern educational program. The Memphis Convention of 1853 demanded the employment of native teachers, the encouragement of a home press, and the publication of books adapted to the educational wants and the social conditions of the section.[10] The following year, the Charleston Convention passed a resolution which urged the production of textbooks by Southern men " with express reference to the proper

---

[7] *De Bow's Review*, Vol. XXVIII (1860), p. 435 *et seq.*
[8] " Southern School Books," *De Bow's Review*, Vol. XIII (1852), pp. 258–266.
[9] *Ibid.*, p. 265.
[10] *Ibid.*, Vol. XV (1853), p. 268.

education of the Southern youth." [11]   The resolution declared that "this Convention earnestly recommends all
parents and guardians within these states, to consider well,
that to neglect the claims of their own seminaries and colleges, and patronize and enrich those of remote states, is
fraught with peril to our sacred interests, perpetuating our
dependence on those who do not understand and cannot
appreciate our necessities and responsibilities; and at the
same time fixing a lasting reproach upon our institutions,
teachers and people." [12]

In 1856, the Savannah Convention issued to " The People
of the Slaveholding States " an address advocating joint
action on the part of the Southern legislatures.   " It will be
well, at least, to look to our school books," they declared.
" Can the making of these be entrusted exclusively to those,
who by instilling an occasional heresy, dangerous to our
repose, imagine that they serve at the same time God and
Mammon — their consciences and their pocket?   The State
Legislatures at the South alone are competent to heal this
mischief.   Property will submit to any amount of taxation
for such a purpose.   A system can and ought to be matured
at the South by which the most ample encouragement shall
be given to its educational system and its press.   Withdraw
at once the contributions which are returned too often to us
now in contumely and insult." [13]

At the same convention the committee upon the subject
of " Text Books for Southern Schools and Colleges " reported that " the books rapidly coming into use in our
schools and colleges at the South are not only polluted with
opinions adverse to our institutions, and hostile to our con-

[11] *Ibid.*, Vol. XVII (1854), p. 508.
[12] *Ibid.*
[13] *Ibid.*, Vol. XXI (1856), p. 553.

stitutional views, but are inferior in every respect, as books of instruction to those which might be produced amongst ourselves, or procured from Europe. . . ."[14] The Committee proposed that the convention take the matter " under their auspices and select or prepare such a series of books, in every department of study, from the earliest primer to the highest grade of literature and science, as shall seem to them best qualified to elevate and purify the education of the South."[15] The Committee further recommended that " when this series of books shall have been prepared, the Legislatures of the Southern States be requested to adopt them as text-books."[16]

The committees appointed at the Southern conventions evidently failed to obtain results, for *De Bow's Review* of 1858 querulously remarked that the committees seemed to have dropped into repose after their appointments.[17] Newspaper agitation, however, continued without abatement, *The Constitutionalist* suggesting, in 1858, that Georgia by law should compel her schools to use Georgia school books in which information was given regarding the early history of the state, and which contained " eloquent and patriotic emanations from the gifted pens " of some of their " ablest writers."[18]

·History textbooks held a conspicuous place in most of the discussions. Peter Parley's *History*, extensively used at this time, came in for much adverse criticism because, in the opinion of the Southerner, it " insulted " and " misrepre-

[14] *Ibid.*, Vol. XXII (1857), p. 104. Committee was composed of J. D. S. De Bow, of Louisiana; H. Gourdin, of South Carolina; and D. McRae, of North Carolina.

[15] *Ibid.*

[16] *Ibid.*

[17] *Ibid.*, Vol. XXV (1856), p. 117. Article on "Southern School Books."

[18] *Ibid.*, p. 597.

sented " the institutions of the South.[19] " If it is important for us to have a home literature of our own in the lighter departments of reading and knowledge," one critic remarked, " how much more vitally essential it is to our best interests that the books from which our children imbibe their earliest lessons in history and political economy should be written by those who are able to expound and vindicate, instead of misrepresenting and defaming the institutions under which they are to live and be educated." [20]

Further criticism of the same textbook is found in an article on " Wants of the South " in *De Bow's Review* for 1860. " Our schools have long been groaning under the burden of questionable orthodoxy, and in some instances decided hostility to the institutions which her public instructors, of all others, may reasonably be expected to advocate and defend," said one writer. " . . . no teacher or pupil who has used Peter Parley's Histories, or any of the popular ' Readers ' and ' Orators ' from which juvenile disciples of Demosthenes have learned to spout so glibly eloquent invectives against slavery, the slave trade, will fail to recognize the long-deplored existence of this deadly evil." [21]

Other books of an historical nature, which were especially obnoxious to the South, were Gilbert's *Atlas* and Appleton's *Complete Guide of the World,* which contained " hidden lessons of the most fiendish and murderous character that enraged fanaticism could conceive or indite." [22] " This book and many other northern school books scattered over the country come within range of the Statutes of this State

[19] Peter Parley was the pen-name of S. G. Goodrich.
[20] " Education at the South," by " A South Carolinian," *ibid.,* Vol. XXI (1856), pp. 651–652. Peter Parley's (Goodrich's) *Pictorial History of the United States* was also criticized. *Ibid.,* p. 657.
[21] *Ibid.,* Vol. XXIX (1860), p. 219.
[22] *Ibid.,* Vol. XVIII (1855), p. 661.

[Louisiana], which provide for the imprisonment for life or the infliction of a penalty of death upon any person who shall publish or distribute such works . . . ," declared one writer.[23]

Whelpley's *Compend of History* was also considered heretical in nature because of its discussion of slavery, which inculcated "improper precepts in the minds of our children."[24]   The writer in his diatribe against this book quoted the following passage from Whelpley to prove his point: "But for what purpose was he [the slave] brought from his country?   Why was he forced from the scenes of his youth, and the cool retreats of his native mountains?   Was it, that he might witness the saving knowledge of the gospel? . . . No. He was deprived of his *freedom,* the dearest pledge of his existence. *His mind was not cultivated and improved by science! . . . He is detested for his complexion, and ranked among the brutes for his stupidity.* His laborious exertions are extorted from him to enrich his purchasers, and *his scanty allowance is furnished, only that he may endure his sufferings for their aggrandizement.*"[25]

The discussion of slavery in the Northern textbooks was not the only cause for irritation.   Equally distasteful to the Southerner were the invidious comparisons made between North and South.[26]   The histories produced by the North, one writer pointed out, " are filled with praise and glorification of the New England and Northern states generally, as a set of incorruptible patriots, irreproachable moralists, and most exemplary models for future imitation, and their descendants are depicted as fully equalling the standard set

[23] *Ibid.,* p. 663.
[24] *Ibid.,* Vol. XXI (1856), p. 653.
[25] *Ibid.,* p. 653. The italics are supplied by the transcriber.
[26] *Ibid.,* Vol. XXII (1857), p. 557. Criticism of Willson's *Outlines of History* and his *American History.*

for them by their distinguished ancestors, of unexceptionable demeanor. On the other hand, the individuals who organized society in the Southern States are pictured as a race of immoral reprobates, who have handed down all of their vices and evil habits to their descendants of this day. While the institution of slavery and its introduction into our country are made the occasion of much violent invective, there is but a slight effort at rebuke, and a large amount of apology is offered, for the amusements of burning witches, hanging Quakers, and banishing Baptists, formerly so very popular in New England. While we, who now support and defend the institution of slavery, are either denounced or pitied, the residents of the Northern States, who have always been the chief prosecutors of the slave trade are allowed to pass uncensured. Such is the state of the histories." [27]

To Willson's *Historical Series* objection was raised because "the author has elected to make himself sectional and therefore must expect sectional support." "Why say of the odious Hartford Convention," a critic remarked, "'Its proceedings were not as objectionable as many anticipated,' or why use comparisons between the different sections as invidious, and as we believe and know, as false as these: 'In Virginia and the southern colonies, where the inhabitants guided in the selection of their dwelling places chiefly by consideration of agricultural conveniences, dispersed themselves over the face of the country, often at considerable distances from each other, schools and churches were necessarily rare, and social intercourse but little known. The evils of the state of society thus produced still exist to a considerable extent in the southern portions of the Union. The colonization of New England was more favorable to the improvement of human character and morals.'" Further

[27] *Ibid.*, Vol. XXVIII (1860), p. 438. "Our School Books."

cause for complaint lay in the following passage: " Of the state of manners and morals in Maryland, Virginia and the southern colonies generally, we cannot give so gratifying an account. While the upper classes of inhabitants among the southern people were distinguished for a luxurious and expensive hospitality, they were too generally addicted to the vices of card playing, gambling and intemperance, while hunting and cock-fighting were favorite amusements of persons of all ranks. . . . It cannot be denied, however, that New England colonial history furnishes, on the whole, the most agreeable reminiscences, as well as the most abundant materials for the historian." [28]

So common was a biased presentation of controversial questions in the books of the time that William Howard Russell, The [London] Times correspondent during the Civil War, declared that he was unable to obtain " a single solid, substantial work " on the controversy between the North and the South, for there was not one published which was " worth a cent." [29]

Little response to the exponents of "home education " seems to have been made at this time by the state legislatures, although, in 1859, the Louisiana legislature adopted a resolution endorsing the movement " to encourage the pro-

[28] *Ibid.*, Vol. XXII (1857), p. 557. Again in an article on " Southern School Books," Vol. XXV (1858), p. 117. Geographies and readers received similar criticism, because they, too, contained " invidious " comparisons or sought to " inculcate improper precepts " in the minds of the children on the subject of slavery. In 1868 Willson's *Intermediate Readers* were condemned because the fourth of the series declared: " The Great Rebellion was a war set on foot for the purpose of destroying the government of the United States."

[29] Russell, William Howard, *My Diary North and South* (Boston, 1863), p. 25. " Mr. Appleton sells no less than one million and a half of Webster's spelling-books a year; his tables are covered with a flood of pamphlets, some for, others against coercion; some for, others opposed to slavery, — but when I asked for a single solid, substantial work on the present difficulty, I was told there was not one published worth a cent."

duction of and introduction into the schools of Louisiana of a series of school books written by citizens of the State, published in the South, not contaminated by the fanaticism of Northern authors." [39] Other Southern states since the Civil War have prescribed the type of histories to be used in their schools, but they have had for their chief intent a "proper presentation of the War of the States."

Since the Civil War the most active exponents of a pro-Southern history have been Southern veterans' associations and kindred groups. Especially vigilant have been the United Confederate Veterans who, since 1892, with few exceptions have announced in annual convention their advocacy of "a true and reliable history." In 1892, the first historical committee, composed of "comrades skilled and experienced in such matters," was appointed to "select proper and truthful histories of the United States to recommend for use in the public and private schools of the South." [31] No meeting of the Veterans was held in 1893, but the following year the Historical Committee offered an extensive and elaborate report.[32] This report suggested the establishment of a chair of American history in Southern universities with time for research; that the Association recommend to the legislatures of Southern states that provision be made in the public school course for the teaching of history of the native state for one year, and for the establishment and support of a chair of American history in the state university or some suitable state institution, and that the preparation of school histories of the state be en-

[30] *Acts* of Louisiana, 1859, No. 244, p. 190.
[31] *Minutes of the Third Annual Meeting and Reunion of the Confederate Veterans* . . . 1892, pp. 98–99.
[32] *Minutes of the Fourth Annual Meeting and Reunion of the United Confederate Veterans* . . . 1894, pp. 3–12.

couraged; that all private schools and academies teach the history of the state one year and devote the same amount of time to United States history; and that state legislatures be memorialized in order to gain their coöperation in securing "a different presentation of the narrative of facts for the truth of history of our common country." [33]

The Committee, besides their recommendations, classified school histories in three groups. In the first class were those issued in the first ten or fifteen years following the close of the War, "dictated by prejudice and prompted by the evil passion that time had not then softened." Secondly came those Northern histories apparently fair, either through a revision of an earlier edition or emasculation, in an "effort to curry favor with the text-book patrons of both sections"; also those histories with separate editions for North and South, as well as those "written and published at the North in which an honest effort is made to do justice to the South" but which failed to emphasize the distinctive features of the South or to emphasize the place of the South in the history of the Union. The third group contained a list of textbooks acceptable to the Veterans, including *Hansell's Histories* by H. E. Chambers of Louisiana, *History of the American People* by J. H. Shinn of Arkansas, *History of the United States* by Alexander Stephens of Georgia, *History of the United States* by George F. Holmes of Virginia, *History of the United States* by Blackburn and McDonald of Maryland, *Grammar School History* by L. A. Field of Georgia, and *History of the United States* by J. T. Terry of Georgia.

The report of the Committee of 1894 was accepted unanimously and the resolution, passed to continue the committee, urged that it "do everything in its power to encourage the preparation of suitable school histories and especially to

[33] *Ibid.*

encourage their publication by the building up of Southern publishing houses. . . ." [34]

The Reports of 1895 and of 1896 manifested the same spirit and offered substantially the same recommendations as those made by the Committee of 1894. Both desired a " vindication for the Southern people and a refutation of the slanders, the misrepresentations and the imputations " which they had " so long and patiently borne." [35] The Report of 1895 pointed out that " while the South has always been prominent in making history, she has left the writing of history to New England historians " whose chief defect was " lack of catholic sympathy for all sections of the country." [36] The importance of the work of the Historical Committee was recognized in 1895 by increasing its membership from seven to fifteen to include a representative from each Southern state.[37]

By 1897 the agitation for sectional histories had become so stormy that the Nashville reunion took under advisement a suggestion of the Grand Army of the Republic of Wisconsin, which proposed the appointment of a " commission of distinguished educators from the ranks of the contending armies " who should write a history of the period 1861 to 1865 which should be satisfactory to both sections.[38] The

[34] *Ibid.* The meeting of the Veterans was at Birmingham, Alabama.

[35] *Minutes of the Fifth Annual Meeting and Reunion of the Confederate Veterans* . . . 1895, p. 13.

[36] *Ibid.*, p. 15. The Committee of 1895 added to the list of acceptable textbooks drawn up in 1894 the *History of the United States* by Susan P. Lee.

[37] In the meeting held in 1896 the following histories received endorsement: *School History of the United States*, by J. William Jones, D. D. of Virginia, *Brief History of the United States*, by Susan Pendleton Lee of Virginia, *Our Country, A History of the States*, by Oscar H. Cooper and others of Texas. *Minutes . . . of the United Confederate Veterans, . . .* 1896, pp. 28–50.

[38] *Minutes . . . of the United Confederate Veterans* . . . 1897, p. 49. See also *Journal . . . of the Grand Army of the Republic* . . . 1897, p. 233. The activities of the G. A. R. are discussed later.

Historical Committee of the Confederate Veterans, however, deemed it inadvisable to undertake such a project, believing that a history textbook could not be written as well by a commission as by one person. However, the Committee pointed out that "the destiny of the South is now inseparably bound up with that of this great republic and that it is to the interest of the whole nation and its citizens everywhere that coming generations of Southern men should give to the Union the same love and devotion which their fathers gave to the United States and then to the ill-starred Confederacy; . . . ."[39] And, although they realized that "no sectional history is wanted in the schools of this country," yet the Southern people desired in their histories "to retain from the wreck in which their constitutional views, their domestic institutions, the mass of their property, and the lives of their best and bravest were lost, the knowledge that their conduct was honorable throughout, and that their submission at last . . . in no way blackened their motives or established the wrong of the cause for which they fought."[40]

Among the points at issue in the adoption of Northern textbooks was the use of certain opprobrious terms. At the Atlanta reunion in 1898, a resolution was adopted which gave voice to such objections. It requested the substitution of the term "the civil war between the States" for "the war of the Rebellion," because such an expression reflected "on the patriotism of the Southern people and the cause for which they so heroically fought. . . ."[41] The Historical Committee at the same time indicated their aversion to other "offensive epithets" in Northern histories, such as "rebels" and "arch-traitors."[42] They recommended, among other things, that "Boards of Education and all

[39] *Minutes . . . of the United Confederate Veterans . . . , op. cit.,* p. 46.
[40] *Ibid.*
[41] *Minutes . . . of the United Confederate Veterans . . .* 1898, p. 87.
[42] *Ibid.,* pp. 44–52.

others having charge of the selection of histories, geographies, speeches, readers, etc., be careful to exclude works that show the partisan, sectional and unpatriotic spirit." [43]

Yet the need of a "broad American patriotism" was recognized by the United Confederate Veterans regardless of their attacks on Northern produced histories. Such an attitude manifested itself in the committee report of the reunion of 1898 which quoted with favorable comment an extract from an address of Commander John W. Frazier of the Fred Taylor Post, G. A. R., of Philadelphia. The Confederate Veterans especially approved the spirit of Mr. Frazier when he declared: "We must under the blending influence exerted by the new order of things, undo that which sectional feelings led both North and South to do in regard to the publication of public school histories — certain to create and foster lasting and bitter prejudices — and use our influence in behalf of a public school history of the late war and the causes leading to it, that will be used in common in all the public schools of the country, ..." [44]

The suggestion of Mr. Frazier reflected the welding influence of the Spanish-American War upon all factions in America. In 1899, the Historical Committee of the Confederate Veterans announced that its duty was " little more than to keep watch upon the histories of the day " for " the prospect for fairness and candor in historical writing " seemed " much improved since the Spanish War," because " a new perspective," had been afforded the historian. [45] Yet the same report evidenced a watchfulness on the part of the Southerner to prevent the use of books which " either pervert or fail to do justice to the history of the people of this

[43] *Ibid.*
[44] *Ibid.*
[45] *Minutes . . . of the Confederate Veterans . . .* 1898, pp. 144–154.

section." [46] The reunion further endorsed the recommendation of the Historical Committee for the appointment in
each state of a sub-committee of three to examine " every
history taught in the schools of the state with especial reference to ascertaining whether said books contain incorrect or
inaccurate statements or make important omissions of facts,
or inculcate narrow or partisan sentiments." [47] In the event
that any defects were found in any of the histories used in
the schools, the Committee suggested that each sub-committee should " enter into friendly correspondence with the
authors and publishers of such books, with a view to correcting such errors, or supplying such omissions." In addition,
it became the duty of each sub-committee " annually, one
month before each reunion to make a report" to the Historical Committee, showing what histories of the state and
of the United States were used in the schools of the state;
and further " to make such suggestions with regard to school
histories and with regard to the teaching of history " as
might seem appropriate.[48]

The reports of the next few years show a slackening
vigilance on the part of the historical committees. At each
meeting of the Veterans a report and suggestions as to the
improvement of historical instruction in the South were
offered, but much of the recriminatory tone of the reports of
the 'nineties had disappeared. In 1900, the Committee
recommended again that the term " the war between the
states " be substituted for other terms, and that money be
appropriated in order that the Historical Committee could
carry on their campaign, through the press and public
meetings, for the use of histories doing " full justice " both
to the South and the North.[49] The Reunion of 1902 sanc-

[46] *Ibid.*, p. 147.   [47] *Ibid.*, p. 152.   [48] *Ibid.*
[49] *Minutes . . . of the Confederate Veterans . . .* 1900, pp. 78, 80.

tioned the suggestion of the Historical Committee dealing
with the preparation of a source book portraying the " character, the ideals and the leadership of the South," and called
favorable attention to Thomas Dixon's novel *The Leopard's
Spots.*[50]

The historical reports presented to the reunions held in
1908, 1909 and 1910 still discussed the need for " true history " although commending the fairness of most historians.
Yet the Committee hesitated to relax its watchfulness because " the history of the Confederate period as it is told in
many books that may be used in our schools, . . . demands
and deserves undiminished vigilance." [51]

The Report of 1910 expressed, however, a sanguine satisfaction in the condition resulting from the agitation about
history textbooks. " We do not fear the bookmaker now,"
the Veterans declared. " Southern schools and Southern
teachers have prepared books which Southern children may
read without insult or traduction of their fathers. Printing
presses all over the Southland — and all over the Northland
— are sending forth by thousands ones which tell the true
character of the heroic struggle. The influence and wealth
of the South forbid longer the perversion of truth and the
falsification of history." [52]

In the reports of the historical committees two history
textbooks received specific criticism for their treatment of
Southern institutions and life. In 1903, attention was called

[50] *Minutes . . . of the Confederate Veterans . . .* 1902, pp. 54–59. The
Report of 1901 pointed out that " one of the most favorable omens of
our times is the catholicity with which thoughtful men, both North and
South, now speak and write of the issues of the war between the States."
Minutes . . . of the Confederate Veterans . . . 1901, p. 61. A similar
sentiment was expressed at the Reunion of 1904. *Minutes . . . of the Confederate Veterans . . .* 1904, pp. 32–33.

[51] *Minutes . . . of the Confederate Veterans . . .* 1909, pp. 30–38.

[52] *Minutes . . . of the Confederate Veterans . . .* 1910, p. 101.

to a paragraph in *The Young People's Story of the Great Republic* by Ella Hines Stratton, in which "a most false and misleading account" was given of the capture of Fort Pillow by General N. B. Forrest.[53] The Report of 1911 devoted considerable space to an attack on Elson's *History of the United States*. "One of the most extraordinary happenings in regard to the history of the South occurred in Virginia in the last few weeks," chronicled the Report. "Elson's History of the United States had been selected as a textbook by Roanoke College. Miss Sarah Moffett, one of the students of the college, refused to attend the history class or use this history where it referred to the South and its people. For this she suffered reprimand."[54] The Southern Cross Chapter of the United Daughters of the Confederacy thereupon undertook an investigation and issued a circular which was "widely distributed."[55] The circular was addressed: "To the Daughters of the Confederacy, the Camps of the Confederate Veterans, the Sons of Veterans, and to all Who are Loyal to the Southland, and Love Her Traditions and Desire a truthful History of Her Social and Political Life."[56]

The charges brought against Mr. Elson rested upon "the partisan spirit that prompted the writer to slander a people who had reached the pinnacle of high ideals, refinement and culture, and to which it has never been the fortune of many to attain."[57] To the Southerner was especially abhorrent the portrayal of slave life in the South in which it was said:

[53] *Minutes . . . of the Confederate Veterans . . . 1903*, p. 164. The Southerners felt that Northern histories failed to recognize any successes of the Confederate forces. The objectionable points in Stratton's book were found on pages 257–258, according to the *Minutes*.

[54] *Minutes . . . of the Confederate Veterans . . . 1911*, p. 11.

[55] *Ibid.*

[56] *Ibid.* This appeared in large black-faced type in the *Report*.

[57] *Ibid.*, p. 12.

" ' Often the attractive slave woman was a prostitute to her master,' " " ' an evil ' " that " ' was widespread at the South.' " [58]   Further objections arose to the statement: " ' A sister of President Madison declared that though the Southern ladies were complimented with the name of wife they were only the mistresses of Seraglios ' "; and that " ' a leading Southern lady declared to Harriet Martineau that the wife of many a planter was but the chief slave of his harem.' " [59]   Mr. Elson was also regarded as misrepresenting the cause of the Civil War, which he attributed " to slavery and slavery alone " and not to state rights, which he declared " in the abstract had nothing to do with bringing on the war." [60]

In response to the circular of the United Daughters of the Confederacy, the Veterans adopted a resolution indicating that it could not be " too earnestly pressed upon the attention of those in charge of our educational institutions the supreme importance of excluding from our schools and colleges all histories that do not in their reports of the great struggle for constitutional liberty . . . fairly and impartially represent the facts."   The Reunion further resolved that there be used " only such histories as will recognize the justice of that cause [of 1861–1865] in support of which so many of our brave comrades shed their blood and gave their lives." [61]

In 1912 the agitation regarding history textbooks had lost much of its bitterness and the line of cleavage between the Northerner's history and that of the Southerner seemed less apparent.   Under the fusing influence of the World War, the Confederate Veterans held their reunion in 1917 in the city of Washington where Confederate and Union flags waved together.[62]   But the spirit of sectional interest had

[58] *Ibid.*, p. 13.   [59] *Ibid.*   [60] *Ibid.*   [61] *Ibid.*
[62] *Reunion of the United Confederate Veterans Proceedings of the Twenty-Seventh Annual Reunion.*

too long enslaved them and, in 1921, the Reunion favorably adopted a report of the Rutherford Committee. Chief among the achievements for a "true history" which the Committee were able to report was the adoption of satisfactory histories in the states of Mississippi and Texas. The Committee predicted similar action in North Carolina where there were "true histories by Southern authors and published by a home house," thereby eliminating any necessity for even considering "any Yankee books." [63]

A revival of propaganda for sectional histories since 1921 is due in some degree to the appearance of two pamphlets which set forth the need of a distinct type of history for the South: *The Truth of the War Conspiracy of 1861*, by H. W. Johnstone, and *Truths of History*, by Mildred Lewis Rutherford, state historian for the United Daughters of the Confederacy. These pamphlets received the unanimous endorsement of the United Confederate Veterans at their meeting in Richmond, Virginia, June, 1922, in a resolution recommending their use in the public schools. [64] Among other things, these writings purported to establish the fact that Lincoln began the Civil War. The committee report declared: "This [*The Truth of the War Conspiracy of 1861*] presents the official evidence gathered principally from the United States Government archives, which proves the Confederate War was deliberately and personally conceived and its inauguration made by Abraham Lincoln, and that he was

---

[63] *Minutes . . . United Confederate Veterans,* 1921, p. 11. Report of the Rutherford Committee, October 24, 1921, C. Irvine Walker, general chairman.

[64] *The New York Times,* June 21, 1922. Miss Rutherford's ideas had been endorsed by the United Confederate Veterans in Atlanta, October 7-11, 1919. See *A Measuring Rod for Text-Books* prepared by Miss Rutherford (Athens, Georgia). This pamphlet sought to establish some of the facts later brought out in *Truths of History.*

personally responsible for forcing the war upon the South." [65]

The endorsement of this ultra-Southern viewpoint caused a storm of protest, particularly in the North. Under the caption "The Confederate Veterans' New Glands," the *Chicago Daily Tribune* observed: "We are moved to wonder, 'What is history?' The Standard Dictionary defines it as 'a systematic record of past events.' No better definition in six words occurs to us. But more or less recent events in world politics, coupled with the current action of the Confederate Veterans, indicates [*sic*] that that definition is in error. History is becoming, if it has not already reached that stage, a medium of propaganda. That became evident in the world war, when European histories were combed for evidence of the innate barbarity of the German people. It was more evident in the efforts to arouse the American people to the point of intervention and actual warfare to free Ireland. It is now emphasized through the efforts of the Confederate Veterans to impose upon the children of the south their own interpretation of the Civil War, regardless of accuracy or the effect upon the nation. The Veterans are attempting to pass on their old hates and rancors to their descendants. They have not yet surrendered to Grant. They are a trifle feeble, to be sure, but apparently becoming less so. They are busily engaged in swapping their old glands for new." [66]

The New York Times expressed equally strong disapproval of an effort to revive the bitterness of the past and attempt "a revocation of beatification or canonization" of Lincoln. [67]

---

[65] *Ibid.*

[66] *Chicago Daily Tribune*, June 23, 1922, editorial.

[67] *The New York Times*, June 23, 1922, editorial. The *Times* felt that "quite the gravest of Miss Rutherford's charges against Lincoln, . . . is

No less resentful at the attempted disparagement of Lincoln's services were the officers of the Grand Army of the Republic, who assailed Miss Rutherford's statement that Lincoln began the war as a " lie." [68]   Mrs. John A. Logan, representing the Dames of the Loyal Legion, also offered objections to such " a perversion of facts," and declared that all patriotic societies would be urged to seek the suppression of any such histories.[69]

Protests against this revival of sectional animosity were not localized in the North. *The Macon* [Georgia] *Telegraph* suggested to Miss Rutherford that she would find better employment were she to bring to public view the virtues, the generosities and heroisms which were in the Old South and should be carried over in the New South. The *Telegraph* also believed that it would prove fruitful of good were she to dwell on the cordial tributes paid by the North to Lee as a man and as a general; and as for Lincoln, with much less research than she used in unearthing dubious evidences of his antagonism to the Southerners, she could find almost innumerable and indubitable proofs of his goodwill. The *Telegraph* concluded that " the whole nation looks upon its Lincolns and its Lees as Americans, and humanity looks upon them as its own." [70]

Beside the allegation that Lincoln began the Civil War, Miss Rutherford, following the impulse given her by the Johnstone pamphlet, *Truths of the War Conspiracy of 1861*,[71]

---

that he wanted a civil war and forced the South to begin one that inevitably would end in her defeat and ruin." Objection was also raised to Miss Rutherford's charge that Lincoln's Gettysburg address was worthless. Rutherford, Mildred, *Truths of History* (Athens, Georgia, 1921).

[68] *The New York Times*, June 28, 1922.

[69] *Ibid.*, June 24, 1922.

[70] *Ibid.*, November 4, 1922.

[71] Written in 1917 and sent to Miss Rutherford who added to the contents and produced her *Truths of History*.

offered quotations to show that Lincoln was not a fit example for children, nor was he given his rightful place in history. Such quotations as the following are indicative of the character of her remarks: "People found in Lincoln before his death nothing remarkably good or great, but on the contrary, found in him the reverse of goodness or greatness. Lincoln as one of Fame's immortals does not appear in the Lincoln of 1861 (Schouler's *History of the United States,* Vol. VI, p. 21)."[72] "Lincoln signed the liquor revenue bill and turned the saloon loose on the country, thus undoing the previous temperance work of the churches."[73] "Mr. Lincoln went to church, but he went to mock and came away to mimic."[74] "The people all drank, and Abe was for doing what the people did, right or wrong."[75] Miss Rutherford also presented evidence designed to prove that Lincoln was a tricky politician,[76] and that the Emancipation Proclamation was unconstitutional.[77]

In contrast with these characterizations of Lincoln are the "spotless integrity, controlling conscience" and "sincere religious convictions" ascribed to Davis. Even a Northern historian, Ridpath, according to Miss Rutherford, testified that Davis had bitterness toward no man.[78]

Eighty-one per cent of the schools and colleges in the South, according to Miss Rutherford, were using, in 1921, "text-books untrue to the South," and "seventeen per cent" were "using histories omitting most important facts concerning the South."[79] As written, the histories "magnify

[72] Rutherford, *op. cit.*

[73] *Ibid.,* p. 64. Miss Rutherford gave no source for this quotation.

[74] *Ibid.,* p. 70. Miss Rutherford ascribed this quotation to Lamon's *Life of Lincoln.*

[75] *Ibid.,* from Lamon's *Life of Lincoln.*

[76] *Ibid.,* pp. 77–78. Quoted from Charles Francis Adams, Lamon's *Recollections of Lincoln,* Mr. Everett, and Mr. Seward.

[77] *Ibid.,* p. 71.   [78] *Ibid.,* p. 57.   [79] *Ibid.,* p. 1.

and exalt the New England colonies and the Mayflower crew, with bare mention of the Jamestown Colony, thirteen years older, and the crews of the *Susan Constant*, the *Discovery*, and the *Goodspeed*." [80] Other objectionable features in most school histories were the "extended account" generally given to the "religious faith and practice" of New England with no mention of Sir Thomas Dale's Code in the Jamestown Colony, "which enforced daily attendance upon Divine worship, penalty for absence, penalty for blasphemy, penalty for speaking evil of the Church, and refusing to answer the Catechism, and for neglecting work." [81]

Other Southerners than Miss Rutherford have criticized the customary presentation of history. "We owe it to our dead, to our living, and to our children, to preserve the truth and repel the falsehoods, so that we may secure just judgment from the only tribunal before which we may appear and be fully and fairly heard, and that tribunal is the bar of history," asserted Benjamin H. Hill.[82] Likewise Thomas Nelson Page declared: "In a few years there will be no South to demand a history if we have history as it is now written. How do we stand today in the eyes of the world? We are esteemed 'ignorant, illiterate, cruel, semi-barbarous, a race sunken in brutality and vice, a race of slave drivers who disrupted the Union in order to perpetuate human slavery and who as a people have contributed nothing to the advancement of mankind.' " [83]

Among the textbooks designated by Miss Rutherford for special criticism were Davidson's *History of the United States*, Montgomery's *Beginner's American History*, and Muzzey's *An American History*.[84] Davidson was criticized

[80] *Ibid.*, p. 11.   [81] *Ibid.*   [82] *Ibid.*   [83] *Ibid.*, p. v.
[84] Davidson, William M., *History of the United States* (Chicago, 1903); Montgomery, David, *The Beginner's American History* (Boston, 1899, 1920); Muzzey, D. S., *An American History* (Boston, 1920).

because he asserted that " the Jamestown colonists were vicious idlers and jail birds picked up on the streets of London," and because of the statement that " side by side the two civilizations had grown up in America — the one dedicated to progress and kept up with the spirit of the age — the other a landed aristocracy with slavery as the chief excuse for its existence." [85]

Condemnation was meted out to Muzzey's textbook because it was alleged that he said, " The cause for which the Confederate soldiers fought was an unworthy cause and should have been defeated," and because " it is impossible for the student of history today to feel otherwise than that the cause for which the South fought was unworthy." [86] Montgomery was placed in the objectionable group because he described the settlers of Georgia as " filthy, ragged, dirty prisoners taken from the 'Debtor's Prison' by Oglethorpe." [87]

[85] Rutherford, op. cit., p. 104.

[86] Ibid., p. 110. This quotation from Muzzey's is incorrect in Truths of History. Muzzey, eulogizing the Southern women, adds this statement: " It is impossible for the student of history today to feel otherwise than that the victory of the South in 1861–1865 would have been a calamity for every section of our country. But the indomitable valor and utter self-sacrifice with which the South defended her cause both at home and in the field must always arouse our admiration." Muzzey, An American History, pp. 372–373.

[87] Rutherford, op. cit., p. 104. In her chapter entitled " Reconstruction was not just to the South. This injustice made the Ku Klux Klan a necessity," Miss Rutherford, pursuing a policy peculiarly inharmonious for a writer of Truths of History, allowed herself again to become negligent as to the accuracy of her quotations. Citing Muzzey as one authority for the title of her chapter, she ascribed the following statement to him: " The rules of these negro governments of 1868 was an indescribable orgy of extravagance, fraud and disgusting incompetence — a travesty on government. Unprincipled politicians dominated the States' government and plunged the States further and further into debt by voting themselves enormous salaries, and reaping in many ways hundreds of thousands of dollars in graft. In South Carolina $200,000 were spent in furnishing the State Capitol with costly plate glass mirrors, lounges, armchairs, a free bar and other luxurious appointments for the use of the negro and scalawag

On the other hand, R. G. Horton's *A Youth's History of the Civil War* presents a point of view acceptable to Miss Rutherford, for it declares that "the withdrawal of the Southern States from the Union was in no sense a declaration of war upon the Federal government but the Federal government declared war on them, as history will show." [88]

Doubtless the most prejudiced discussion of mooted questions since the Civil War appears in the textbooks produced before the opening of the twentieth century. This period, in general, characterized by a spirit of intense local patriotism, reflected itself clearly in the history textbooks. During this period were published such Southern textbooks as Venable, *A School History of the United States*, Lee, *New School*

---

legislators. It took the South nine years to get rid of these governments." In reading Muzzey's book, the reader cannot but wonder at the reason for the inaccuracy of the quotation, for precisely the same end would have been accomplished had Miss Rutherford quoted verbatim: "The Reconstruction governments of the South were sorry affairs. For the exhausted states, already amply 'punished' by the desolation of war, the rule of the negro and his unscrupulous carpetbagger patron was an indescribable orgy of extravagance, fraud, and disgusting incompetence, — a travesty on government. Instead of seeking to build up the shattered resources of the South by economy and industry, the new legislators plunged the states further and further into debt by voting themselves enormous salaries and by spending lavish sums of money on railroads, canals, and public buildings and works, for which they reaped hundreds of thousands of dollars in graft." In a footnote Muzzey adds the following from which Miss Rutherford has culled the idea for part of her quotation: "The economic evils and social humiliation brought on the South by the Reconstruction governments are almost beyond description. South Carolina, for example, had a legislature in which 98 of the 155 members were negroes . . . ; in one year $200,000 was spent in furnishing the state capitol with costly plate-glass mirrors, lounges, desks, armchairs, and other luxurious appointments, including a free bar for the use of the negro and scalawag legislators. It took the Southern states from two to nine years to get rid of these governments." See Rutherford, *op. cit.*, p. 87; Muzzey, *op. cit.*, pp. 387–388.

[88] Horton, Rushmore G., *A Youth's History of the Great Civil War in the United States from 1861–1865* (New York, 1866).

History of the United States, Chambers, *A School History of the United States,* and Taylor, *Model School History.*

Susan Pendleton Lee's *New School History of the United States* can be quoted as typical. " The Constitution of the United States recognized slavery. . . . The opinion that it was a moral wrong did not prevail before the days of Garrison and his followers who pronounced it to be the sum of all ' iniquity.' . . . The outcry against slavery had made the Southern people study the subject, and they had reached the conclusion that the evils connected with it were less than those of any other system of labor. Hundreds of thousands of African savages had been Christianized under its influence. The kindest relations existed between the slaves and their owners. . . . The bondage in which the negroes were held was not thought a wrong to them, because they were better off than any other menial class in the world." [89] The same author justified the Ku Klux Klan because " no high spirited, courageous people could patiently submit to such a government." " As open resistance was impossible," she declares, " they, too, had recourse to secret organizations. They were at first local, and were intended for self-protection against the barn burnings and worse outrages committed by misguided negroes." [90]

As a result of this desire to present the history of their section in terms of their own convictions, the Southerners have always agitated for textbooks different from those used in Northern schools. Northern textbook companies whose enterprise was much condemned during the *ante-bellum* period have capitalized this sectional preference and produced for Southern consumption, among others, Evans' *The Essential Facts of American History,* Chambers' *A*

[89] Lee, *New School History of the United States,* p. 261.
[90] *Ibid.,* p. 357.

School History of the United States, and Stephenson's *An
American History.*[91] On the other hand, for the North, the
same book companies have published textbooks satisfactory
to that section.   Today, in substantially all of the states
which formed the Confederacy, specific textbooks in American history are prescribed, a practice not so universal in the
North, where local adoption is sometimes found.[92]   An analysis of these Southern textbooks, however, discloses a very
temperate presentation of controversial questions.   Upon the
points of contention between the North and the South, there
is a natural bias in favor of the South, a tendency to attempt
justification and exoneration.   Evans, in *The Essential Facts
of American History,* for example, in discussing " reasons
for secession," lays greater stress than the textbooks of the
North on the right of secession, a " right which had been
asserted by other than the Southern States." [93]   Stephenson,
in *An American History,* dubs John Brown as " that terrible
John Brown," [94] and characterizes the carpet-bag govern-

[91] Evans, Lawton B., *The Essential Facts of American History* (Benja-
min H. Sanborn and Company, 1920) ; Evans is from Augusta, Georgia.
Thompson, Waddy, *History of the People of the United States* (D. C.
Heath and Co., 1919) ; Chambers, Henry Edward, *A School History of the
United States* (American Book Co., 1895) ; Stephenson, Nathaniel Wright,
An American History (Ginn and Co., 1913, 1921) ; Estill, Harry F., *The
Beginner's History of Our Country* (Southern Publishing Co., Dallas, Texas,
1919).

[92] Alabama, James and Sanford's *American History;* Arkansas, Evans'
The Essential Facts of American History; Florida, Stephenson's *An American History;* Georgia, Evans' *First Lessons in American History* and Evans'
Essential Facts of Lessons in American History; Louisiana, Estill's *Beginner's History of Our Country,* Evans' *Essential Facts of American History*
and Stephenson's *An American History;* Mississippi, Estill's *Beginner's
History of Our Country* and Mace-Petrie's *History of the People of the
United States;* Texas, Cousin and Hill's *American History;* Virginia, Andrew's *United States History.* These data were secured from a questionnaire. North Carolina reported state adopted textbooks but did not name
them; South Carolina failed to report.

[93] Evans, *The Essential Facts of American History,* p. 364.

[94] Stephenson, *An American History,* p. 399.

ments as insolent, dishonest and violent.[95]   The terms " rebellion " and " civil war " are employed by Northern, not Southern, histories, the "war of the states " and the "war of secession " being used in the South.

ATTEMPTS OF THE GRAND ARMY OF THE REPUBLIC TO CONTROL HISTORY TEXTBOOKS

Six years before the Confederate Veterans in reunion accepted the report of their first historical committee regarding the " false " histories used in Southern schools, the Grand Army of the Republic learned through a similar channel that the history textbooks of the North " signally " failed " to comprehend the causes that resulted in the war of the rebellion." [96]   Much cause for complaint arose from the fact that textbooks were "compiled for a national system of education, South as well as North," — a condition held sadly unacceptable, it would seem, by the patriotic organizations of this period.[97]

In the Report of 1888, the G. A. R. undertook to point out statements in textbooks used in the South which appealed to them as indicative of " a thoroughly studied, rank, partisan system of sectional education." [98]   As a case in point Davidson's *School History of South Carolina*, "published at Columbia, South Carolina, by one W. J. Duffie, copyrighted in 1869," was examined.   This history, so the Report declared, in Chapter 195 ascribed " the cause of

---

[95] *Ibid.*, p. 486. However *cf.* Muzzey, *op. cit.*, p. 387 *et seq.;* Guitteau, William S., *Our United States* (Boston, 1919), p. 47 *et seq.;* West, Willis M., *American History and Government* (Boston, 1913), p. 627.

[96] *Journal of the Twenty-Second Annual . . . Encampment Grand Army of the Republic*, 1888, pp. 210–217. The U. C. V. Committee first reported in 1894, no reunion being held in 1893.

[97] *Journal . . . op. cit.*, p. 210.

[98] *Ibid.*

secession, which was the cause of the war," to the fact that
" Congress kept passing laws which it had no right to pass
according to the Constitution." [99] Further, in speaking of
the withdrawal of South Carolina from the Union the author
asserted that " she had a right to do this; that is, if the
States rights party of the South was correct in its
doctrine." [100]

The Report condemned another history textbook, written
by Blackburn and McDonald, because of the following passage: " The second year of the war now commenced; it
found each section preparing with terrible earnestness for
the conflict. The South was straining every nerve to resist
the Northern multitudes; . . . . To fill her armies the
North had a better and more successful mode, she offered
immense bounties and high pay. Induced by these, thousands of European mercenaries enlisted. The South had
nothing but her gallant children to put in the field and thus
she was condemned to stake her most precious jewels against
the trash of Europe." [101]

Other grounds for criticism were found in Alexander
Stephens' common school history which was guilty of an
effort " to indoctrinate the youth" of the South with the
" monstrous heresy " of state rights and secession.[102]

" These Southern histories do not fail to make known
their side of this question. They are full of it," concluded
the Committee. " What we deem treason is there made
respectable. While our histories on the same subject are
comparatively silent, indeed are so lamentably deficient upon

[99] *Ibid.*
[100] *Ibid.*
[101] *Ibid.*, pp. 212–213. Criticism of a history " By J. S. Blackburn,
Principal of the Potomac Academy, Alexandria, Virginia, and W. N. Mc-
Donald, A. M., Principal of the Male High School, Louisville, Kentucky,
Twelfth Edition Revised."
[102] *Ibid.*

this question that it were far better to discard all history of our country during the epoch of 1860–5 than to admit them to our schools as now compiled. It is indeed time to cease toying with treason for policy, and to cease illustrating rebels as heroes, as in the case of some of our school histories." [103]

The Report of 1888 inaugurated a practice extending over a period of more than twenty years. The Report of 1892 laid its emphasis upon the fact that the textbooks in history " slandered the North and the cause of the Union, . . . depreciated the value of our troops, and represented that the South was in the right, and that the army which saved the Union was a wicked aggressor. . . ." [104]

In 1895 the Encampment, meeting at Louisville, had its attention called by the Department of Indiana to the character of history textbooks used in Northern schools. In that state alarm had been excited by Montgomery's *Leading Facts of American History,* " the authorized history " for the public schools of the state. Under the auspices of the local G. A. R. an investigation of this book had been conducted. As a result, seven charges were presented against it, the indictment stating that Ellis' *Eclectic Primary History* and Barnes' *History* were believed to be " equally objectionable." [105]

The objections of the Indiana G. A. R. received the endorsement of the national encampment, and Montgomery's history was found guilty on the following counts: first, it contained " no suggestion or intimation that the men who fought for the preservation of the Union were right "; sec-

[103] *Ibid.,* p. 215.
[104] *Journal of the Twenty-Sixth National Encampment Grand Army of the Republic . . . 1892,* p. 207.
[105] *Journal of the Twenty-Ninth National Encampment Grand Army of the Republic, . . . 1895,* p. 230.

ond, there was "a general unfairness of treatment of the people of the North, of the officers and soldiers of the Union armies and the battles fought by them"; third, it was "calculated to give the student false impressions as to the relative courage, heroism and achievements of the contending armies, and of the endurance, devotion and sacrifices of the people of the two sections of the country engaged in the conflict"; fourth, "the accounts of the victories of the Confederates" were "exaggerated, while those of the Union armies" were "dwarfed and made insignificant by comparison"; in the fifth place, "all statements of a commendatory and eulogistic character" were "reserved for the Confederates, while nothing of like character" was said "in favor of the Union soldiers or people"; sixth, that it was "unpatriotic and partisan in statement, tone and sentiment"; and seventh, that it was "unreliable in its statement of facts." [106]

Among objectionable history textbooks "written by Southern authors, for the avowed purpose of giving a history of the War of the Rebellion from a Southern standpoint," was that of "Reverend Dr. D. W. Jones, published in 1896." [107] This book was taken "as a fair sample of its class" by the Committee on School Histories reporting in 1897. The Veterans rested their case upon such a statement as: "The seceding states not only had a perfect right to withdraw from the Union but they had amply sufficient cause for doing so." [108]

[106] *Ibid.*, p. 331. Montgomery's books were disapproved by the South. *Cf.* page 159.

[107] *Journal of the Thirty-First National Encampment of the Grand Army of the Republic* . . . 1897, p. 233. This book was endorsed by the Confederate Veterans in 1896, but the author's name is given as J. W. Jones. *Minutes . . . of the Reunion of Confederate Veterans* . . . 1898, p. 31.

[108] *Journal, op. cit.*

In the "careful examination" to which the school histories of the North were subjected by the Committee of 1897 no book was found which deserved "unqualified endorsement." [109] This was due to the "one vital defect" common to all the histories — that all of them treated the War "as a contest between the sections of the country . . . and not as a war waged by the Government for the suppression of rebellion against National authority and meant to destroy National existence." [110] Indeed, the Committee had reached their conclusions regarding the "histories in general use in all sections" after "two days of examination." [111] During this time they had found in "many of these works extravagant expressions as 'this crushing defeat'" in speaking of the Northern army, and such a statement as "'the Confederates could not be conquered until they were destroyed,'" — all equally obnoxious and uncomplimentary to the North.[112] Such a condition, the Committee felt, arose from "a commercial spirit" which "largely controls and inspires these publications." [113]

In view of the situation as it then existed, the Committee asked that the "Encampment record a solemn and emphatic protest against the further use of any history of the Civil War in the public schools of this country which does not teach that this war was a war waged by the National Government for the suppression of rebellion and the preservation of National existence; that there was a right side and a wrong side, . . . that in the decision of this question the victors were right and the vanquished wrong." [114] They further recommended that the agitation for "improved text-books" be continued, that a permanent committee on the teaching of patriotism in the schools be appointed, and that the Grand Army of the Republic and its allied organizations "give direct and persistent attention to the removal and exclusion of improper histories . . . in use."[115]

The results of the agitation for "unbiased" histories which the Confederate Veterans felt had been achieved by 1896 in the South, the G. A. R. through their activities failed to accomplish in the North before 1898. However, at that time they felt "justified to report substantial improvement in the tone and sentiment" of textbooks, particularly in "the more recent publications."[116] Yet they urged "a continuance of effort . . . to place before the children of the Republic truthful and patriotic histories" of the Civil War, and registered a "solemn and emphatic protest" against the proposal that the struggle of 1861 to 1865 be called "the Civil War between the States."[117]

The following year the Committee report rang with a spirit of optimism because of the changed character of history writing and instruction brought about by "our organization." As proof for their gratification they pointed out that "in one of the leading works in use more than fifty substantial changes of the text have been made in that portion presenting the history of the rebellion."[118] Yet regret was expressed that no history known to them made "it clear in statement that the war for the preservation of the Union was prosecuted on the one side by the National Government and on the other by those in armed rebellion against its authority."[119] To insure continued vigilance the Encampment approved the appointment of an "aide" to each de-

[115] *Ibid.*, p. 238.

[116] *Journal of the Thirty-Second National Encampment of the Grand Army of the Republic* . . . 1898, p. 192.

[117] *Ibid.*, p. 194.

[118] *Journal of the Thirty-Third National Encampment of the Grand Army of the Republic* . . . 1899, pp. 244–246. The textbook was not named.   [119] *Ibid.*

partment to keep in touch with the school histories in his state, and to " confer with school authorities and endeavor through them to secure the best obtainable school histories in the schools and the exclusion of such as are unfit." [120]

The satisfaction expressed by the Committee of 1900 was reiterated at the encampment the following year. But the Committee were robbed of much of their gratification when they considered the " avowedly sectional standpoint " of histories in the South, where it was still taught that the Confederate States were " a lawful government." [121]

The agitation to investigate history textbooks lost much of its vigor and aggressive anxiety with the opening of the twentieth century. In 1904 the chairman of the school history committee suggested " in view of the utter want of interest exhibited throughout the whole country in regard to this matter " that the committee " be abolished." [122] Warren Lee Goss, national patriotic instructor, reporting at the forty-first encampment in 1907 declared it his belief that the G. A. R. were " not called upon to interfere in any way with the regular instruction in the schools in United States history, but rather to supplement that instruction by special observances." [123] Two years later the portion of the report on patriotic instruction devoted to " histories " merely listed the textbooks most commonly used,[124] and in 1910 a similar report eulogized " the loyalty and patriotism of the

[120] *Ibid.*

[121] *Journal of the Thirty-Fourth National Encampment of the Grand Army of the Republic* . . . 1900, p. 145.

[122] *Journal of the Thirty-Eighth National Encampment of the Grand Army of the Republic* . . . 1904, pp. 244–246.

[123] *Journal of the Forty-First National Encampment of the Grand Army of the Republic* . . . 1907, p. 173.

[124] *Journal of the Forty-Third National Encampment of the Grand Army of the Republic* . . . 1909, p. 164. The list included McLaughlin's *History of the American Nation*, Montgomery's *Leading Facts of American History*, Mace's *School History of the United States*, McMaster's *History of the United States*, Gordy's *History of the United States*, Eggleston's

majority [of those living] who wore the gray." [125]   This sympathetic and tolerant attitude seems to have remained unchallenged in the successive encampments of the G. A. R., and unlike the Confederate Veterans of the last few reunions, the Grand Army of the Republic have not sought to rekindle old animosities.

TEXTBOOKS FOR ROMAN CATHOLICS

As early as 1834 the Roman Catholics of New York urged upon the schools textbooks which would show agreement with their point of view.   In 1828 the Public School Society, an organization designed to educate poor children not provided for by any religious society, was allowed to levy a local tax for its support.   To this the Roman Catholics raised objections, since they were permitted to dictate neither the kind of instruction offered nor the textbooks adopted.   Among the points in controversy was the request of the Catholic clergy that no book should be used but such as had been submitted to the Bishop and declared " free from sectarian principles or calumnies against his religion." [126]   In those books where

---

" *History*," Johnson's " *History*," Barnes' " *History*," Fiske's " *History*," Scudder's " *History*," Anderson's " *History*," and in the South "Waddy Thompson's *United States History*, revised and improved by the late General John B. Gordon."

[125] *Journal of the Forty-Fourth National Encampment of the Grand Army of the Republic* . . . 1910, p. 219. The Phil Sheridan Post No. 4, G. A. R., joined with the Sons of the American Revolution in 1922 in an effort to eliminate West's *History of the American People* from the acceptable textbooks of the Boise, Idaho, schools. In addition to criticisms regarding West's discussion of the American Revolution and the War of 1812, the Veterans objected to the treatment of the Civil War period. See p. 265 and the *Idaho Statesman*, December 9, 1922.

[126] The controversy related to Public School Number 5. The Public School Society was organized in 1805 and gradually extended its activities until 1853, when it gave its buildings and property to the City Board of Education. See Bourne, William Oland, *History of the Public School Society of the City of New York* (New York, 1870), p. 324 *et seq.*

objectionable statements were found, it was suggested "that such passages be expunged or left out in binding."[127] The censorship requested was not granted, and in 1840 the agitation regarding textbooks was renewed. Again it was charged that some books contained passages not merely displeasing to the Roman Catholics, but hostile to their faith; whereas others indulged in statements which were both "defamatory" and "false."

The trustees of the Public School Society, avowedly anxious to dissipate these objections, took measures to secure information from various sources, including both laymen and clergy, with the hope that a removal of the complaint might be effected. They adopted a resolution declaring that they would submit for examination, to the Reverend Felix Varela, some textbooks used in Public School Number 5. As further proof of their desire for harmony, the trustees appointed a committee of five to see whether the books in the schools or libraries contained passages derogatory to the Roman Catholics.[128] Following their action Reverend Mr. Varela pointed out certain objectionable features in some of the textbooks. In one geography he discovered a passage in which the Catholic clergy were characterized as having great influence but being opposed to the diffusion of knowledge. He also disapproved of the description of Italy in which were statements which would "tend to diminish the consideration that a Catholic child has for the Catholic Church."[129] In another textbook, the discussion of the character of Luther proved objectionable, for, although it might please the Protestants, he felt that there was implied an attack on the Catholic Church.

---

[127] *Ibid.*, p. 324. No action was taken at that time, but a Roman Catholic teacher was employed for Public School Number 5.

[128] *Ibid.*, p. 325.   [129] *Ibid.*, p. 328.

On July 9, 1840, John Power, vice-general of the diocese of New York, wrote a letter to the editor of *Freeman's Journal*, in which he voiced his disapproval of the textbooks employed to instruct children. Odium, he felt, was attached to the Catholic clergy because they were represented as keeping the people in ignorance to promote their own interests, and libraries contained books with " most malevolent and foul attacks on their religion . . . no doubt with the very laudable purpose of teaching them [Catholic children] to abhor and despise that monster called popery." [130]

With failure attending their efforts at censorship, the Roman Catholics resorted to an address to their " fellow citizens of the city and state of New York " in which they appealed for a redress of their grievances. " We are Americans and American citizens. If some of us are foreigners," they declared, " it is only by the accident of birth, ... But our children, for whose rights as well as our own we contend in this matter, are Americans by nativity." [131]   Repeating the assertions of the priests, the address remonstrated against the false "historical statements respecting the men and things of past times, calculated to fill the minds of our children with errors of fact and at the same time to excite in them prejudice against the religion of their parents and guardians." [132]

In answer to the exceptions raised by the Catholics, the trustees of the Public School Society expressed doubt as to the wisdom of expurgation, for they believed " nothing of a mere negative character " would be acceptable. " The books selected for the children," they stated, " have, from the first, been those used and most highly esteemed as school-books. The passages objected to, or nearly all of them, are historical, and relate to what is generally called

[130] *Ibid.*   [131] *Ibid.*, p. 331.   [132] *Ibid.*

the Reformation. The writers were Protestants, and took a view of the men and incidents of that excited and eventful period directly opposed to those entertained by the members of the Roman Catholic Church. These portions, must, of course, be offensive to Catholics, and they furnish just cause for complaint. . . . The objectionable passages are not numerous, but the books are not to be found without them. . . . The difficulty of procuring books entirely exempt from objection cannot perhaps be more forcibly illustrated than by the fact that one work containing passages as liable to objection as almost any other, is now used as a class-book even in the Catholic schools. It is the intention of the trustees, nevertheless, to prosecute the work of expurgation until every just cause of complaint is removed." [133]

As a result of the agitation, revised and expurgated books appeared; in some instances the objectionable passages were stamped out with ink from a wooden block or the leaves pasted together or removed. In some cases the books under criticism were prohibited in the libraries and the schools. Yet this failed to satisfy the Roman Catholics. When the expurgated editions were worn out, they were replaced by new books without changes, and gradually this discussion over textbooks subsided.

During the 'eighties it again became a matter of speculation with the Roman Catholics whether they should be taxed to support schools from which their children got " no benefit," or, if attending, suffered " positive injury and injustice." [134] They were indeed skeptical as to the merits of a non-sectarian education which they held " professedly non-Christian," — a system that occupied itself " as little with the mission, history, and teachings of the divine Founder

[133] *Ibid.*, p. 342.
[134] Deshon, George, " A Novel Defence of the Public School," *The Catholic World*, Vol. L (February, 1890), pp. 677–687.

of Christianity " as it did " with the life and doctrines of
Confucius or Buddha." [135]

A storm center of the agitation was Boston, where the
Catholics formed a considerable number of the population.
Here a denunciation of public school instruction included
both teachers and textbooks, resulting in the removal of
Swinton's *History* and the dismissal of a teacher (a Mr.
Travis) for "erroneous and misleading " statements about
the granting of indulgences.

" It is very hard," declared one writer on the controversy,
" that a young man who teaches only what he has been
taught himself, only what thousands of young men and
women have been taught and are teaching, should be singled
out and set aside for penalty while others go scot free. . . .
While the Roman Catholics were weak they could not help
themselves, and we went on saying what we pleased. Now
they are numerous enough in some places to hold the balance
of power, and they hold it with a mighty grasp. . . ." [136]

In an effort to prevent the exclusion of the textbook from
the schools, the Protestants advanced various arguments:
that it had been in use ten years without protest, that " the
outcry " was not " honest," and that the agitation was
" simply the opening wedge for riving our school system
and dividing the public school money between Catholics and
Protestants." [137]

Other histories than Swinton's were in like manner placed
by the Catholics in the objectionable list. It was alleged
that Prescott's works " swarm[ed] with Puritan prejudice
against all things Catholic " and that Macaulay's *History of
England* emphasized the worst traits of Catholic personages

[135] *Ibid.*
[136] Hamilton, Gail, " Catholicism and Public Schools," *North American
Review*, Vol. CXLVII (1888), pp. 572–580.
[137] *Ibid.*

and gave little credit to the Jesuits.[138] So far as Macaulay was concerned, one Catholic objected to sending his children to school to study history from a book acknowledged by the Protestants to be "a gloriously Protestant book," by which his children would be "gloriously indoctrinated into Protestantism and a hatred of their parents' religion."[139]

As a means of settling the controversy it was suggested that all history or the parts relating to the Protestant and Catholic churches be omitted from the curriculum. This could be done, one writer maintained, "without missing anything of value to our common school system or to our other cherished institutions." Moreover, it was also held that there were "plenty of undisputed topics" to be studied in the schools which were looked upon with "entire unanimity" by "all creeds," such as two and two make four. For "nothing should ever be taught in schools supported by common funds except that which is accepted by the common faith."[140]

With the great expansion of the Catholic Church in the United States since the Civil War and the growth of parochial schools in all parts of the country, the particular needs of the Catholics have been met by the enterprise of publishers in supplying special textbooks for their use.[141] As a result today there are found in parochial schools such social study textbooks as McCarthy's *History of the United States*, O'Hara's *A History of the United States*, *A History of the United States for Catholic Schools* by the Franciscan Sisters of the Perpetual Adoration of St. Rose Convent, La

[138] "The Anti-Catholic Spirit of Certain Writers," *The Catholic World*, Vol. XXXVI (February, 1883), pp. 658–667.

[139] Deshon, *loc. cit.*   [140] Hamilton, *loc. cit.*

[141] In 1815 there were "about 70,000 Catholics to be found in the United States, ... In 1918, . . . its Catholic population had increased to 17,416,303, ..." McCarthy, Charles H., *The History of the United States for Catholic Schools* (New York, 1919), p. 421.

Crosse, Wisconsin, Lawler's *Essentials of American History,* Betten's *The Ancient World,* Betten and Kaufman's *The Modern World,* and Burke's *Political Economy.*[142]

The desire to present events in American history in such a way as to show the importance of the Catholic Church has led to the preparation of textbooks like McCarthy's *History of the United States.* In this book it has been " made clear that Catholics discovered, and in a large way, explored these continents, that Catholics transferred civilization hither, that they opened to the commerce of Europe the trade of the Pacific, and that they undertook the conversion of multitudes of dusky natives, of whom few had risen to the upper stages of barbarism." [143] Although the " war for independence " was begun largely by Protestants, the author avers the help of Catholic nations like France and Spain gave " undoubted assistance to the New Republic." Norse settlement and discovery are treated extensively, and Columbus' missionary spirit receives considerable attention. Catholic notables like Governor Dongan, the Calverts, Captain John Barry, and Thomas Macdonough are given more space than ordinarily allotted in school histories. " The winning of the West, in which Catholics acted an important part," the war on the sea in which are enumerated " the exploits of the O'Briens of Machias, Maine," " the beginnings of the Catho-

---

[142] McCarthy, Charles H., *The History of the United States for Catholic Schools* (American Book Co., 1919); O'Hara, John P., *A History of the United States* (The Macmillan Company, 1919); *A History of the United States for Catholic Schools* prepared and arranged by the Franciscan Sisters of the Perpetual Adoration (Scott, Foresman and Company, 1914); Lawler, Thomas B., *Essentials of American History* (Ginn and Company, 1918); Betten, Francis S., *The Ancient World* (Allyn and Bacon, 1916); Betten, Francis S., and Kaufman, Alfred, *The Modern World* (Allyn and Bacon, 1919); Burke, E. J., *Political Economy, designed for use in Catholic Colleges, High Schools and Academies* (American Book Company, 1913).

[143] McCarthy, *op. cit.,* preface, p. iii. Professor McCarthy is Knights of Columbus Professor of American History at the Catholic University of America.

lic Church in America " and " Washington's patriotic letter
to his Catholic countrymen " are other unique features.[144]

Similar in point of view is the textbook written by the
Franciscan Sisters of the Perpetual Adoration. Its contents,
announces the *Foreword,* are not immured within the bounds
of " the usually taught historical facts," but include " the
too often forgotten efforts of the Church in American History." Not only is the story of " the venturesome explorer,
the intrepid colonizer, the hardy pioneer, the noble warrior,
the eloquent statesman " narrated, but there is also depicted
" the quiet heroism of the loyal sons and daughters of the
Catholic Church." " Our country is justly proud of the
liberty she offers to all her children," affirm the authors,
" but these children are many in faith, and diversified in
race peculiarities. Common interests may seem to unite
them from time to time, but there can be no true, permanent
union except where the spirit and the faith are dominating
forces. But where is such a bond of unity except in the
Catholic Church? Mother Church folds her arms about all
her children and questions not their color or their race." [145]

To the teachers, the authors offer certain aids and direc-
tions. The importance of a " proper setting of United
States history with a knowledge of the threefold chronological divisions of world history " and an insight into the " difference between Sacred history and Profane, or Secular
history " are indicated. In the period of colonization, teachers are urged to make clear, among other things, " how the
Catholic Church, like the mustard seed of the Gospel, has
flourished and grown, as it were, into a mighty tree." The
Sisters urge, also, a thorough delineation of the growth of
the educational system of the United States including an

[144] *Ibid.,* preface, p. iv.
[145] The Franciscan Sisters of the Perpetual Adoration, *A History of the
United States for Catholic Schools* (Chicago, 1914), pp. 3-4.

understanding of " how our cherished parochial schools grew from humble beginnings into the splendid system which now labors so zealously for the spiritual and intellectual welfare of our country." [146]

The Betten-Kaufman histories, *The Ancient World* and *The Modern World*, are typical of Roman Catholic textbooks in the field of European history. Based upon West's *Ancient World* and his *Modern World*, the authors have introduced changes desirable for the purpose of " promoting the great cause of Catholic education." [147] The chief departure from the traditional European history textbook used in the public schools is in the discussion of Luther and the Reformation. Although Tetzel's use of the theory of indulgences is criticized in the Betten and Kaufman textbook as " ill advised," [148] Luther's theories regarding the remission of sins are characterized as " monstrous." [149] The Church

[146] *Ibid.*, pp. 5–6.

[147] Betten, *The Ancient World*, preface.

[148] " This much maligned priest [John Tetzel], personally of blameless character, undoubtedly went too far in his endeavors to procure financial success. He insisted indeed on the necessity of contrition and confession for all those who wished to obtain the remission of temporal punishment for themselves; but his teaching concerning the indulgence for the dead was not free from serious errors. To secure this benefit for a soul which has, of course, departed this life in the state of grace, nothing, according to him, is required but the alms. This doctrine, though at his time actually taught by some irresponsible preachers, has never been supported by ecclesiastical authority. Tetzel's own brethren in religion openly reproached him for his ill-advised tactics, which soon became the talk of the whole country." Betten and Kaufman, *The Modern World*, p. 376.

[149] " At least he [Martin Luther] imagined that he had made the discovery that the doctrine of the Church concerning the remission of sins was altogether wrong. He thereby implied that Christ, contrary to His solemn promise, had allowed the Church to fall into a most disastrous error. The new system, which gradually developed in Luther's mind, confused the nature of sin with concupiscence, which is a consequence of original sin, and while it makes man inclined to sin is no sin in itself. By the sin of Adam, he thought human nature was corrupted beyond recovery; man's acts can only be bad; but Jesus Christ covers the soul with His infinite merits, which, as it were, conceal all trespasses from the eye of the

as an agency for good and for promoting the civilization of the world is given significant attention; the " Catholic view " of social evils is set forth in opposition to other theories, and a discussion of " harmonious coöperation " between church and state is intended to disclose the influence of the Church in the solution of the world's evils.[150]

In an allied field Father Burke has written his *Political Economy designed for use in Catholic Colleges, High Schools, and Academies.* Here political economy is discussed not only from the standpoint of " the merely concrete, material things that enter into the science, but also with reference to the personalities of the members of society whose activity is exercised on these concrete, material things." [151]

---

just God; if sinful man expresses his firm 'belief' in this merciful dispensation, God will not punish him, though the sin is not taken away, but merely covered; the sinner therefore remains a sinner; . . . It is evident that such a justification is no justification at all, and it will always remain a riddle how Luther could maintain that he had found such a monstrous doctrine in the Bible." *Ibid.,* pp. 377-378.

[150] " The causes of the social evils are *not only economic, but moral and religious as well.* It is true that present economic conditions are far from satisfactory. Though production, on account of the introduction of machinery, has increased enormously, wages have not kept pace with that increase. . . . But the moral and religious causes are not to be overlooked. The breaking loose from practical Christianity, so characteristic of the last two centuries, has developed an intense selfishness, a struggle for wealth in which each one seeks his own material advantage at the expense of his neighbor. . . . What, then, are the remedies proposed by Catholics? Certainly not the adoption of Socialist views. . . . The Socialists deliberately ignore, yea exclude, religion from coöperation in the solution of the great social problem. They forget that man's happiness here below is not his ultimate end, that the Creator did not want equal wealth and equal material advantages for all. . . . The state having at heart the temporal welfare of its citizens, should by wise legislation protect the workers, their health, and morals, and that of their family. But the change of hearts which is so necessary for the cure of modern evils is the principal task of religion. Hence the Church should be free to carry out her mission." *Ibid.,* pp. 639–641.

[151] Burke, E. J., *Political Economy designed for use in Catholic Col-*

Father Burke's book is divided into twenty-three chapters with titles common to the usual economics textbook. Its unique feature lies in the treatment of various economic theories from the point of view of the "Catholic School." The doctrine of Malthus is rejected for moral and economic reasons, which take their course in "human injustice and selfishness in the spirit of greed that closes the hearts of men to the dictates of charity and fairness," and which lead to "improper methods of the distribution of wealth." [152] The author expresses a belief in the inequality of man, through which comes inequality of distribution. Such a hardship is due, in no small degree, Father Burke declares, to the "fallen state" of man. Because of the sin of his first parents he is "subject to death, to sufferings, to misery, and to labor." This can be proved, it is averred, by the Book of Revelation. "Hence," asserts Father Burke, "evils may exist in this world, injustice and oppression may go on, and the equilibration of things may never take place here; the wicked may prosper and the honest and just may be oppressed, and no adequate remedy may appear; yet the moment of compensation, of perfect justice, will come, if not in this life, then in the life of eternity." [153]

Such a presentation of economic theories has been ac-

---

leges, High Schools, and Academies (New York, 1913), p. 1. According to Bullock's *Elements of Economics,* one textbook used in the public schools, "Economics is the science which deals with the efforts of mankind to secure the material commodities and personal services which are needed to support life and to make a civilized existence possible." Bullock, Charles J., *Elements of Economics* (Boston, 1913), p. 4.

[152] Burke, *op. cit.,* p. 57.

[153] Burke, *op. cit.,* p. 386. Although "followers of the Catholic School do not deny that much of the evil existing in society is due to defective methods of distribution, they suggest no such drastic action as the Socialists. . . . They appeal to the influence of the Church's teaching and the power of Christian doctrine to bring about a spirit of charity and justice in the mutual dealings of capitalists and labor." *Ibid.,* p. 392.

claimed highly satisfactory in Catholic reviews, for, "since ethics as a science directing human actions according to right reason embraces of necessity all of man's activities, it follows that political economy is rightly subject to the laws of ethics." [154] "This clear understanding of the state of the question . . . enables us at once to detect the errors and dangers of many of the high sounding economic theories which occupy so much space in the literature of the day," declares one reviewer.[155] Another reviewer in *Extension* believes that an accurate knowledge of economic principles is impossible "from an examination of the text-books used in some of the secular colleges and universities" in which not only are "some of the so-called principles false, but the resultant deductions, where they are not entirely fallacious, are frequently misleading."[156]   *The Pilot* offers its endorsement of the textbook because "in these days of industrial and economic unrest, when so much that is false and misleading is written on political and social problems, a book on political economy for Catholic schools is most welcome. Catholic philosophy sets forth sound and unimpeachable principles bearing upon the rights of the individual and of the family, and upon the powers and functions of 'the State.'"[157]

The purpose of these books is to place emphasis upon Catholic contributions and the power of the Church. As indicated in a textbook written in the later nineteenth century, whose content is much the same as the more recent Catholic textbooks, it is "the manifest duty of those who are entrusted with the education of our children to see that in learning the history of the country they do not lose sight of the rise, progress, and social influences of the Church in

[154] Advertising pamphlet entitled "The Hospitality given Father Burke's Political Economy."
[155] *Ibid.*, p. 6.   [156] *Ibid.*   [157] *Ibid.*, p. 4.

the United States. . . .[158] And finally, as religion is always the sweetest inspiration and support of patriotism, the breaking down of religious beliefs in various modern nations, and notably in our own, is accompanied by a loss of patriotism. . . . Reverence for authority is lost, and society, in order to protect itself, is driven to appeal to force. Nothing can avert the danger but the influence of a great moral power endorsed with all the attributes which create respect and encourage obedience. The Catholic Church is this power. . . ." [159]

In turn, these textbooks have been criticised because of the amount of space given to the Catholic Church in comparison with that allotted other churches. One critic has asserted that the history by the Franciscan Sisters does not mention a single Protestant body after the period of the Revolution, and that "one ignorant of the true situation and reading this particular history would imagine that the United States was a Catholic nation." [160] Further criticism has arisen because, in the critic's mind, facts of history are

[158] Hassard, John R. G., *A History of the United States of America* (New York, 1878), p. vi.

[159] *Ibid.*
The National Lutheran Council had, in 1923, a committee on history textbooks, whose purpose was to make known any "flagrant or actual misrepresentations" of their church in history textbooks used in the United States. Letter from Lauritz Larsen, President of the National Lutheran Council to the author under date of January 13, 1923. No report of the committee was given. The writer of the letter also stated that there had been no "organized effort to suggest the content of history textbooks in the public schools, not even as this might pertain to the teaching of the history of the Reformation in the public schools."
According to Werner, Brigham Young "insisted that the school-books should be published in Utah, and written there if possible, rather than imported at unnecessary expense from the East. The teachers, too, he wrote should be Latter-day Saints, so that the children might learn only what they ought to know." Werner, M. R., *Brigham Young* (New York, 1925), p. 451.

[160] Sweet, W. W., "Religion in Our School Histories," *The Christian Century*, Vol. XLI (November 20, 1924), pp. 1502–1504.

mixed with " acts of Catholic piety." As proof of this objection is cited an excerpt from a Catholic textbook in which is given a description of the death of Pizarro: " Just before he died he called upon his Redeemer and tracing with his bloody finger a cross upon the floor, he kissed the sacred symbol and expired." [161]

Further evidence of this is seen by the same writer in the statement that " as the missionaries made their way westward, the worship of St. Mary marked their path till the great Mississippi, the River of the Immaculate Conception, bore them [down] toward those Spanish realms where every officer swore to defend the Immaculate Conception." [162] To this objector of a separate history for Catholic schools, " it is the very evident purpose of these texts . . . to propagate Catholic ideas and not to give a true picture of the development of America." [163]

TEXTBOOKS IN CIVICS, ECONOMICS AND SOCIOLOGY

Criticism of public school textbooks and teaching is not confined solely to the subject of history but includes in its ever-widening circle books in the allied fields of civics, economics and sociology. Especially is this true of those in government or civics. Since the close of the World War a movement for the teaching of the Constitution has closely paralleled that for the study of American history. Organizations and individuals with the avowed purpose of inculcating patriotism have urged that more attention than formerly be given the study of the machinery of government. To this end influence has been exerted for the passage of laws re-

[161] The textbook is not named in the article.
[162] The title of this book is not given in the article but such a statement appears in *A History of the United States* by the Franciscan Sisters of the Perpetual Adoration, p. 68.   [163] *Ibid.*

quiring the subject of civics in the schools, and many books on the Constitution have appeared to meet an increased demand.

Among the organizations which have sponsored the movement for instruction in the Constitution have been the American Bar Association, the National Security League, The Constitution Anniversary Association, and the Better America Federation. Organizations such as the Sentinels of the Republic are engaged in a similar program in adult education.

In 1922 in pursuance of a resolution adopted by the executive committee at Tampa, Florida, the American Bar Association appointed a Committee on American Citizenship " to devise ways for promoting the study of and devotion to American institutions and ideals." This resolution was interpreted as laying upon the Committee " the duty to prepare a program under which the lawyers of the United States, coöperating with every patriotic society and organization, and with every true American man and woman, shall be urged to join in an earnest effort to stem the tide of radical, and often treasonable, attacks upon our Constitution, our laws, our courts, our law-making bodies, our executives and our flag, to arouse to action our dormant citizenship, to abolish ignorance, and crush falsehood, and to bring truth into the hearts of our citizenship." [104]

The Committee recommended the appointment of a standing committee on American Citizenship, the appointment of local committees " to see that the Constitution of the United States is taught in every school . . . to report to the bureau the courses in each state, the textbooks used, and the qualifications of teachers for teaching American citizenship." In

[104] *Report of the American Bar Association*, Vol. XLVII (1922), pp. 416–423.

addition it was suggested that the coöperation of Commissioners on Uniform State Laws be enlisted " in an effort to have enacted in each state suitable laws making a course each year in the study of and devotion to American institutions and ideals part of the curriculum in all schools and colleges sustained or in any manner supported by public funds." [165]

The Reports of 1923 and 1924 again envisaged " the need of activity " because of " the socialistic doctrines . . . taught in many of our schools and colleges," and pointed out that efforts of the Bar toward laws requiring the teaching of the Constitution had received encouragement from legislators and the public in general.[166]   In 1923, according to the Report of that year, twenty-four states had definite laws, in five states laws had been introduced and in nineteen states there was no such statute.   The principal difficulty which the Committee had encountered in having such a law passed had arisen out of " the conservatism of school authorities," who appeared " fearful that the mere requirement " would " not necessarily be the best means of promoting the teaching of the Constitution," and who were " slow to change from long established methods that had been used in connection with the school curriculum."

In their advocacy for a wider-spread knowledge of the Constitution the American Bar Association received the coöperation of other organizations interested in the same work, such as the American Legion, patriotic societies, women's organizations, the Masonic Service Association, the Knights of Columbus, Chambers of Commerce, the

[165] *Ibid.*

[166] *Report of the American Bar Association,* Vol. XLVIII (1923), pp. 442–451. The committee was composed of R. E. L. Saner, chairman, Walter George Smith, Andrew A. Brice, Wallace McCamant, John Ford O'Brien.

Rotary, Lions, and Kiwanis. Yet they felt that "the most powerful influence" that they could evoke "undoubtedly would be the association of teachers," for they wished "to reach the mind of the child while it is still plastic." They affirmed as their "ultimate aim" that "no child should leave even the common schools without an elementary knowledge and appreciation of our Constitution and what it means to every individual." [167]

By 1924, the Committee reported the existence of a law requiring the teaching of the Constitution in thirty-one states, and in other commonwealths regulations of the state department of education effecting the same purpose.[168] One of the aspects of the situation which appeared to the Committee as more important even than properly qualified teachers was "the proper attitude toward our government and the spirit in which the teaching is performed" — a teaching which should be grounded "on bed-rock Americanism" and "imbued with a desire to communicate such spirit to their pupils." [169] Indeed, it was held that "the schools of America should no more consider graduating a student who lacks faith in our government than a school of theology should graduate a minister who lacks faith in God." [170]

According to the Report the educational activities of the Committee were many, "even going so far as to suggest to the ministers appropriate texts for Thanksgiving Day which should call attention to the blessing of our form of government." [171] Members of the Bar had written special articles for several periodicals on good citizenship as well as furnishing cartoons for the press of the country. The Committee

---

[167] *Report of the American Bar Association*, Vol. XLIX (1924), pp. 255–269.
[168] *Ibid.* Chapter IV discusses laws since 1917.   [169] *Ibid.*
[170] *Ibid.* The Reports of 1923 and 1924 are similar.
[171] *Ibid.*, pp. 262–263.

had aided in the display and sale of books on the Constitution, they had sponsored " a nation-wide celebration of Constitution week," they had appeared as speakers on community programs and otherwise had helped in the celebration of national holidays. In addition they had prepared a " citizenship creed." This creed stressed the obligations of citizenship and a faith in the American government, "the best government that has ever been created — the freest and most just for all the people." To uphold and defend the government was at all times a duty of the citizen. " Just as the ' Minute Man of the Revolution ' was ready upon a moment's notice to defend his rights against foreign usurpation " so it was the citizen's duty " as a patriotic American to be a ' Minute Man of the Constitution ' ready at all times to defend the long-established and cherished institutions of our government against attack, either from within or without," and to do his " part in preserving the blessings of liberty " for which his " Revolutionary forefathers fought and died." [172]

The National Security League is likewise engaged in the movement for teaching the Constitution in the schools. Through the Committee on Constitution Instruction and its Civic Department, the League has campaigned " for over three years " to have passed a bill requiring definite courses in the Constitution in all public schools.[173] According to literature circulated by the League, the Committee was rewarded by the passage of such a requirement in thirty-six states, in most cases the legislatures taking over verbatim the bill drafted by them.[174]

[172] *Ibid.*, p. 271. The entire creed appears in the Appendix.
[173] Printed statement from the National Security League, 25 West 43d Street, New York.
[174] For the statement of the American Bar Association as to their activities see page 187.

To the League's program opposition to a mandatory legislative control of education occasionally arose from educational authorities in states where the bill had been introduced. But the chairman of the Committee was " glad to say that state legislators generally, representatives of the public will, have not agreed with these gentlemen and their arguments, and have looked upon a knowledge of the Constitution as an essential in citizen making." [175]

In addition to legislation which requires the study of the Constitution, thirty-three states by May, 1925, made mandatory a teacher's examination on the Constitution.[176] So far-reaching were the results of their activities, that the League's Committee on Constitutional Instruction estimated that 200,500 teachers were required to teach the Constitution of the United States to a total of over 4,000,000 school children.[177]

To find suitable textbooks became a problem, for the Committee held that " while there are many books which satisfactorily explain the Constitution to advanced students and adults, there is practically nothing which suitably transmits the basic principles of our government to the minds of children." For this " short stories " on the Constitution were necessary in order that facts concerning the history of the document would be " readily understood by the average child," because when " eloquently taught and interpreted in story form by a teacher who knows it and reverences its provisions, it will rouse any class to enthusiasm." [178]

Besides the " nation-wide popularization of the Constitution " through the distribution of almost a million copies of

[175] *Ibid.*
[176] *The National Security League,* " Report to Members for the Month Ending May 15, 1925."
[177] Printed statement quoted previously.
[178] *Ibid.*

a " Catechism of the Constitution," the National Security
League endeavors to assist teachers in passing their examinations for licenses by publishing a Course on the Constitution
for Normal Schools.[179]   Its literature on the Constitution has
been sent by request to 2038 teachers, to whom was also
made available Dr. Jean Broadhurst's book, *Verse for
Patriots to Encourage Good Citizenship*, " of special value
in teaching English literature and patriotism " and for holiday program materials.[180]   In the campaign for education,
Beck's *The Constitution of the United States: Yesterday,
Today and Tomorrow* was also sent " to the governors of all
the States where the bill requiring the compulsory teaching
of the Constitution has become a law, . . . with the advice
that the book is available for all teachers and instructors in
their states upon application." [181]   A teachers' manual
" which is attracting wide attention under the title ' Our
Constitution in My Town and My Life ' which contains 115
questions and answers on the Constitution for classroom
use " has been written by Miss Etta V. Leighton, Civic
Secretary.[182]

As an " evidence of the value " and of the influence of the
Security League's educational program, the " Report " for
November 15, 1925, recounted " that the Professor of Politi-
cal Science in a large western university will use our sug-
gestions in revising her text book on the State and National
Constitution." [183]

The Constitution Anniversary Association, incorporated
March, 1923, is another organization engaged in promoting

[179] *The National Security League*, " Report to Members for the Month
Ending May 15, 1925."
[180] *Ibid.*, October 15, 1925.
[181] *Ibid.*, May 15, 1925.
[182] Printed statement quoted previously.
[183] *The National Security League*, " Report to Members for the Month
Ending November 15, 1925."

a study of the Constitution in order to familiarize to a greater degree the people of this generation with " those historic days incident to the writing of the Constitution," that they may " recognize their value " and understand " the danger of our drifting during recent years away from representative government toward direct action; from individual property rights to socialism; from individual responsibility for individual conduct toward class consciousness, class agitation and class legislation, ..." A purpose of the Association is " to arouse interest in the men who wrote the Constitution . . . to make clear that they were governmentally-minded as Edison and Marconi are electrically-minded; as Emerson and Socrates were philosophically-minded; as Shakespeare and Longfellow were literary-minded; as Mozart and Mendelssohn were musically-minded; and that in the light of all that history and experience could teach, they were making a contribution as important to the science of government as was [sic] the ten digits to the science of mathematics, the scale to music, or the alphabet to language." [184]   A further aim of the organization is " to urge upon educational institutions that in the teaching of History, Civics and Political Science the Constitution be given the place of prominence and importance which it deserves." [185] The observance of Constitution Week, as the name of the Association attests, is of primary interest to the organization.

Harry F. Atwood, author of *Back to the Republic, Safeguarding American Ideals* and *Keep God in American History,* directs the activities of the Constitution Anniversary Association.   Since 1918 Mr. Atwood " has spoken in all parts of the country to various types of audiences on the Constitution." [186]   While addressing a Los Angeles gathering under the auspices of the Better America Federation in May,

[184] *Constitution Anniversary Association,* " A Statement of the Expanding Activities."   [185] *Ibid.*   [186] *Ibid.*

1922, Mr. Atwood sowed the seed for the National Oratorical Contest on the Constitution. It was at this meeting that Mr. Harry Chandler, of the *Los Angeles Times*, conceived the idea " of developing interest in the Constitution " by conducting such a contest in the schools of the state. As a result, " the school year of 1922–23 witnessed the preparation of over 8000 orations," and " the final contest was held in Los Angeles where prizes aggregating $5000 were awarded." [187]   This led to similar contests in other states, supported by " the American Bar Association, the Constitution Anniversary Association and other patriotic organizations." [188]   The contest became nation-wide, the final meeting being held at Washington. In the second contest (1924–1925) over 18,000 schools entered; the awards amounted to $45,600, and 1,500,000 high school students competed. Twenty-eight daily newspapers across the continent conducted this contest." [189]

Mr. Atwood carries his advocacy of a knowledge of the Constitution and of representative government to the people not only through his addresses delivered throughout the country but also by means of his writings. It is his belief that " we have drifted from the *republic* toward democracy; from statesmanship to demagogism " in " an age of retrogressive tendencies." [190]   He holds that a republic provides the " golden mean " of government, autocracy and democracy offering " undesirable extremes." To make clear his

[187] *Constitution Anniversary Association,* " Bulletin Number 10."
[188] *Ibid.*
[189] *Constitution Anniversary Association,* " Bulletin Number 9." The first prize in the Second Annual Contest was $2000, and was awarded to Robert Sessions of Birmingham, Alabama, a boy of fifteen years. See *Constitution Anniversary Association,* " Bulletin Number 10."
[190] Atwood, Harry F., *Back to the Republic the Golden Mean: the Standard Form of Government* (Chicago, 1918), p. 20. The italics are in the original.

meaning parallels are drawn between " the realm of nature and of human activity " and the realm of government, attributing to each " two extremes and the golden mean." For instance, he believes that " what thirst is to the individual, autocracy is to government; what drunkenness is to the individual, democracy is to government; what temperance is to the individual, the *republic* is to government." [191]

According to Mr. Atwood " the most defective portion of our thinking and teaching in the schools is that phase of education which pertains to civics, economics and history." [192] So far as textbooks are concerned, Mr. Atwood was convinced that " there are comparatively few who will contend that there has ever been written a good history of the United States of America." The same statement holds true for textbooks in civil government, for none makes clear " to the average student the form of government that was established here under the Constitution." [193] Mr. Atwood was concerned still more with the fact that so few students had read the Constitution, — students who had received from twelve to sixteen years' education at the expense of the state. " So long as the expense of the public schools and State universities is paid by the government," Mr. Atwood declared, " one object at least should be to turn out well informed and patriotic citizens, and the best possible way to do that is to give them an understanding of the meaning of the Constitution and a high regard for its wise provisions." Mr. Atwood is, moreover, sympathetic with those who maintain that " teachers in the public schools should

[191] *Ibid.*, pp. 36–40. Mr. Atwood draws ten parallels to autocracy, democracy and the republic from religion, domestic life, food, drink, music, thought, sleep, light, moisture, and the number of wheels most serviceable on vehicles.

[192] Atwood, Harry F., *Safeguarding American Ideals* (Chicago, 1921), p. 34.

[193] *Ibid.*, pp. 29–32.

be impressed with the fact that their salaries are paid at public expense." [194]

The sentiment of the Better America Federation of California regarding the study of the Constitution in the schools is not unlike that of the Constitution Anniversary Association.   Mr. Woodworth Clum in " America is Calling," a pamphlet to the students in high schools and colleges, sets forth the tenets of his organization, in his declaration that he would like to see " every school and college student in America not only learn the *Preamble* to the Constitution so that they could repeat it verbatim at any time or any place, but . . . also have them know its *meaning* so well that when they repeat it they would recall the entire philosophy of the American government." [195]   Much apprehension was felt by the Better America Federation because of " groups of free thinkers or radicals " agitating for some other form of government under which there would be " no profits . . . in business." [196]

In accord with an interest in education evident in its earliest meetings, the American Federation of Labor has carried on investigations as to the character of teaching and the content of textbooks in the social studies.   In 1903, the Executive Council was directed " to secure the introduction of textbooks that will be more in accord with modern thought upon social and political economy, books that will teach the dignity of manual labor, give due importance to the service that the laborer renders to society, and that will not teach the harmful doctrine that the wage-workers should be content with their lot, because of the opportunity that may be afforded a few of their number rising out of their

[194] *Ibid.*
[195] Clum, Woodworth, " America is Calling," The Better America Federation of California, Los Angeles.
[196] *Ibid.*

class, instead of teaching that the wage earners should base their hopes upon the elevation of the conditions of the working people." [197]

In 1919, the Executive Council was instructed "to appoint a committee to investigate the matter of selecting, or of preparing and publishing textbooks appropriate for classes of workers," because the convention found "one of the chief difficulties in securing appropriate classes for the workers is the dearth' of unbiased and suitable textbooks." [198]

The committee thus appointed reported in 1920 an insufficient and inaccurate teaching of industrial growth and of the trade union movement. The responsibility for this condition was assessed upon the economists of the past " whose teachings still largely dominate in the educational institutions of our time," — teachings " which have failed to stand the test of experience and of unbiased investigation." Ideas held faulty were thought, furthermore, to be in no small measure the outgrowth of ideas gained from books failing to " state accurately and interpret correctly economic laws and their application to our modern industrial society." [199] The Committee therefore recommended the preparation of a textbook by a competent trade unionist under the direction of the executive officers of the American Federation of Labor with a special committee for this purpose, and " the teaching of unemasculated industrial history embracing an accurate account of the organization of the workers and of the results thereof, the teaching of principles underlying industrial activities and relations, and a summary of legislation, state and federal, affecting industry." [200]

[197] " Education for All," *Official Record of the American Federation of Labor in the Struggle to Bring Knowledge to the Masses* (American Federation of Labor, Washington, 1922), p. 4.
[198] *Ibid.*   [199] *Ibid.*   [200] *Ibid.*, p. 5.

The attention of the convention was focussed in its educational program the following year upon a proposed investigation of textbooks in civics, economics and history. The committee to whom this task was delegated reported in 1922. Their report, published in 1923, pointed out the importance of " instruction in social and economic studies," because such studies are " vitally concerned with wide-spread understanding of our social and economic institutions and forces." [201] Yet the American Federation of Labor expressly denied a desire to have their point of view " stressed to the exclusion of all others." They wanted merely " an emphasis commensurate with its significance." Nor did they wish " public education to be influenced by partisan bodies of any kind." For they esteemed " the persons most competent to judge in detail what should be taught and how it should be taught . . . those who are themselves engaged in the educational profession." [202]

Inasmuch as " there are no more important determining factors than the economic fabric to which the majority of citizens contribute the larger share of their creative energy " the Federation considered essential a knowledge of the trade-union movement and " of all other social problems having to do with the welfare of the working people." [203] The information held important for the worker they felt should be taught in the junior as well as in the senior high school, in order to reach those students who leave school early.[204]

[201] *Report of the Proceedings of the Convention of the American Federation of Labor at Cincinnati, June, 1922.* Eighth Day Proceedings. *Report of the American Federation of Labor,* Committee on Education on Social Studies in the Public Schools, " Labor and Education " (The American Federation of Labor, Washington, 1923), pp. 1–13.

[202] *Ibid.,* pp. 3–4, 7. *The New York Times,* August 25, 1921.

[203] *Report of the American Federation of Labor, op. cit.,* pp. 3–4, 9.

[204] *Ibid.,* p. 21.

In the consideration of the textbooks most commonly used in the public schools, the Federation's committee held it " obvious that old-fashioned didactic methods of teaching are not suitable to the new treatment," that " subjects should be presented not in the form of finished judgments and dogmatic rules . . . but rather as observations of the world about us, concerning which the pupil must to a great extent exercise his own judgments; " and that " in the case of highly controversial subjects, important dissenting views should be fairly and adequately presented." [205] Although special pleaders for some change in common educational practice, they asserted that " the labor movement, unlike selfish interests, does not and cannot depend for public favor upon narrow propaganda; what it wants and needs is the light of day and freedom of opinion. The more people know, and the more they think, the better in the long run for working men and women, and for all our citizenship."

As a consequence of their premises, the Committee applied to the textbooks considered the following tests: " In the first place, is the book of old, narrow type, or of the newer and broader type?   In the second place, is its general method that which inculcates certain fixed principles which may have been acceptable some time in the past, or, on the other hand, that which portrays society as a group of growing and changing institutions?   In the third place, does it include adequate information about important subjects, particularly subjects of concern to the wage-earning population, such as trade-unionism, collective bargaining, standards of living, hours of work, safety and sanitation, housing, unemployment, civil liberty, and the judicial power?   And in its treatment of these subjects, does it fairly present labor's point of view as well as that of others? " [206]

205 *Ibid.*, p. 23.   206 *Ibid.*

The application of these tests to one hundred twenty-three textbooks — forty-seven histories, forty-seven civics, twenty-five economics, and four sociologies, revealed that fifty-five per cent were of "the newer type dealing with the broader aspects of government, and the social and industrial life of the people rather than with forms of organization, military events and abstract themes." Sixty per cent were found to be "dynamic rather than static in their method of treatment" in that they recognized "to a greater or less degree the power for growth in our institutions."

On the other hand, the Committee decided that "a majority of texts fell short of the standards in one or more important respects," [207] although, on the whole, "the newer type of text" attempted "to give the labor movement in the problem of industry adequate and just consideration." [208] Failure to do so the Committee attributed either "to ignorance of the author or to a hesitancy to deal with this difficult subject, rather than to a deliberate attempt to keep the facts of industry out of the schools." The survey found "no evidence that text books are being used for propaganda purposes." [209]

[207] *Ibid.*

[208] *Report of Proceedings*, Eighth Day (1922), p. 356.

[209] *Ibid.* According to the Committee the "modern textbooks in most frequent use are: civics, Ashley's *The New Civics*, Beard's *American Citizenship*, Dunn's *The Community and the Citizen*, Forman's *The American Democracy*, Hill's *Community Life and Civic Problems*, Hughes' *Community Civics*, Magruder's *American Government in 1921*, and Reed's *Forms and Functions of American Government;* in economics, Burch's *American Economic Life*, Burch and Patterson's *American Social Problems*, Hughes' *Economic Civics*, Laing's *An Introduction to Economics*, Marshall and Lyon's *Our Economic Organization*, and Thompson's *Elementary Economics;* in sociology, Burch and Patterson's *American Social Problems*, Ellwood's *Sociology and Modern Problems* [sic], Towne's *Social Problems*, and Tuft's *The Real Business of Living;* in history, Ashley's *American History*, Beard and Bagley's *A First Book in American History*, Beard's *History of the United States*, Bourne and Benton's *History of the United*

The Public Service Institute through its chairman also has urged a more extensive study of "labor civics," and commended the New York course in civics for older grammar grade children and first year high school pupils.[210] Still others have become censors of the character of social study instruction in the public schools. Books treating the modern problems of race, labor and capital, immigration, private property, and topics of like nature have been examined with a critical eye. The portrayal of facts relating to races and nationalities in the United States has proved a fruitful source of attack. Authors have been asked to omit or make colorless references to controversial topics in the preparation or the revision of textbooks which would discuss, for example, the Chinese and Japanese in America, the Italians and the Jews. In one city the negroes protested the use of a textbook because of a statement to the effect that the Southern white man tried to keep the negro from voting, the protest carrying enough weight to cause a special edition of the book to be printed for use in that city.

Its presentation of the subject of private property was the source of an attack upon Berry and Howe's *Actual Democracy*, " an elementary discussion " of present-day problems in America. Exception was taken to children being taught that "private property is one of the fundamental institutions of American democracy . . . an unmistakable index of social progress . . . [which] cannot be destroyed with-

---

States, Cousins and Hills' [*sic*] *American History,* Evans' *The Essential Facts of American History,* Forman's *A History of the United States for Schools,* and *Advanced American History,* James and Sanford's *American History,* Mace's *School History of the United States,* Muzzey's *American History,* Thompson's *History of the United States, Political, Industrial and Social,* and West's *History of the American People.* " Labor and Education," p. 28.
[210] *The New York Times,* September 3, 1923.

out destroying also the ideals of liberty and democracy in which Americans believe." [211]

Its method of discussing trade-unionism [212] and immigration likewise met disfavor.   In the case of the latter subject, the critics were disturbed because, among other things, the authors concluded " that the immigration situation has rendered necessary a profound change in the very structure of our government.   [For] in order to control the turbulent non-American elements, we have been compelled to modify, many of our earlier democratic ideals and to adopt centralization of authority, which is far different in spirit from American traditions . . . [and] that [due to immigration] American democracy is facing a life and death struggle with Marxian socialism." [213]

In treating freedom of speech the author of the secondary school textbook is to no less degree upon slippery ground, for here again critics have acclaimed partisanship and bias evident in discussions.   On this charge A. T. Southworth has been adjudged guilty in his *The Common Sense of the Constitution of the United States* in that he says, " This amend-

[211] Herskovitz, Melville J., and Willey, Malcolm M., " What Your Child Learns," *The Nation*, Vol. CXIX (September 17, 1924), pp. 282–284.   The book referred to is Berry, Margaret K., and Howe, Samuel B., *Actual Democracy* (New York, 1923).   The quotation is found on page 63.

[212] In the discussion of trade-unionism objection was raised to the classification of unions as " business unionism — which is trade conscious but not class conscious, . . . the friendly or uplift union which may be either trade or class conscious, and is conservative, . . . ' predatory unionism ' . . . secret, either radical or conservative, class or trade conscious, and has two wings; ' hold-up unionism,' the corrupt type recently exposed in our great cities, and ' guerrilla unionism ' which never combines with employers, but engages in a secret and violent warfare with capital . . . a fourth and more objectionable type of unionism . . . calls itself ' revolutionary unionism.' It may be either socialistic as was the Western Federation of Miners, or anarchistic like the Industrial Workers of the World. . . ." Berry and Howe, *op. cit.*, pp. 73–74.

[213] *The Nation, loc. cit.*   The quotation which was objectionable to the writers of the article was found on pages 167–169 of the textbook.

ment [the first amendment] also guarantees the right of free speech. There can, of course, be no such thing as absolute free speech. The only persons who say exactly what they think every minute of the day are babies and fools. . . . There is reason in all things, and on general principles a person may say in this country anything he pleases, provided what he says is not libelous or slanderous, or contrary to the public morals; and provided that he does not advocate the overthrow of the government by force. In this country where we have a government, not of men but of laws, it is not reasonable that anyone should preach the overthrow of the government by force. If B says, ' Murder A, throw him out of office, and let me rule,' then it is perfectly logical for C to advocate the murder of B after B has set himself up as a ruler. This is anarchy." [214]

The allegation that textbook-making has been directed by " Big Business " has also been made. As a case in point, Hughes's *Text-Book in Citizenship* has been cited as one which carries many illustrations printed " by courtesy " of such corporations as the Carnegie Steel Company, the International Harvester Company and the Baltimore and Ohio Railroad.[215] " And," according to the critic, " it is not pictures of blast furnaces with sweating men . . . but pictures of Americanization schools . . . factory gardens . . . model factory buildings . . . and a group of twenty-four elderly men, who having labored for thirty-five years each in the employ of the Carnegie Steel Company are posed at the annual picnic given to the employees as a reward for services rendered." [216] A section in the same textbook, " Employers

[214] *The Nation, loc. cit.* See Southworth, A. T., *The Common Sense of the Constitution of the United States* (Boston, 1924), pp. 91–92.
[215] *The Nation, loc. cit.* Hughes, R. O., *Text-Book in Citizenship* (Boston, 1923).
[216] *The Nation, loc. cit.*

of the Right Sort," in which is discussed profit sharing by the employees of the United States Steel Company, also met with disapproval. Equally disliked was Mr. Hughes's discussion of the I. W. W. because he said: "It is hard to see how a right-thinking American can possibly indulge in such performances or hold such theories. A decent man finds it difficult to sympathize with even oppressed people who use any such means to have their grievances corrected."[217] The textbook was further adjudged biased in its discussion of Lenin and Trotsky as "two able and unscrupulous leaders" and of the anarchists whom "no civilized people can tolerate."[218] On the other hand, the same author's book *Economic Civics* was attacked by a member of the American Car Company of Berwick, Pennsylvania, on the ground of being "Bolshevistic."

Other books have incurred the disapproval of business interests. *American Economic Life* by Henry Reed Burch has been charged with being "unfair" in its treatment of monopolies for saying: "Trolley lines, subways and 'bus companies often possess great monopoly power. For example, in a city of one million and a half the competitive cost of transportation perhaps does not exceed three or four cents a passenger, yet the actual price paid by the passenger is usually from five to eight cents. This difference between the price paid and the competitive price represents the extent of the monopoly power."[219]

Many business organizations have interested themselves in a program for education not only among their own employees but among the people in general. Pamphlets and

[217] *The Nation, loc. cit.* Hughes, *op. cit.,* pp. 510–511.

[218] *The Nation, loc. cit.* Hughes, *op. cit.,* pp. 510–511.

[219] Letter under date of December 7, 1925, from the editor of "Service Talks," published by the Philadelphia Rapid Transit Company. Burch, Henry Reed, *American Economic Life* (New York, 1921), p. 330.

other published materials have in this way been distributed to set forth the point of view held desirable. Such a motive doubtless led to a survey of books dealing with the subject of banking in 1919 by the American Bankers Association. The examination of the books induced the Association through their Public Education Commission to publish and distribute a series of talks to be given in the schools, since the books examined were, on the whole, found to be "prepared from the standpoint of bankers, and not the standpoint of the mass of students who attend high school." [220] The talks were designed to be delivered by bankers to pupils in the eighth grade, the senior year of the high school, and to civic, business and fraternal organizations in order to acquaint people more thoroughly with methods of banking.[221]

During the World War the preparation of a series of lessons entitled *Lessons in Community and National Life* under the auspices of the Bureau of Education and the Food Administration provoked adverse criticism from the National Industrial Conference Board. In the lessons topics pertinent to a study of community civics were treated, and included discussions on international trade relations, manufacturing methods, labor organizations and similar subjects. To these, exception was taken, and it was asserted that "opinions on controversial subjects are frequently introduced into the Lessons by suggestion rather than by direct statement, and through the whole fabric is woven a thread of propaganda in favor of the eight-hour day, old age pensions, social insurance, trade-unionism, the minimum wage

[220] American Bankers Association, "Books devoted wholly or in part to the subject of Banking." The books mentioned were not all social study books, arithmetic and bookkeeping textbooks being included.

[221] "Talks on Banking and Elementary Economics," prepared by the Public Education Commission, American Bankers Association, New York.

and similar issues." [222] A " partisan " attitude was said to
to expressed in such a statement as: " We are told that in
the United States somebody is injured while at work every
fifteen seconds, and somebody is killed every fifteen minutes.
We cannot wonder at this when we realize how many dangers there are in modern industry." [223] According to *The*
[New York] *World*, Magnus N. Alexander, managing director of the National Industrial Conference Board, alarmed
a convention of the National Boot and Shoe Manufacturers'
Association when he told them that these lessons were
spreading " insidious, unwarranted propaganda, particularly
injurious for reading by youth in the plastic age when youth
is inclined to take for granted and as proved all that is
said through the medium of the books in his class-room." [224]

These criticisms caused editorial comment in different
periodicals throughout the country. *The Capital Daily
Press* of Bismarck, North Dakota, declaring that " for gen-

[222] Educational News and Editorial Comment, "Social Studies in
Public Schools," *The School Review*, Vol. XXVII (1919), pp. 205–212.
National Industrial Conference Board, *A Case of Federal Propaganda in
Our Public Schools*, pp. 4, 11. The lessons were prepared under the direction of Charles H. Judd, Director of the School of Education of the University of Chicago, and Leon C. Marshall, Dean of the School of Commerce and Administration in the same university.

[223] The National Industrial Conference Board in connection with this
remarked: " Such a statement indicates a studied effort to present to the
immature mind an exceedingly distorted picture of factory life. It sug-
gests an almost constant maiming and mangling of industrial workers,
whereas, as a matter of fact, most industrial accidents are of a minor
character such as slight cuts, scratches and slivers. Take, however, at its
face value the statement that somebody is killed every fifteen minutes
while at work. On the basis of a 54-hour work-week, approximately the
average in this country, this means a total of 11,250 deaths in industry
per year . . . the scholar should also be given an idea of the millions of
workers to whom this total of deaths is related. He should in fairness
also have pointed out to him the hazards of non-industrial pursuits which
cause annually more fatal accidents than occur in industry." The National
Industrial Conference Board, *op. cit.*, p. 11.

[224] *The School Review, loc. cit.*

erations the reactionaries have maintained their grip on the control of our educational institutions, and from the kindergarten to college the ' plastic minds of our youth ' have been sedulously taught the superior sacredness of private property and the supremacy of dollar rights over human rights. This is one thing which has made political and industrial progress so slow." [225]

To the editor of *The School Review* the whole discussion furnished " a legitimate opportunity to call attention to the fact that the schools have been very deficient in times past in their treatment of social problems." He felt that the time had come " when there ought to be a very clear and explicit assertion on the part of educational people that they will not be dominated by such criticism as here presented," for he believed " the schools of a democracy have a right to discuss democratic and popular matters." [226]

[225] Quoted in *The School Review, loc. cit.*
[226] *The School Review, loc. cit.* Instances of criticism of textbooks might be multiplied. Authors have met objections to their works because there were no " Republican illustrations in the book," because of quotations from Münsterberg and other Germans, and because of the discussion devoted to prohibition. In this last case a member of the Board of Education of Chicago is reported to have criticised the use of an arithmetic as looking like " a bartender's friend " in that it was full of problems of " how much did this wine merchant order his sherry or how many barrels of whiskey could the man purchase for such an amount." *Iowa City* [Iowa] *Press-Citizen*, November 13, 1924.

CHAPTER VII

THE ATTACK ON HISTORY TEXTBOOKS SINCE 1917

Since the World War, an ardent patriotism has swept the country, resulting in a widespread investigation of the teaching and writing of history. Sponsored by various groups, the movement has gained considerable momentum, until history teaching and history textbooks are in danger of being an expression of certain religious, racial or other partisan opinions. These groups hold, in common, that American histories, as now written, neglect heroic characters in American history, especially in the Revolutionary War, and that they are distorted by a pro-British bias. Propaganda, indeed, makes strange bed-fellows. In this new praetorian guard of the temple of American patriotism are found the Hearst newspapers, an element of the Knights of Columbus and of the Irish-Americans, the German-Americans, and finally patriotic societies of this country.

The charge of " Anglicization," usually enlivened by mysterious references to " British gold," arises in part from the new trend of American historical scholarship in the last twenty-five years. Historians employing scientific methods have done much to revise the traditional ideas concerning our relations with Great Britain. Important contributions of this character have been made, for instance, by such historians as George Louis Beer, Charles M. Andrews, Herbert L. Osgood, Sydney George Fisher, and Claude H. Van Tyne.

These investigations were going forward at the same time that conscious efforts were being made by the publicists of the two countries to reveal to the two English-speaking peoples their common ties and responsibilities in the world today. Many books were printed and organizations formed to promote Anglo-American concord; among the latter, such bodies as the Sulgrave Institute, the Anglo-American League and the English-Speaking Union.

To suspicious onlookers the work of the historians in their cloisters took on the appearance of deliberate propaganda favorable to Great Britain — a suspicion, it need hardly be said, entirely unwarranted. It needed only an appeal such as that of Herbert Adams Gibbons that we solidify an amicable relationship with Great Britain through our common language, common ideals and common interests, to confirm the credulous in their suspicions.[1]   Furthermore, suggestions from men like Albert Bushnell Hart that our history textbooks be rewritten to encourage better international relations seemed to afford additional proof that pro-British agencies were in control of history textbooks.[2]   The writings of special pleaders like Owen Wister strengthened this impression.[3]   Indeed, Charles Edward Russell has gone so far

[1] In an article, "The Anger of the Anglophiles," Edward F. McSweeney of the Knights of Columbus Historical Commission discussed the "Anglo-Saxon myth." In his discussion he ascribes to Gibbons the point of view that an "over emphasis upon Anglo-Saxonism is positively harmful to Anglo-Saxon solidarity, that it is a stimulus to the enemies among Americans of friendship with Great Britain," [and] "that the idea that a better understanding with Great Britain can be effected by rewriting our history textbooks be abandoned." Gibbons, however, points out means of bringing about "the better understanding" by "creating an irresistible public opinion." *Columbia*, April, 1922, p. 10.

[2] Hart, Albert Bushnell, *School Books and International Prejudices* (International Conciliation Bulletin, January, 1911, No. 32). Professor Hart points out that a more favorable attitude toward Great Britain developed in the United States about the time of the Spanish-American War, and urges that the American Revolution be taught American and British youth as "a deep and broad Anglo-Saxon movement in which both sides had some rights and both had some wrong."

[3] A study of the presentation of the American Revolution in history

as to declare that definitely planned attempts to rewrite American history textbooks, for the purpose of encouraging better Anglo-American relations, were launched as early as 1896, and have been carefully carried on since then.[4]

On the other hand, the proponents of revision, conscious of an "agitation for the reintroduction of parochial patriotism into the schools and colleges," have entered a plea for "the truth" in school histories and for the writing and teaching of history by scholars unaffected by the demands of "politicians."[5] To them, the true fount of patriotism does not arise from textbooks of history which are "nationalistic rather than impartial."[6] They would seek, rather, to depict events not as "partisans" but in a "scientific spirit, with the desire to understand rather than to justify."[7]

ATTACKS ON HISTORY TEXTBOOKS BY THE HEARST NEWSPAPERS AND CHARLES GRANT MILLER

In 1921 the Hearst newspapers began the publication of a series of articles designed to arouse "patriotic American

---

textbooks was made by Charles Altschul in 1917. See Altschul, Charles, *The American Revolution in Our School Text-Books* (New York, 1917). Also see Wister, Owen, *A Straight Deal or the Ancient Grudge* (New York, 1920).

[4] Russell, Charles Edward, "Behind the Propaganda Scenes," *Columbia*, September, 1922, p. 5 *et seq.* Mr. Russell declares that the undertaking was financed by Andrew Carnegie.

[5] William Allen Neilson, president of Smith College, in an address before the English-Speaking Union, May 16, 1920. *The Christian Science Monitor*, May 17, 1920; also Bulletin No. 7, June, 1923, of the English-Speaking Union (345 Madison Avenue, New York). Agencies for Anglo-American friendship assert they have made no attempts to combat present-day efforts of anti-English groups. (Letters to the author under date of June 26, 1923, from the Secretary of the Sulgrave Institution, and under date of July 6, 1923, from the Secretary of the English-Speaking Union.)

[6] Eagleton, Clyde, "The Attitude of Our Textbooks Toward England," *Educational Review*, Vol. LVI (December, 1918), pp. 424–429.

[7] Schuyler, Robert Livingston, "History and Public Opinion," *Educational Review*, Vol. LV (March, 1918), pp. 181–190.

parents " to a realization that " the school histories now being taught to their children have been revised and in some instances wholly rewritten in a new and propitiatory spirit toward England." [8] Since that time these articles have appeared at irregular intervals from the pen of Charles Grant Miller. There has been yeast in his statements, and to them may be attributed the origin of much of the criticism directed against history textbooks by individuals and organized groups. With titles set up in large black-faced type these articles captured the eye of those who, consciously or unconsciously, were giving heed to the feverish propaganda which has flourished since the World War. In his articles, Mr. Miller proceeded from the discussion of " United States History Revised in School Books, Belittles Revolution and Thanks England for Bestowing Liberty on America " to a treatment of " Propaganda seeks to Distort American History, British Workers are Being Backed by a Heavily Financed Machine. . . ." [9]

Chief among the historians whom Mr. Miller would characterize as " Anglicized " are found Albert Bushnell Hart, John P. O'Hara, Everett Barnes, A. C. McLaughlin, C. H. Van Tyne, William B. Guitteau, and Willis Mason West. Charges of " Anglicization " have been brought also against C. H. Ward for his edition of Burke's *Speech on Conciliation with America* and upon Helen Nicolay for her *Book of American Wars*. The pro-British point of view which Mr. Miller found expressed has been brought about by " intrigue and treason " and the American school histories which portray it " must be cast out if America is to remain America." [10]

[8] Chicago *Herald and Examiner*, July 3, 1921.
[9] In Chicago *Herald and Examiner*, July 3, 1921, and October 15, 1922. The latter was not the last article written, however.
[10] *Ibid.*, January 14, 1923.

Substantially all of the criticisms of history textbooks in which Mr. Miller has indulged have related to statements regarding the Revolutionary War. He found it especially objectionable when a history like John P. O'Hara's gives " the impression " that " the American Revolution originated not in the colonies themselves, but among the devoted friends of liberty in England," and when " more quotation is given from Pitt than from Patrick Henry." [11] A " wholesome desire for increased friendship and coöperation between the United States and Great Britain," declared Mr. Miller, " creates no justification for the policy of propitiation of England through defamation of America, which offers as sacrifice upon the altar of international comity immortelles snatched from the monuments of our nation's heroic founders. . . . In our own heroes and history our nation has been exceptionally blessed. They have proved unfailing sources of pride and inspiration that have prompted us as a people to stanch character, high endeavor, noble achievements and unparalleled progress." [12]

The second article in the Chicago *Herald and Examiner* lay bare the alleged defects in Barnes' textbook, where the author plays " the part of a flunky apologist to England for

---

[11] *Ibid.*, July 3, 1921. In O'Hara's *History of the United States,* thirteen lines are given to Patrick Henry's opposition to the Stamp Act, over four of which are devoted to the words by Henry: " ' Tarquin and Caesar each had his Brutus; Charles I his Cromwell; and George III — (here cries of " Treason! Treason! " from the Speaker and others were heard) — may profit by their example. If this be treason make the most of it.' " pp. 124–125. On the other hand, six lines are allotted to a discussion of Pitt's reaction toward the repeal of the Stamp Act, and approximately three lines to direct quotation from him. ("When the question of repeal came up in the House of Commons, Pitt ' rejoiced that America had resisted.' He was glad that Americans were not ' so dead to all the feelings of liberty as voluntarily to submit to be slaves.' ") p. 126. (O'Hara, John P., *History of the United States,* New York, 1919). There has been only one edition of this history textbook.

[12] *Ibid.*

the independence established by our fathers," and in which he "burlesques its world affecting results." [13] Barnes, furthermore, Mr. Miller pointed out, ignores such patriots as "Nathan Hale, whose only regret on the British scaffold was that he had but one life to give to his country, . . . Ethan Allen, Mad Anthony Wayne and the battle of Stony Point," while, on the other hand, "there is a full page of praise for the traitor Benedict Arnold whom ' Congress had treated unfairly.' " [14] In addition to other faults, Mr. Miller cited the statements that " the first signer of the Declaration of Independence was a smuggler," " that the Continental Congress ' was a scene of petty bickerings and schemings ' among ' selfish, unworthy, short-sighted, narrow-minded, office-seeking and office-trading plotters,' that ' half the colonists were loyal to England '; that the rest were united in resistance only ' because they dared not be otherwise,' and that if in England the wise course had only prevailed against the ' foolish ' King, ' this great country would probably now have been a great branch of the British empire.' " [15]

Barnes was also condemned because he calls the War of 1812 "a mistake," the burning of Washington "an act of reprisal " for the burning of buildings in Canada, and Jackson's victory at New Orleans "a wasted battle; a needless victory." [16] How different to Mr. Miller was "this new Barnes " from the Barnes' *Brief History of the United States* which spoke " always from the American viewpoint, with American interests and sympathies at heart! " [17]

The next authors to arouse his ire were McLaughlin and Van Tyne, who with other historians were " reshaping " American history " to serve international interests under

---

[13] *Ibid.*, July 17, 1921.   [15] *Ibid.*   [17] *Ibid.*
[14] *Ibid.*   [16] *Ibid.*

whose hypnotism of propaganda American public opinion has been goose-stepping for five years in the direction of a return to English subjection."[18]   Charged with omitting Hale, Decatur, Faneuil Hall, the Green Mountain Boys, Betsy Ross and the flag, the quartering of troops and "the British attempts to bribe," they were declared guilty also of "strictly minimizing the patriot valor at Lexington, Bunker Hill and New Orleans." Such omission in the school histories Mr. Miller compared with "an ancient custom to remove the viscera and brain before embalming a body." Indeed, Mr. Miller found it extremely objectionable that the "leading founders of our liberties are characterized by McLaughlin and Van Tyne as follows: 'It is hard to realize how ignorant and superstitious were most of the colonists of America' — p. 134; 'Patrick Henry, a gay, unprosperous and hitherto unknown country lawyer' — p. 141; 'Smuggling was so common that even a leading Boston merchant was known as 'the Prince of Smugglers' — p. 140; . . . and 'Adams and Hancock stole away across the fields' — p. 153."[19]

Besides these grievances the Hearst papers objected to the omission of "such famous slogans as 'We have met the

[18] *Ibid.*, July 24, 1921. The article is entitled "Declaration of Independence is Censored: England's Guilt for Revolution Disputed in New United States Histories."

[19] *Ibid.* This characterization of the colonials as "ignorant and superstitious" is in a chapter devoted to "Life in the Colonies" in which are discussed, among other things, "Colonial Ignorance and Superstition" and "The Salem Witchcraft." In the paragraph on "Colonial Ignorance and Superstition," the following sentence is indicative of the trend: "Hornets were thought to come from the decaying bodies of horses, and honey bees from cattle." The quotation regarding Henry is as follows: ". . . Patrick Henry, a gay, unprosperous, and hitherto unknown country lawyer, who made his reputation by declaring with marvelous eloquence that there was a limit to the legal control which the King might exert over Colonial lawmaking," page 141. McLaughlin, Andrew C., and Van Tyne, Claude Halstead, *A History of the United States for Schools* (New York, 1911).

enemy and they are ours' and 'Don't give up the ship'";
and McLaughlin and Van Tyne "go further [even] than
their fellows and seek to destroy these inspiring slogans by
disputing their authenticity." [20]

This attack on the McLaughlin and Van Tyne textbook
provoked a protest from C. H. Ward, whose edition of
Burke's *Speech on Conciliation with America* the Hearst
papers also had criticized. " Mr. Miller," declared Ward,
" skillfully quotes with a sneer from the McLaughlin and
Van Tyne book " (regarding Patrick Henry). " Yet this
book," he asserted, " does in fact give more than usual
prominence and praise to Patrick Henry: 'Who declared
with marvelous eloquence' (p. 141); 'With burning words
he denounced the tyranny' (p. 142); 'Patrick Henry
again electrified the Virginia leaders by his daring prophecy'
(p. 150); 'Securing a commission and money from the
Governor of Virginia, Patrick Henry' (p. 182)." Notwithstanding this treatment of Henry, Mr. Ward averred that
" Mr. Miller so quotes as to imply that the authors have
slandered Henry; but the two adjectives 'gay and unknown' are the only two words that convey aught but
praise." [21] Further, Mr. Ward showed that, in the account
of Lexington, the statement that " Adams and Hancock
stole away " is taken out of its context. Ward, likewise,
found that Miller has " misrepresented " Hart's history, for
he was unable to discover some of the statements attributed
to that author.[22]

[20] *Ibid.* In the 1911 edition of McLaughlin and Van Tyne's textbook,
" We have met the enemy and they are ours " appears on page 247. The
quotation " Don't give up the ship " is on page 248, but a footnote sug-
gests that Lawrence's real words seem to have been, " Fight the ship until
she is sunk," while those usually given are the words of the boy who took
the message on deck.

[21] *The New York Times,* September 28, 1921.

[22] *Ibid.*

On November 20, 1921, the Chicago *Herald and Examiner* devoted an article to an attack not only upon Barnes, Hart, McLaughlin and Van Tyne, but also upon William B. Guitteau, who, too, had fallen victim to " the snobbish spirit of apology and subserviency to England." [23]   This attitude, according to Mr. Miller, " the publishers, Silver, Burdett and Company, boldly proclaim in their advertisements " in saying: " This book has been written in the light of recent events in which a new atmosphere has been created for the study of our national life. . . .   The revolutionary war and subsequent Anglo-American difficulties hitherto distorted in our school books through an unthinking adherence to traditional prejudice, have been restated by Dr. Guitteau in their true light." [24]

One of the objectionable points urged against Guitteau and other historians was the ignoring of Irish patriots.   In large, bold-faced type Mr. Miller called attention to " the elimination of German and Irish assistance to the colonists in the Revolution, as well as the Dutch of New York and Pennsylvania, the French of Carolina and the Swedes of New Jersey and Delaware, while the help given by France is minimized and charged to selfish, scheming motives." [25] In his earlier editions, declared Mr. Miller, Professor Hart had the " frankness to say ' Germans, Irish, Scotch-Irish, French, Dutch, Negroes and Englishmen stood side by side in the ranks, ' " but in the revised edition of 1920 " he has magically transformed so eminent a hero as Baron De Kalb from a German to a Frenchman." [26]

[23] Chicago *Herald and Examiner,* November 20, 1921.
[24] *Ibid.*   [25] *Ibid.*
[26] *Ibid.*   Mr. Miller quotes thus: " France shut her eyes when some gallant French officers, especially Marquis De Lafayette and Baron De Kalb, went to America as volunteers, p. 136." In Professor Hart's book the quotation is as follows: " Agents were sent to Paris to ask help; the French secretly gave them military supplies and money and shut their eyes when

"Home grown motives might be imagined for carrying back a century and a half the cancellation of friendly relations with the Germans," was Mr. Miller's observation, "but whence comes the motive for a sudden change in attitude toward Irish heroes of the Revolution?" Such a situation revealed to Miller a significant animus, for certainly "it is not our own country that has had the trouble with the Irish." To him it was conceivable that hidden forces were actuating the "recent revisions," for "by the early historians" the high regard in which George Washington held Irishmen was "glowingly recognized." [27]

The publication of this "series of articles written for the Hearst newspapers by Charles Grant Miller . . . aroused a wave of indignation all over the country," according to the Chicago *Herald and Examiner* for May 14, 1922. As a result, "patriotic societies have taken up the battle and various organizations have started movements to stop such perversion of American traditions." As an example of one who was aroused to the situation described in the articles, the *Herald and Examiner* published a letter from Senator William E. Borah, "who raises a clarion voice against the insidious effort to falsify the glorious story of the American fight for independence and to cheat the youth of this day of the heroic inspiration and sturdy manhood of the days of the Revolution." [28]

Although Senator Borah did not desire "to have our histories do any injustice to Great Britain," yet he did not want

---

some gallant young French officers, especially Marquis de Lafayette and De Kalb, went to America as volunteers." (Hart, Albert Bushnell, *School History of the United States*, New York, 1920, p. 136.)

[27] *Ibid.*

[28] Chicago *Herald and Examiner*, May 14, 1922. Letter from William E. Borah to P. B. Arnell, Manager *Oregon Teacher's Monthly*, Salem, Oregon.

" facts concealed nor events ignored in order to satisfy those
who now seem to regret that their ancestors ever came to this
country." [29] He presumed that the next step would be " an
expurgated edition " of the Declaration of Independence,
which would be read " with appropriate apology " on the
Fourth of July " should that continue to be observed." All
of this led him to remark that in " due time some sycophantic intellectual interloper will feel constrained to urge that
we withhold from our young men and women the unjust
attack so long made upon the American-English gentleman
known as Benedict Arnold." [30]

Under the caption " Let United States History Teach
Patriotism," Wallace McCamant, one-time president of the
Sons of the American Revolution, announced his approval
of the stand taken by Charles Grant Miller. "What think
you of a school history," queried Judge McCamant, " which
begins the story of the American Revolution with this sentence? ' There is little use trying to learn whose fault it
was that the war began, for, as we have seen, such a long
train of events led to disagreement between England and
America, that we should have to go back and back in the
very founding of the colonies. As in most quarrels, the
blame is laid by each party on the other.' " [31] When an
author, in discussing taxation without representation declares that " there was here an honest difference of opinion,"
it was evident to Judge McCamant that he " has certainly
not been called of God to write American history." [32]

To those " who say that history should not stress war,"
Judge McCamant admitted that " there are important chapters in our peace history which should be adequately covered," but he suggested that there is " nothing else " which

[29] Ibid.   [31] Chicago Herald and Examiner, May 21, 1922.
[30] Ibid.   [32] Ibid.

"will grip the imagination of the young like the story of the soldier or the sailor who fights and dies that his country may be free." [33] The inculcation of patriotism, which is the chief value in the teaching of American history in Mr. McCamant's mind, can best be attained in setting forth " sacrifices in winning freedom." [34]

The next angle from which Mr. Miller criticized American school histories is in " the magical transformation of King George III from a born Briton into a German." [35] Such, he asserted appears in the 1916–17 edition of the school history by Hart, a plain evidence of " the forces of British propaganda " which " were increasing their influences to quicken an American hatred of Germany and to hurry us into war and into permanent alliance. . . ." [36] To prove his contention regarding the nationality of King George III, he quoted the " English historical authority, Macaulay," thus: " ' The young King was a born Englishman. All his tastes and habits, good and bad were English.' " [37]

As a result of the " many forces actively at work " Mr. Miller observed that the " Anglicized revisionists, like ten automatons worked by one will, begin to teach American school children: ' that the American revolution was made in Germany; . . . ' that ' the American revolution was a contest between German tyranny and English freedom, although neither party in the struggle knew that this was the issue '; . . . ." [38] On the other hand, Mr. Miller found in John Bach McMaster's history " an excellent summary " where " the venomous quality of English comments upon America is vividly described." [39]

Another victim of " Anglicization " Mr. Miller held to be

[33] *Ibid.*
[34] *Ibid.*
[35] *Ibid.*, September 10, 1922.
[36] *Ibid.*
[37] *Ibid.*
[38] *Ibid.*
[39] *Ibid.*

Matthew Page Andrews, " director of the English-Speaking Union and Anglicized author of three American school histories " whose source of information was Greg's *History of the United States*, published in London in 1887.[40] It was the belief of Mr. Miller that it was Greg's *History* from which Mr. Andrews adduced the conclusion that " Lincoln was controlled by fanatics and through perfidy and broken pledges forced our Civil War." [41] In his discussion of Greg's book, Mr. Miller failed to mention Greg's characterization of Townshend's work. In this latter case it would seem that Greg ought to have met with approval, for he described Townshend's part in the Revolution as " folly," as well as saying that Townshend " pledged himself to a series of petty customs imposts." [42] Furthermore, he mentions Ethan Allen, Stark, Wayne, St. Clair, Putnam, Sumter and Marion, and in that regard should prove acceptable to those desiring the inclusion of heroic characters in textbooks.[43]

On October 15, 1922, the Chicago *Herald and Examiner* sought to expose the agencies which ranged " all the way from the cultivation of ' more friendly relations ' to the fulfillment of the Carnegie prophecy of the Reunited States, the British-American Union and the Cecil Rhodes Design," [44] and which were responsible for textbook revision. Besides the " elaborate and well-oiled British propaganda machine established by Sir Gilbert Parker and the late Lord Northcliffe," Mr. Miller had discovered " at least a full half dozen of strong propaganda organizations " all of whose methods were " sinister and to the one end." Among these were the

[40] *Ibid.*
[41] *Ibid.*
[42] Greg, Percy, *History of the United States from the Foundation of Virginia to the Reconstruction of the Union.* 2 v. (London, 1887), Vol. I, p. 134.   [43] *Ibid.*, pp. 165, 168.
[44] Chicago *Herald and Examiner*, October 15, 1922.

"Sons of St. George, an old organization of British-born residents of this country " who, " within the last few years," had " emerged from obscurity through a hard drive for increased membership and vigorous assertion of British spirit," and who had offered " the only open opposition which the Sons of the Revolution in California have encountered in their winning fight against Anglicized school histories. . . ." In the California case, the opposition was directed by " the American-born wife of a son of St. George and from a daughter of the American Revolution who is a member of the English-Speaking Union," which exemplified " the favorite policy of all of these British propaganda organizations " in which they " push their American-born women to the front to do their open fighting." [45]

The English-Speaking Union is another of the organizations of which Mr. Miller spoke. Its magazine, *The Landmark,* has " bitterly attacked as ' demagogic ' and ' narrow-minded' the movement to restore true American history to our public schools "; — and " it arranges for the granting of degrees by English universities to American collegiates who teach to our youth the imperialistic interests of Great Britain." [46]

The third agency for Anglicization, according to Mr. Miller, is the Sulgrave Institute " founded upon the idea that George Washington has loomed too large throughout the world ever to be belittled, and so must be claimed as an Englishman, who established in this western world English freedom." A like fate Mr. Miller prophesied for Lincoln

[45] *Ibid.* According to a pamphlet of the English-Speaking Union " it is an organization based on individual membership, and is non-political and non-sectarian. It aims at no alliance, and is not connected with governments. It takes for granted that the growth of friendship between English-speaking peoples in no way implies or produces unfriendly relations between English-speaking peoples and those of other lands and tongues."
[46] *Ibid.*

" for whom there is now being provided an English lineage
and an English ancestral home, as a shrine where expatriate
Americans may bend the sycophantic knee in foolish worship
of supposed English influences that are said to have freed
our slaves and saved our Union." [47]

Other forces of like design Mr. Miller found in the " Cecil
Rhodes Scholarship, the Cecil Rhodes Secret Society and
the Rhodes Scholarship Alumni Association of America," all
influences for Rhodes' dream — " the ultimate recovery of
the United States of America as an integral part of the
British Empire." [48]   Of like character are " the multiform
Carnegie institutions, supported by the $200,000,000 fund
of the Carnegie Corporation, and designed to influence and
direct the spirit and methods of the scholastic, public school
and library forces of the country," as well as the religious
through the " Church Peace Union." [49]   The World Alliance
for Promoting International Friendship through the
Churches and The American Association for International
Coöperation are among the various influences named by
Mr. Miller, which seek to " Briticize " America.

One of the chief endeavors of " all of the propaganda
organizations," according to Mr. Miller, is the substitution
of the observance of Magna Charta Day, June 15, for that
of July the fourth.   Such an effort led him to conclude that
" the international mind is a British mind throughout.
While insidiously seeking to denationalize America, it is
insistently striving to strengthen the nationalism of Great
Britain." [50]   Mr. Miller held as chiefly responsible for
" this de-Americanizing ' dope ' " Nicholas Murray Butler
and " more than a score of college presidents and professors,
other educators and preachers, who readily are traced into

[47] *Ibid.*   [49] *Ibid.*
[48] *Ibid.*   [50] *Ibid.*

other British propaganda organizations and are officially identified with various British secret services in this country "; who through a system of pensions are " securely subsidized into keen sympathy with the Carnegie design of ' the Reunited States— the British-American Union.' " [51]

The inclusion in American history textbooks of statements designed to show that American constitutional practices had their source in English institutions caused Mr. Miller to criticize not only Barnes, O'Hara, McLaughlin and Van Tyne, against whom he had other grievances, but also David Saville Muzzey and Willis Mason West. " Such is not American history," he declared, " it is British propaganda," for even an Englishman, Gladstone, has said, " The American Constitution is the most wonderful work ever struck off at a given time by the brain and purpose of man." [52] " Such disparagement in revised school history is not mere unintentional error," asserted Mr. Miller. " . . . , these and other gross alterations recently made in ten of our school histories, are a direct result of definite design and organized propaganda " conducted by " propaganda associations pussyfooting among us . . . to deaden our respect for our own birthright, inoculate us with contempt for our free institutions and fit us for coercion of re-colonization." [53]

On November 4, 1923, however, the *New York American* carried a retraction of an attack on West's *History of the*

[51] Chicago *Herald and Examiner*, January 14, 1923. This article names others than educators as open to the charges of " Anglicization." Among these are Rev. Dr. James E. Barton, George E. Roberts, a Magna Charta Day Committeeman, vice-president and publicity manager of the National City Bank, New York and " propaganda expert of the International Banking Corporation," who, with " Henry S. Pritchett, president of the Carnegie Foundation, conducts a correspondence school in ' Economics for Business Executives,' another spacious channel for special privilege."

[52] *Ibid.* Edwin Greenlaw's book, *Problems of Democracy*, was condemned also by Mr. Miller. It is not a history textbook, however.

[53] *Ibid.*

American People which " was printed in such a way as to lead readers to believe . . . that the statements [objected to by the Hearst papers] . . . were made without qualification." The *American* apologized for " inadvertently " publishing part of a discussion in such a way as to distort " the meaning of both paragraphs when read together." [54]

As a result of the agitation of the Hearst newspapers the "treason texts " were being revised, according to the Chicago *Herald and Examiner* of April 20, 1924. Among the authors attempting to " re-Americanize " their histories were David S. Muzzey, who already had made " three mincing revisions," Andrew C. McLaughlin and C. H. Van Tyne who have " at last submitted to the irresistible force of nation-wide protest against treason texts and have strikingly reversed their views. . . ." [55]

[54] The *New York American,* November 4, 1923. The article for which apology was offered appeared in the issue of April 1, 1923, under the caption of " U. S. Histories made up of British Slanders." The article criticized certain characterizations of heroic characters in American history as: " Englishmen of that day believed sincerely that the Revolution was the work of a group of ' soreheads.' George Washington, as a youth, had been refused a coveted commission in the British Army. Sam Adams' father had been ruined by the wise British veto of a Massachusetts ' Land Bank.' The older Otis had failed to secure an appointment on the Massachusetts bench. Alexander Hamilton was a penniless and briefless law student with no chance for special advancement unless by fishing in troubled water." The statement of the *American* follows in part: " The fact is, that the paragraph referred to immediately preceded the following qualifying paragraph: ' All this of course as an explanation of the part played by Washington, Adams, Otis and Hamilton, was as absurd as was the view of many Americans that high-minded men like Chief Justice Oliver and Governor Hutchinson of Massachusetts were loyalists simply to cling to office and salary. But had the British charge been true, what greater condemnation could be devised for the old colonial system than that under it George Washington could not get a petty lieutenant's appointment and that a genius like Hamilton had practically no chance for advancement unless taken up by some great gentlemen.' " West, Willis Mason, *History of the American People* (Boston, 1918).

[55] Chicago *Herald and Examiner,* April 20, 1924. According to Mr. Miller the McLaughlin and Van Tyne textbook, among other " corrections "

However, Mr. Miller has not confined his activities solely to the publication of articles in the Hearst newspapers, but has resorted to other means for preaching his gospel. Through the agency of an organization called the Patriot League for the Preservation of American History he has endeavored to carry on his war against the " British propagandists " and "to purge the public schools of the Anglicized school histories and establish in their stead textbooks that teach the true American annals and inculcate the true American spirit." [56]   The slogan for the Patriot League is taken from Washington's *Farewell Address:* " Against the insidious wiles of foreign influence, I conjure you to believe me, fellow citizens, the jealousy of a free people ought to be constantly awake; since history and experience prove that foreign influence is one of the most baneful foes of republican government." [57]   Charges against " ten " Anglicized school histories reincarnating " the spirit of Benedict Arnold " have been made by the Patriot League in a pamphlet entitled " *Treason to American Tradition.*"   These charges have been indorsed and the accused books condemned, in formal resolutions unanimously adopted in their national conventions by the American Legion, the Descendants of the Signers of the Declaration of Independence, the Grand Army of the Republic, the Knights of Columbus, the Sons of the American Revolution, and the United Span-

---

made, included in the latest edition " Nathan Hale, who had been omitted entirely . . . as one who ' risked all for his country's cause.' "   These authors also have, according to Mr. Miller, " improved the picture of Patrick Henry " by describing him thus: " A hitherto unknown country lawyer, but a sincere lover of liberty." " Such corrections and many others in this one book and all the innumerable corrections that have been made in five other texts can have but one significance," concluded Mr. Miller. " The Anglicized authors have come to realize that the American people will not tolerate Anglicized histories in our public schools."

[56] *Bulletin of the Patriot League* (Charles Grant Miller, Organizing Director, Rosebank, New York City, 1922).   [57] *Ibid.*

ish War Veterans.[58]   The proscribed list includes books
under the authorship of Matthew Page Andrews, Albert
Bushnell Hart, John P. O'Hara, C. R. Ward, David Saville
Muzzey, Willis Mason West, William B. Guitteau, A. C.
McLaughlin and C. H. Van Tyne, Everett Barnes, and
Edwin Greenlaw.   The Patriot League concludes that " the
heroic history of a nation is the drum and fife music to
which it marches," and that " it makes a mighty difference
whether America continues to quickstep to ' Yankee Doodle '
or takes to marking time to ' God Save the King.' " [59]

In commenting upon Mr. Miller's pamphlet *The New
York Times* declared: " Mr. Miller attempts in this pamphlet, through the quotation of isolated sentences and passages,
to prove that the authors whom he criticized have no reverence for the Revolutionary leaders, preach the doctrine that
the colonists had no grievance against England, suppress all
the thrilling stories of valorous achievement on which our
youth used to be nourished, and make no use of authorities
other than British in commenting on the Revolution.

" What Mr. Miller does prove by all his toil is quite
different, namely, the undenied fact that our recent textbooks dealing with the early days of the Republic have been
compiled by men whose purpose, so far as they had a purpose in addition to that of supplying accurate information,
has been to promote friendship between Great Britain and
the United States rather than to perpetuate their ancient
animosities.   That is a crime in Mr. Miller's eyes, for he
holds and avows the strange belief that school histories
should be different for the children of different countries. . . .

---

[58] *Ibid.*
[59] Miller, Charles Grant, *Treason to American Tradition* (New York),
p. 6. The books by Ward and Greenlaw are literature textbooks. West's
History of the American People was attacked on much the same basis as
other histories in the Chicago *Herald and Examiner*, March 5, 1922.

" To argue with an upholder of that grotesque theory would be worse than waste of time. Fortunately, Mr. Miller is alone in holding it, except, perhaps, for the company of those whose hatred of England is so fierce that for them any stone is good enough to throw at her. . . ." [60]

AGITATION BY CATHOLICS AND IRISH

A desire to combat the tendency of recent textbooks to depict our relations with England from a viewpoint not violently anti-British has led an element of the Knights of Columbus to join in the movement for expurgating textbooks. Their chief cause for complaint lies in the narration of events of the American Revolution, the War of 1812, and in England's attitude toward the Federal Government during the Civil War. Joseph T. Griffin, in a pamphlet, *American History Must It Be Rewritten to Preserve Our Foreign Friendships?* regretfully remarks that with the present-day presentation of the Revolutionary War in our histories, " it will soon require more courage for Americans to believe the Declaration of Independence than it did for Jefferson to write it." [61] Such a condition has arisen, according to Mr. Griffin because of the fear of exciting antagonism toward Great Britain, whereas " the only consideration which should guide the American writer of a history text-book is whether the material he is to present . . . is true as to facts, ennobling as to sentiment, and stimulating to the morale of the nation; and that while we are eager to preserve friendly relationships with other nations, we are

[60] *The New York Times,* November 26, 1921. Editorial " Appealing Now to Teachers." The editorial first discussed the mailing of the pamphlet to many teachers in New York's public schools.

[61] Griffin, Joseph T., *American History Must It Be Rewritten to Preserve Our Foreign Friendships?* (Knights of Columbus Historical Commission, Boston, 1922), p. 4.

not willing to forego one iota of our national glory or consign to oblivion any part of our historical traditions." [62]

The charge that a definite campaign of British propaganda had been carefully inaugurated, Edward F. McSweeney, one-time head of the Knights of Columbus Historical Commission, set forth in a pamphlet entitled *America First*.[63] " According to our modern Tories in their propaganda Campaign," declared Mr. McSweeney, " Washington and his colleagues were wrong, and only the leaders of an ignorant, criminal, and cruel mob. American independence was only a sudden thought, and not the result of long growth and development."

In proof of the conspiracy charge the author showed by actual figures the increase in the area of the English dominions during the past three hundred years. This expansion he ascribed to the wrecking " of every nation that aspired to be her competitor for any considerable share of the world's commerce or for equality of political power among the States of the world "; for by " intrigue, propaganda and alliance " Great Britain has " destroyed the commercial power of Spain, Holland, Denmark, France, and as a result of the great world-war, of Russia, Austria-Hungary and Germany." Today, Mr. McSweeney pointed out, there remain only two nations " which are real competitors of England — Japan and the United States," the former annexed by secret treaties and alliances, the latter, in reality, being the sole competitor.[64]

It was Mr. McSweeney's belief that the first effort of the pro-British propagandists " *to undermine the foundations of our national life* " was " *by tampering with the children in*

---

[62] *Ibid.*, p. 3.
[63] McSweeney, Edward F., *America First* (Boston, Mass.).
[64] *Ibid.*, p. 4–5.

the public schools "; a movement which had " made substantial progress," for " the history of the Revolution has been re-written to make it appear that the objections to a connection with England, so important a hundred years ago, have been to a large extent set aside, and that the time may come when through some application of the Federal principle . . . [the English-speaking people] may come together into a vaster United States, the pathways to whose scattered parts shall be the SUBJECTED seas." [65]

This movement, he held, had been aided by some of the great publishing houses of the United States, citing the words of George Haven Putnam, " the head of one of the largest publishing houses in the country," in a Fourth of July speech made in London: " The feelings and prejudices of Americans concerning their trans-Atlantic kinfolk were shaped for my generation as for the boys of every generation that had grown up since 1775 on textbooks and histories that presented unhistorical, partisan and often distorted views of the history of the first English colonies, of the events of the Revolution, of the issue that brought about the war of 1812–15, and the grievances of 1861–65. . . . Textbooks are now being prepared which will present a juster historical account of events of 1775–83, 1812–15, and 1861–65. . . . It is in order now to admit that the loyalists had a fair cause to defend, and it was not to be wondered at that many men of the more conservative way of thinking should have convinced themselves that the cause of good government for the colonies *would be better served by maintaining the royal authority and by improving the royal methods, than by breaking away into the all-dubious possibilities of independence."* [66]

[65] *Ibid.*, p. 5. He cites Hosmer, *Samuel Adams*, p. 263.
[66] *Ibid.*, pp. 5–6.

Some of the British proselytism, Mr. McSweeney attributed to a propagandist campaign inaugurated by Lord Northcliffe, who left " one hundred and fifty million dollars " and " ten thousand agents " in this country.[67]   " Local societies should be formed in every center to foster British-American good-will, in close coöperation with an administrative committee," Lord Northcliffe is alleged to have said. " *Important articles* should be broken up into *mouthfuls* for *popular consumption,* and booklets, cards, pamphlets, etc., distributed through organized channels to the public.   Advertising space should be taken in the press, on the hoardings, and in the street cars for steadily presenting terse, easily read and remembered mind-compelling phrases and easily grasped cartoons *that the public may subconsciously* absorb the fundamentals of a complete mutual understanding."   According to Mr. McSweeney, the influence of this campaign is already evident in textbooks for primary grades " in which more than ninety per cent of the pupils are children of foreign born parents, or are themselves foreign born." [68]   Authors of such textbooks, writers like Owen Wister, Ex-President Taft, George Haven Putnam, Professor William L. Cheney, Albert Shaw, President Judson of the University of Chicago, Admiral Sims, and others are arraigned by McSweeney and charged with un-Americanism.[69]   The condemnation of Wister is based, in part, on his statement that our school histories have been responsible for keeping George III's memory green, but that " A movement to correct the school books has been started and will go on." [70]

[67] *Ibid.,* p. 5.   [68] *Ibid.,* pp. 6–7.

[69] These men, with the exception possibly of one, have written no history textbooks although they may have written books and articles for the general reader favorable to an Anglo-American understanding.

[70] *Ibid.,* p. 9. Quoted from *The* [London] *Times,* July 4, 1919. Many

Of all the propagandist arguments set forth by England "the most dangerous and un-American " in the opinion of the writer is that about " Anglo-Saxon civilization." " By dint of iteration and reiteration," declared Mr. McSweeney, " this uncontradicted falsehood has actually brought about in the United States the subconscious acceptance of a misleading idea, which during the last fifty years has grown, until it is commonly used, yet nobody even knows what it means. . . . The Anglo-Saxon tradition is a pure myth. To verify it is like looking at midnight in a dark cellar for a black cat that isn't there." Nor did he believe " the Anglo-Saxon impulse . . . in the least responsible for the progress of the United States. It had nothing to do with the Spanish in Florida; the Huguenots in Virginia; the Swedes in Delaware and New Jersey; the Dutch in New York and Pennsylvania, and the Celts in Maryland and Pennsylvania." [71]

Furthermore, this antagonist of Great Britain sought to controvert some of the statements which would show that American institutions sprang largely from England. He contended that never was there " a greater falsehood " than the claim that the English were the founders of the New England town meeting, for it arose from the Teutonic " folk mote "; that it was unquestionably true that there is in the United States scarcely a political or legal institution of English origin; that the doctrine of the Declaration of Independence that " all men are created equal " was of Roman not English law; that the United States could not get religious liberty from England, " because religious lib-

---

of the " reformed " schoolbooks, according to Mr. McSweeney, attempt to picture George III as a German monarch, and " consequently the fight of the colonials was against Germany," thereby leaving an erroneous impression. *Ibid.*, p. 10.

[71] *Ibid.*, pp. 11–12.

erty did not exist there "; that popular education, freedom of the press, the secret ballot, the vast machinery of public charitable, reformatory and poor administration were derived from other than English sources.[72]   With such an exposition, Mr. McSweeney arrived at the conclusion that the part of " our legal system which is consistent with natural justice comes from Rome; the incongruous, absurd and unjust features " from England.[73]

The place of the Irish race in the making of America, Michael J. O'Brien, chief historiographer for the American Irish Historical Society, sought to establish in *A Hidden Phase of American History*.   It proposes to set forth " Ireland's Part in America's Struggle for Liberty " and to lay bare " the heart of the Irish race in Ireland during the War of Independence as beating in sympathy with the revolted colonies in America," to narrate the story of Irish contributions to the Revolutionary army, and to establish a place of preëminence for the Irish in the building of the Republic.[74]   It runs, in its twenty-four chapters, the gamut of the history of most of the colonies, depicting the part played by the Irish.   It is offered as an antidote to Bancroft, Henry Cabot Lodge, and other American historians, and concludes its narrative with a chapter on " America's Debt to Ireland " in which is set forth the plea for American aid for Ireland in her struggle for independence.[75]

[72] *Ibid.*, p. 12.

[73] *Ibid.*, pp. 12–13.

[74] O'Brien, Michael J., *A Hidden Phase of American History*.   Published by Dodd, Mead and Company, 1919.

[75] O'Brien, *op. cit.*   The chapters are entitled: Attitude of the People of Ireland toward the American Colonists, Benjamin Franklin's Visits to Ireland, Irish Sympathy for the Revolting Colonies, Efforts to Conciliate the Irish Catholics, History by Suppression, Ireland's Share in America's Fight for Freedom, False Statements Refuted, Irish Names in American Muster-Rolls, The Friendly Sons of Saint Patrick, " The Line of Ireland," More History by Suppression, Marion, Lacey, and McClure, Irishmen Flock

Of this book the *Irish World* speaks with enthusiasm: "The most repulsive snake in popular opinion is the cobra, famous in stories of East Indian life. . . . Yet a little animal of the ferret type can kill him in a brief fight, . . . a frail but daring creature known as the mongoose. . . . In the historical order we have the cobra, the repulsive serpent who makes history a fountain of lies, whose fangs poison the human race for centuries, whose history of the so-called Reformation is the cobra of the past four centuries. The Anglo-Saxon history of this continent is a cobra of the same species. It has poisoned the life of the American people. . . . All the Anglo-Saxon writers from Bancroft on, suppressed, ridiculed where they could not suppress, mutilated where they could neither suppress nor ridicule, everything Irish in American history. The Universities of Harvard, Yale and Columbia have been conspicuous in spreading the poison, for that matter in cultivating and intensifying its virulence, as their historians are the best illustrations of the cobra's viciousness and malignity. The Catholic faith at this moment cannot get a hearing from them. . . . It is pleasant to announce that the mongoose has arrived and is already at work. His name is Michael J. O'Brien . . . [who] has brought out a book . . . called 'A Hidden Phase of American History.' " His first battle is with George Bancroft, "looked upon as our great historian, our most dignified, honest and truthful writer. . . .

---

to the Standard of Washington, Irish Immigration Prior to the Revolution, Vast Irish Immigrations to Pennsylvania, The " Scotch-Irish " Myth, Early Irish Settlements in New York, The " Irish Donation," Early Irish Settlers in Virginia, More Light on the " Scotch-Irish " Myth, Early Irish Settlers in the Carolinas, Pre-Revolutionary Irish in Georgia, The First Census of the United States, America's Debt to Ireland. The obscurity which envelops the Irish in American history, Mr. O'Brien believes, is because of the " premeditated suppression of facts " due to the influence of the " Anglo-Saxon cult." *Ibid.*, pp. 241–242.

Saturated with the poison of the cobra George Bancroft could no more see and tell the truth about the Catholics and the Irish than Sir Edward Carson or Tom Watson," but O'Brien " will kill the Anglo-Saxon cobra in this country. He is more important than twenty cathedrals and one million orators. He should be provided with a pension of one hundred dollars a week and let loose upon the libraries and records of the Anglo-Saxon. . . ." [76]

During 1921 and 1922 the Knights of Columbus, acting through an Historical Commission, promoted a movement for original studies in American history by offering prizes for original research. The purpose of the society was " to encourage investigation into the origins and achievements and the problems of the United States, to interpret and perpetuate the American impulse, the impulse of the patriots who founded and who through their successors, have preserved the Republic; to promote American solidarity; and to exalt the American ideal." [77]   The session of the Supreme Assembly which launched this project was held May 28, 1921, at Chicago. According to John H. Reddin, Supreme Master, it was their " aim to enlist a commission of leading historians of diverse racial extraction and religious denominations " to prepare twenty-four pamphlets " covering critical periods in the nation's history; the matter to be written direct from original sources," and the pamphlets to be distributed " in millions of copies to schools and colleges, legislators and newspapers throughout the country." [78]

The Thirty-Ninth International Convention of the

---

[76] McClure, S. S., " Some Delusions about Ireland," *McClure's Magazine*, Vol. LII (June, 1922), pp. 93–103. Quoted from the *Irish World*, August 23, 1919.

[77] Reddin, John H., " The American History Contest," *Columbia*, September, 1921, p. 12.

[78] *The New York Times*, May 29, 1921.

Knights of Columbus, with twenty thousand delegates in attendance, met at San Francisco on August first. Among the activities which were endorsed was the movement for a "propaganda proof" history at the cost of one million dollars,[79] by which, if necessity demanded, every town in the country could be flooded with pamphlets telling "the true tale of America's great origin and America's greatness" and "stripped of all manner of European or Asiatic coloring."[80]

Shortly following this announcement of the plan of the Knights of Columbus, Edward F. McSweeney, Chairman of the Historical Commission, issued the following statement: "The Knights of Columbus history movement aims at only one thing — the preservation of truth in the writing of American history. Many of the textbooks used in our schools are utterly unreliable on important phases of the nation's story and totally disregard many cardinal events and personages. The Knights of Columbus oppose the cause of no other nation, they are simply aligning the 800,000 members of the order in the production and distribution of a straight-forward story, free from propaganda of any kind as to the origin and development of this country."

"An attempt is even now being made," continues the statement, "and Dr. Nicholas Murray Butler, President of Columbia University, announced his advocacy of it recently in London, to promote the celebration of the signing of the Magna Charta in English-speaking countries. The anniversary of the Magna Charta coming late in June, and being

[79] *The New York Times*, August 1, 1921.
[80] *Ibid.*, August 4, 1921. Remarks of Supreme Master John H. Reddin, of Denver. According to Charles Grant Miller, the Knights of Columbus took the matter up after "my first series of exposures of Anglicized alteration" proposing "to produce a new school history." Opposition led them "to withdraw from this project," but to issue "historical brochures to the general public." Letter, under date of November 23, 1922, from C. G. Miller to the author.

the object of the celebration as the basis of liberty, which it is not, would necessarily eclipse our own Independence Day, which, I believe, is the ultimate object of the movement. . . . The Knights of Columbus believe that the Declaration of Independence is an infinitely more important and conclusive document than the Magna Charta." Under the compulsion of this belief they registered their opposition to " this and other forms of un-American propaganda." [81]

In December the movement for " Americanized " histories was furthered at a meeting held at Washington, D. C., and the announcement was again made that the Knights of Columbus would offer $7500 in prizes for monographs in American history, the first prize to be $3000.[82]

According to *Columbia*, the organ of the Knights of Columbus, their history program was attacked with " virulence " by " certain organizations, dedicated to creating better Anglo-American relations." Thus, from the Loyal Coalition of Boston emanated the following protest: " The obvious intention of a certain group, with the approval of the French ambassador, to rewrite the history of the United

[81] *The New York Times*, September 8, 1921. According to the *Times* other members of the Commission besides McSweeney, who were present at the meeting, were Rear Admiral William Benson, Maurice Francis Egan, Professor George Derry of Union College, and Professor Charles H. McCarthy of the Catholic University of America. All signed the statement, the *Times* reported. A trustworthy Catholic authority informed the author that Henry Jones Ford of Princeton and Hannis Taylor, former minister to Spain, were on the Commission. At Taylor's death Dr. Dunne succeeded. Egan early resigned, it is said, due to his fear of anti-British tendencies.

[82] Chicago *Herald and Examiner*, January 1, 1922. The amount of the first prize was $2500, according to an announcement in *Columbia*, September, 1921, p. 12. This prize was awarded to Samuel F. Bemis, a Protestant, of Whitman College, Walla Walla, Washington. According to *The Fortnightly Review* this work was not inspired by the Commission, for " it was practically completed when the prize was announced and would have been published this year anyhow." The *Review* also states that it was " the only scientific study submitted." *The Fortnightly Review*, Vol. XXX (November 1, 1923), p. 422.

States, is an issue of the hour. Our whole educational system is seriously menaced because of the influence of certain instructors who react to aliens of hyphenated influence." [83] The British-American Association also showed their opposition by offering " a prize to be known as the John Adams Gold Medal for the essay best setting forth the most instances of the friendship of Great Britain toward America from 1600 to 1920." This hostility was clearly evident to the Knights in the statement of the organization: " To offset the work of the Fourth Degree Knights of Columbus Historical Commission, whose Chairman, Edward F. McSweeney, has declared that the English people, so far as they had any voice, were substantially unanimous in their attitude, opposing the aspirations of the Colonists for freedom and backed up by the King and Parliament in continuing the fight for Colonial Liberty." [84]

Yet not all Catholics gave unqualified endorsement to the Commission's activities. January 1, 1924, Mr. McSweeney's chairmanship ceased. In commenting upon the changed personnel of the Commission, *The Fortnightly Review*, a Roman Catholic periodical, expressed the hope that reorganization would " result in a more economical programme and one that will really advance the cause of history." [85]

" The organization of this Commission in the first place was a most extraordinary procedure," stated the *Review*. " A man whose work and training had never been in the field of history, was chosen before the members of the Commission were selected, and was given a salary that amounted to more than twice the pay of a full professor of history in

[83] McSweeney, Edward F., " The Anger of the Anglophiles," *Columbia*, April 1, 1922, p. 10. [84] *Ibid.*

[85] " The K. of C. Historical Commission," *The Fortnightly Review*, Vol. XXX (December 1, 1923), pp. 457–458. The Commission is reported to have spent between $80,000 and $90,000.

our larger universities![86] When the personnel of the Commission was announced, it was found to contain the name of but one professional historian. . . .[87] Unfortunately, the early statements appearing under the imprint of the Commission, some utterances of the Chairman, and some articles published in *Columbia*, were not calculated to remove the existing impression that the Commission had no constructive programme, . . . and that the Chairman at least was willing to follow 'the historical expert' of the Hearst syndicate in the unjust, unfair, unmerited, and uncalled for attack on certain history textbooks."[88]

In the course of setting forth their arguments the pro-Irish criticized certain textbooks in common use in the public schools. Albert Bushnell Hart's *School History of the United States* was attacked because it " attempts to show that the American Revolution was not justified " by the following statements: " They [the colonists] were as well off as any other people in the world. They were not desperately oppressed,"[89] and " they enjoyed more freedom and self-government than the people in England."[90] And again, " Thousands of good people sincerely loved Great Britain and were loyal to King George. The loyalists were harshly put down."[91] Hart, moreover, includes statements whose effect may be " unquestionably bad " upon " the impressionable minds of the young," according to one critic.[92]

[86] According to a reputable Catholic authority, Mr. McSweeney's salary was $12,000 and expenses.

[87] *The Fortnightly Review, loc. cit.* The writer of the article was of the opinion that " with Catholic laymen filling chairs of history and political science at Harvard, Columbia, Bryn Mawr, the Catholic University, and elsewhere, and with other Catholics engaged in library and archival work of importance, it is small wonder that the Commission, containing the name of but one engaged in the profession of history, failed to win the confidence of those interested in history."   [88] *Ibid.*

[89] Hart, Albert Bushnell, *op. cit.*, p. 120.   [90] *Ibid.*, p. 126.

[91] *Ibid.*, p. 145. These attacks are found in Griffin, *op. cit.*

[92] Griffin, *op. cit.*, p. 5. " Others were drawn into the army by money,

It was also held that the "National spirit" of the pupils will suffer inevitably from such expressions of a "propaganda of palliation" as appear in McLaughlin's *History of the American Nation*. "And all this means that while we speak, we shall probably always speak, of the struggle between England and America, the war that ensued had many of the features and many of the deplorable effects of a civil war." Besides, an attempt to abase the motives of the Revolutionary patriots was plainly evident to objectors in the assertion that "Trivial offenses on the part of governments cannot justify revolution. Only oppression and serious danger can justify war. It cannot be said that the Colonies had actually suffered much. It might be even seen that the mother country was not at all tyrannical in taxing the Colonies to pay for defending them, and beyond question George III and his pliant ministers had no interest in treating the Colonies with cruelty." [98]

Everett Barnes, too, was found culpable in assuming an "apologetic attitude" toward the Revolution in his statement: "The disputes that brought about the War were not between the Colonists and all the English at home. They were rather between the Tories and the Whigs on both sides of the sea, neighbor against neighbor. Had the great Whig party in England been in power with Edmund Burke as its leader, it would have checked the King in his foolish course. . . . Had there been no war, this great country

---

bounties and promise of land." Hart, *op. cit.*, p. 134. Mr. Griffin asks: "Is this building up or breaking down the morale of a nation? The consideration of such statements may be a painless intellectual question for the adult — but to the impressionable minds of the young the effect is unquestionably bad."

[98] *Ibid.*, p. 6. Quotation from McLaughlin, Andrew C., *History of the American Nation* (New York, 1919), p. 152. McLaughlin goes on to say that the "Revolution was justifiable because the colonists stood for certain fundamental principles that were woven into the very fabric of their lives."

would probably now be a great branch of the British Empire." [94]   Another occasion for grievance was discovered in teaching that the War of 1812 was "a mistake," and "a case in which righteous anger overcame judgment," when, in reality, "the events which preceded the declaration of war were infinitely more humiliating to the young nation than those which caused us to enter the World War." [95]

When "Faneuil Hall, the cradle of liberty," Nathan Hale, the Swedes of New Jersey and Delaware, the Dutch of New York, the Germans of Pennsylvania, the French of South Carolina, the Irish both North and South are not mentioned as a part of the Revolution or are practically ignored in the struggle for American independence, the would-be revisionists feel there is just cause for remonstrance.[96]   Therefore, the Irish "solemnly protest" at "the diluted historical fluid served by Barnes, Van Tyne, McLaughlin, Hart, and others," [97] for "Americans are not yet ready to accept a King." [98]

[94] *Ibid.,* p. 7.   Barnes, Everett, *American History for Grammar Grades* (New York, 1920).   [95] Griffin, *op. cit.,* p. 9.   [96] *Ibid.,* p. 11.

[97] *Ibid.,* p. 8.   Objections were lodged against John P. O'Hara's history although he is a Catholic.   In *The Fortnightly Review,* April 15, 1924, Mr. O'Hara protests against the criticisms directed against him: "As long as the criticisms were confined to the Hearst press and similar secular mediums of publicity I was able to follow the discussion without being greatly disturbed; but when with the blessing of the K. of C. Historical Commission the Hearst 'authority' was allowed a page in *Columbia,* the official K. C. organ, on which to spread his charge that I, among others, was a Benedict Arnold who had sold his country for British gold, and when, in addition, his stuff was widely reprinted in the Catholic press, a different situation was created. . . .   I received letters from various persons complaining . . . that a man of my name should have fallen a victim to British agencies of corruption.   One such letter put me in distinguished company in this fashion:
"'Judas, 30 pieces of silver;
Benedict Arnold, 10,000 pounds and a coronet:
O'Hara???'"
The Fortnightly Review, Vol. XXXI (April 15, 1924), pp. 156–157.

[98] *The Gaelic American,* March 11, 1922, p. 6.   "McSweeney on the Schools."   The pamphlet by Mr. Griffin, from which the author has quoted,

GERMAN-AMERICAN AGITATION

Of similar purport has been the movement to disparage " denatured " histories instituted by the Steuben Society, the successor of the German-American Alliance. This organization has taken its name from " the man that forged the tool which overthrew British tyranny." Its avowed purpose is to battle against " the sinister efforts that threaten to pervert historical truth and independence of thought in this fair country of ours." [99] The membership is composed of men and women of the German race who are citizens of the

---

was published by the Hudson County Federation of the Holy Name Society (1922) " as a guide to RED-BLOODED AMERICANS with the moral fibre strong enough to believe and insist that American History, crimsoned with the blood of our martyrs, shall be maintained in its entirety and shall be elaborated upon by those authors alone, who, as Americans, still believe IN THE MAGNIFICENT STRUCTURE WHICH THE FOREFATHERS OF THIS REPUBLIC HAVE REARED AND WHICH MUST ENDURE."

[99] Jaegers, Albert, *A Brief Sketch of the Life and Character of Baron von Steuben* (Steuben Society Publication, Jacob Leisler Unit), p. 5.

In the hearings in the Senate Judiciary Committee to repeal the charter of the German-American Alliance in 1918, it was revealed that this organization had endeavored to control history textbooks. In conjunction with the Ancient Order of Hibernians in America in 1907, the Alliance had resolved " to recommend a systematic investigation of the share all races have had in the development of our country, in war and in peace, from the earliest days, as the basis for the founding and continuance of an unbiased American history." In the testimony it was declared that it was their purpose " to give credit where credit is due " because " in all of our current school histories, and most others, . . . the Anglo-Saxon has been glorified and exalted to the exclusion of those others who did so much for this country, like the Irish and the Germans and the other countries." " Hearings before the Subcommittee of the Committee on the Judiciary, United States Senate," 65th Congress, 2d Session, *Senate Report* 3529, p. 645 *et seq.* At the same time Professor Samuel B. Harding testified that in 1915 objection was raised to a chapter on the World War which he had written for a high school textbook and that his publishers (the American Book Company) had been warned that such would be " considered obnoxious," and that " the organization no doubt would feel itself obliged to actively oppose the use of such a book in any school anywhere in any state." *Ibid.,* pp. 619–620.

United States, excluding those who were " shifters and trimmers during the War," and " who are known to possess no race pride." [100] The chief medium for the dissemination of information is the *S. S. Bulletin.* An article appearing in the issue of February 15, 1922, set forth the attitude of the Steubenites toward history textbooks, and acknowledged the indebtedness of the Society to the Hearst newspapers for exposing " the conspiracy secretly to alter United States school histories, so as to promote a British-American union." [101] In commenting upon the charge that school histories were being edited by British propagandists, the *Bulletin* pointed out that " the public school is the fountain head of future citizenship. History teaching is the chief source of patriotic spirit and purpose. . . . A nation's history is to its own people an essential force for national pride, morale and solidarity." [102]

Much of the irritation of the Germans toward " de-Americanized " histories arose from the same source from which sprang the dissatisfaction of the Knights of Columbus. Their chief causes for complaint lay in the " defamation " of the nation's " heroic characters," the " misrepresentation " of " the just causes of the American Revolution " and of " the basic principles of the Republic," besides " innumerable inspiring episodes in our history [being] belittled or entirely omitted " because of " the professed interest of Anglo-American amity." [103]

" Every true American," asserted the Steubenites, " naturally resents and resists the teachings in these books to our children that ' the President of the Continental Congress and first signer of the Declaration of Independence was a smug-

[100] *S. S. Bulletin,* Vol. I, No. 13 (February 1, 1922), p. 1.
[101] *Ibid.,* No. 14 (February 15, 1922).
[102] *Ibid.*
[103] *Ibid.*

gler, with no other mention of Hancock from cover to cover,'
that Jefferson was 'deserving of a halter,' and that Hamilton
declared that 'the people are a great beast.' " [104]   And although "nine revisionists give nine different sets of causes
for the American Revolution," which are mutually contra-
dictory and contrary to the causes stated in the Declaration
of Independence, yet the Declaration continues to be " im-
mortal " and " gives the lie to all these anglicized revisions." [105]

In addition to the " emasculation " of many intrinsically
essential historical " truths," the pro-German controversial-
ists found cause for complaint in " the attempt to envelop
the America of today in the myth of Anglo-Saxon origin and
kinship."   Such a procedure " wrongs the colonial Germans
and Dutch of Pennsylvania and New York, the Swedes of
New Jersey and Maryland, the French Huguenots of Carolina, the Irish of all the colonies, [and] the Jews from every
clime." [106]

A confession of kinship of interest with the Knights of
Columbus movement is freely made in the acceptance of
quotations demonstrating the " baleful propaganda." [107]
The German-Americans are one with the Irish-Americans in
their feeling of humiliation at the thought of having " the
history of our national life for one hundred and forty-four
years declared a forgery," and in seeing " it rewritten at the
dictation of the champions of a foreign power who repudi-
ates the stand of their forefathers." [108]

[104] *Ibid.*
[105] *Ibid.*
[106] *Ibid.*
[107] Schrader, Frederick Franklin, " *1683–1920* " (New York, 1920), pp.
22–25.   There are the same quotations from George Haven Putnam, Owen
Wister, and Lord Northcliffe as found in the Knights of Columbus pamphlets. See page 227.
[108] *Ibid.*, p. 25.

It is precisely such a sentiment that influenced the American Turner-Bund, formerly the American Gymnastic Union and made up of Germans, at their annual convention in June, 1923, to endorse the movement of the Sons of the American Revolution, — a movement inaugurated " to revise history textbooks, . . . with a view to eliminating or correcting alleged distortion of facts." [109] The resolution of the Turner-Bund alleged that " many textbooks now in use contain distinctly pro-French and pro-British statements, neglecting throughout American history the work of the German people in its development." [110] The resolution further carried the indictment of a school history which states that " Alsace-Lorraine was stolen in 1871 from France by Germany," whereas, it was asserted, " France stole it from Germany two hundred years before." [111]

Besides the effort of the German-Americans " to put a stop to the prevailing tendency to misuse our public schools for undermining American sentiment in favor of British colonialism," the Steuben Society avowed as one of its purposes the desire to " foster in American children of German blood a proper pride of ancestry as a necessary basis of true American patriotism." [112] Such is the intent of Frederick Franklin Schrader in his book " 1683–1920." His purpose is made clear by the following statement found in the preface:

" A blanket indictment has been found against a whole race. That race comprises upward of 25 per cent of the American people and has been a stalwart factor in American life since the middle of the seventeenth century. This indictment has been founded upon tainted evidence. As is

[109] *The St. Louis Star,* June 27, 1923. The resolution was adopted June 26. It is stated that three hundred delegates were present at the convention. [111] *Ibid.*
[110] *Ibid.* [112] S. S. *Bulletin, loc. cit.*

shown in the following pages, a widespread propaganda has been, and is still, at work to sow the seeds of discord and sedition in order to reconcile us to a pre-Revolutionary political condition. This propaganda has invaded our public schools, and cannot be more effectively combatted than by education." The assertion that a charge of "German propaganda has no terrors for the author," is also included in the preface, for "statements of fact may be controverted; they cannot be disproved by an Espionage Act, however repugnant their telling may sound to the stagnant brains of those who have been uninterruptedly happy because they were spared the laborious process of thinking for themselves throughout the war, or that no inconsiderable host which derives pleasure and profit from keeping alive the hope of one day seeing their country reincorporated with 'the mother country' — the mother country of 30 per cent of the American people. It is to arouse the patriotic consciousness of a part of the remaining 70 per cent that this compilation of political and historical data has been undertaken." [113]

To insure this "proper pride of ancestry" it is the opinion of the author that there should be given greater publicity to German contributions in the making of the United States. Among these contributions, the Germans would have it a matter of more general knowledge that the first iron works in this country were established by a German (Thomas Reuter in 1716); that the first American-printed Bible was printed by a German (Christopher Sauer in 1743); that the first paper to print the Declaration of Independence in America was the *Pennsylvania Staatsboten* of July 5, 1776; that it

---

[113] Schrader, *op. cit.*, pp. 9–10. The place of the German element in American history had been treated by Faust ten years prior to Schrader's book. Faust, Albert B., *The German Element in the United States with especial reference to its political, social and educational influence* (Boston, 1909).

was the Germans who first called Washington "the father of his country"; that General Herkimer of Oriskany was of German extraction; that Steuben formulated the principles and regulations that governed the American army when it was created; that Germans have contributed valuable inventions; that Lincoln was of German descent; that Molly Pitcher was a German; and that of the ideals of liberty and of education the Germans were conspicuous creators.[114]

Nor would the Germans have the Americans forget such incidents as the saving by Germans of American refugees from a "bloodthirsty mob of Mexicans at the Southern Hotel, Tampico, Mexico," through their aid in 1914,[115] the help of Germans in holding Fort McHenry in the War of 1812,[116] and that "the German element furnished nearly 200,000 men, natives of Germany" for the Northern army in the Civil War.[117]

THE CENSORSHIP OF PATRIOTIC GROUPS, FRATERNAL ORGANIZATIONS AND OTHERS

Other agencies than the Hearst newspapers and those groups united by religious and racial bonds have interested themselves in attacking the histories used in the public

[114] Schrader, *op. cit.* Ridder, Victor, *The Germans in America* (New York, 1922), and Jaegers, *op. cit.*

[115] Schrader, *op. cit.*, p. 19.

[116] *Ibid.*, p. 10.

[117] Ridder, *op. cit.*, p. 14.

In 1917, an investigation of the most commonly used textbooks in history was made by Timothy T. Lew to determine the treatment given Chinese-American relations. Mr. Lew's conclusion was that the attitude of Americans toward the Chinese was likely to be one of indifference or prejudice because of the lack of attention given in textbooks, or because many events which would show cordial relations had been overlooked. Lew, Timothy T., "China in American School Text-Books," Spl. Suppl. to *The Chinese Social and Political Science Review*, Vol. VI–VII (July, 1923).

schools. Most active among these censors are various patriotic organizations and individuals, notably newspaper editors. Through such forces many investigations of textbooks have been undertaken, resulting, at times, in the exclusion of the books under criticism from the public schools. During the World War, European history textbooks bore the brunt of attack. Discussions tending to bestow praise upon the Central Powers, or in any way to disparage the institutions or prowess of the Allies, were deemed disloyal to the cause in which the United States was engaged. Not only were history textbooks condemned but also textbooks in foreign language, particularly in German. The same spirit showed itself in many avenues through which public opinion could be affected. Thus a federal judge enjoined the production of " The Spirit of '76," a film depicting the Wyoming Massacre and Paul Revere's ride, because it tended " to make us a little bit slack in our loyalty to Great Britain in this great emergency." [118]

To those who feared a diluted Americanism, it seemed quite apparent that sinister forces were abroad, and in the attacks made upon authors of history textbooks, it was frequently charged that the preparation of school histories was in the hands of German paid agents. Indeed, the activities of pro-German forces to control the content of history textbooks, it was alleged, had been operating for some time, and since 1915 had been directed by Dr. Dernburg, under whom definitely made plans had been perfected.[119] This conclu-

[118] Chafee, Zechariah, " Freedom of Speech," *The New Republic*, Vol. XVII (November 16, 1918), p. 67. Also *Espionage Act Cases with Certain Others on Related Points*, compiled and edited by Walter Nelles (New York, 1918), pp. 33–35. The case is listed as The United States *vs* Motion Picture Film " The Spirit of '76." Southern District of California, Southern Division, November 30, 1917, under Judge Bledsoe.

[119] Harré, T. Everett, " Shadow Huns and Others," *The National Civic Federation Review*, Vol. IV (February 15, 1919), pp. 12–16.

sion was reached by the skeptical when to one of his agents was attributed this statement: " The Americans do not love the British, and they are inclined to like the Germans. By controlling the preparation of school histories, we can begin to make Americans from the time they are children see the German point of view." [120]

Among the organizations which feared the inculcation of disloyalty through a study of history as commonly written was the Fathers of Soldiers and Sailors League. It was through their influence that the James Harvey Robinson histories were excluded from the schools of Des Moines, Iowa, because of the statement regarding Germany contained in these books.[121] Among the objections raised against Robinson's *Medieval and Modern Times* were the characterization of the German government, the failure to fix the responsibility upon Germany for bringing about the World War, and the discussion of the violation of " all laws of humanity as well as of international law " by Germany. In addition to criticisms directed against the 1916 edition of this book, the Des Moines objectors felt that there was a pro-German bias evident in the 1918 Supplement in such a statement as the following: " So while Germany was able, as we shall see, to conquer important portions of Central Europe as the war proceeded, she lost all her colonies. The question whether she is to have them back or not will be one of the great problems to adjust at the end of the war." [122.]

The same organization identified itself with a movement

---

[120] *Ibid.*

[121] *Report of the Committee from the Fathers of Soldiers' League to the Board of Education, Des Moines, Iowa, 1918.* (In manuscript.)

[122] Quoted from Robinson, James Harvey, *Medieval and Modern Times* (New York, 1918). The committee who investigated the textbook hazarded this remark upon the excerpt quoted: " It would seem to your committee that the historian has another guess coming, and that Germany is not liable to get her colonies back or any indemnities." *Report, loc. cit.*

in California to investigate the content of history textbooks. In July, 1918, the State Board of Education directed that all textbooks in American and European history appearing upon the official list of high school textbooks be submitted to a committee of expert historians for review, to determine whether such textbooks were objectionable on the ground of being pro-German or containing matter which might be offensive to the American allies in the World War. On September 18, the committee reported, and the following books were stricken from the official list: Botsford, *A Brief History of the World*, Myers, *Mediaeval and Modern History,* and Myers, *General History.* Robinson's *Medieval and Modern Times,* edition of 1916, was also eliminated from the official list, but the edition with the supplement of 1918 was substituted upon condition that the publishers make certain changes in the revised edition. Robinson and Beard, *Outlines of European History, Part II,* was banned until a specified revision should take place. Of the books examined, the committee found no important objections to Andrews, *Short History of England,* Ashley, *Early European Civilization,* Cheyney, *Short History of England,* Harding, *New Mediaeval and Modern History* (edition of 1918), Robinson and Breasted, *Outlines of European History, Part I,* Webster, *Early European History,* and West, *Modern World.* The committee rendered decisions against the Myers histories because they represented a viewpoint opposed to that of the time. Botsford's textbook was found objectionable because it was " favorable to the acts of Germany and critical to an unjust degree of the acts of the . . . allied nations," and because it presented the causes of the American Revolution in a " bald form." [123]

[123] *California State Board of Education, Special Bulletin No. 4.* Series of 1918. The committee included E. D. Adams, Arley B. Show, W. A. Morris, E. I. McCormac, W. J. Cooper.

Other places, actuated by similar sentiments, interested themselves in the character of history instruction. Seattle, Washington, became the center of a controversy between the school superintendent and the teachers on the one hand, and two of the school directors on the other, regarding Robinson and Beard's *Outlines of European History*.[124] As a result of the discussion, the book was thrown out of the Seattle schools until the expurgation and revision should occur.[125]

In Montana, the State Council of Defense ordered the withdrawal of West's *Ancient World* from circulation in all public and school libraries, because they objected, among other things, to an introductory statement that " the settlement of the Teutonic tribes was not merely the introduction of a new set of ideas and institutions . . . it was also the introduction of fresh blood and youthful minds — the muscle and brain which in the future were to do the larger share of the world's work." [126]

Due to the same point of view and under the same compulsion, the Commissioner of Education of Rhode Island in 1918 undertook an investigation of the textbooks in use in that state, and found objectionable " various text-books designed for sixth grade history according to the report of the committee of eight." In a large number of books [were found] . . . various references to the Germans which, in the light of recent developments, are to be regarded as incorrect or exaggerated statements. . . ." And it was considered " objectionable to place before the children of America statements which are, or which will appear to them to be, laudatory of the people with whom we are at war or ad-

[124] *The Seattle Star,* September 30, 1918, Editorial.
[125] Harré, *loc. cit.*
[126] *Bulletin of the Montana State Council of Defense,* April 22, 1918. West, *Ancient World* (Boston, 1913), p. 570.

versely critical of our own people." [127]   The use of histories considered "offensive" was also discontinued in the states of Arizona, Iowa, Ohio, and Oklahoma, either through the action of the office of the state superintendent or some other official. [128]   Doubtless in other states the action of local boards brought about the same result.

New textbooks, syllabi and other teaching aids appeared. Superintendent William L. Ettinger of the New York City schools, for example, in 1918 issued a syllabus on the War designed to aid teachers in " imparting a correct intellectual understanding of the causes, events and issues of the war," as well as to help them in inspiring " the pupils with a love for the ideals and an appreciation of the sacrifices of our country." For, he held that " the American Army of the future, both men and women, are in our schools today." Dr. Ettinger's letter to the Principals of High Schools declared that " History should be taught so that a deep emotional appeal " should be made in all topics; that " a lasting effect " could " be produced on the ideals, purposes and emotions of the child only by arousing deep feeling in connection with the presentation of the subject matter." In the event of adding new material as the War progressed, it was required that " all such material . . . be approved by the Principal of the School before . . . used in the classroom." [129]

As in all books which were meeting the popular demand of the time, the *Syllabus* made Germany " the only country in

[127] *Forty-Ninth Annual Report of the State Board of Education . . . of Rhode Island*, January, 1919, pp. 77, 81. The history textbooks were not named.

[128] Information gained through a questionnaire sent to the superintendent of public instruction in each state. All states but South Carolina replied.

[129] *A Syllabus of the World War for Use in the High Schools of The City of New York* adopted by the Board of Superintendents (Department of Education of the City of New York, 1918), p. 5.

the world that was prepared and anxious for war " because of her autocratic government, the character of the Kaiser, militarism and navalism, Germany's desire for world domination, and the insidious inculcation of loyalty in the German people through the Prussian system of education.

The insistence of the American people that histories in the schools should not be in any degree " laudatory " of the enemy peoples nor " unfavorable " to our allies in arms led to the revision of many textbooks after April, 1917. Since 1923 these revisions, in turn, have been criticized in the light of recently published documents relating to the origin of the War. Although the question of war guilt is still held by many historians as debatable, it is pointed out in *The Freeman* for June, 1923, that probably " children have already been indoctrinated with a theory that leaves no excuse for uncertainty, no opening for new evidence and no stimulus to free thought." [130]

With this condition in mind, critics have assembled their arguments against certain textbooks in European history found in the public schools. Because it made Germany primarily responsible for the World War objection was raised to *The Story of Human Progress* by Willis Mason West, an author but a short time before criticized for pro-Germanism.[131] Roscoe Lewis Ashley is challenged for saying in his *Modern European Civilization* that " Germany wanted war and determined to rule or ruin . . . and a war which in the true sense had been made ' in Germany ' was a reality "; while Webster, in his *Modern European History,* is criticized for the statement that " There is no longer any need to fix the

[130] " Accepted Fable," *The Freeman,* Vol. VII (June 27, 1923), pp. 366–367.
[131] See page 248. Professor West is author of *Modern Progress* (Boston, 1920) but not of *The Story of Human Progress.* The quotation was not verified.

responsibility for the World War. That the German government planned it and precipitated it has been made evident by the avowal of the Germans themselves." [132]

The interpretation placed upon the causes leading to the War by Charles Downer Hazen in his *Modern Europe* has likewise been condemned. For Hazen " summarizes the case as follows: ' The world was stunned by the criminal levity with which Austria-Hungary and Germany had created this hideous situation. The sinister and brutal challenge was, however, accepted immediately and with iron resolution by those who had done their utmost during those twelve days to avert the catastrophe.' " [133]   A criticism by Professor Harry E. Barnes directed for the same reason at the textbooks of this author provoked a spirited exchange of opinion in the spring of 1924.   Professor Hazen upheld his interpretation as to Germany's guilt, while Professor Barnes asserted that such a point of view was untenable in the light of official documents made known since the War. [134]

Other writers of European histories used in the schools have not escaped. According to *The Freeman*, Robinson and Beard, in their *History of Europe Our Own Times*, seem to have been " more or less taken " with the plan of leaving

[132] "War in the Textbooks," *The Nation*, Vol. CXIX (Sept. 17, 1924), p. 277.
[133] *Ibid.* See Hazen, Charles Downer, *Modern Europe* (New York, 1920), p. 690.
[134] Barnes, Harry Elmer, "Seven Books of History against the Germans," *The New Republic*, Vol. XXXVIII (March 19, 1924), part II, pp. 10–15. Also see Professor Hazen's letter in *The New Republic*, Vol. XXXVIII (May 7, 1924), pp. 284–285. On the question of the origin of the War a series of articles by Professor Barnes appeared in *The Christian Century* for October, November, December, 1925. See also Barnes, Harry Elmer, in *Current History*, Vol. XXII (May, 1924), on the origin of the War; also Fay, Sidney B., " New Light on the Origins of the World War," *The American Historical Review*, Vol. XXVI (October, 1920), pp. 37–53; Fay, Sidney Bradshaw, " The Black Hand Plot that led to the World War," *Current History*, Vol. XXIII (November, 1925), pp. 196–207.

the " readers to draw their own conclusions " in their chapter on the origin of the War. Disapproval arose out of the
statement that " the assertions of the German leaders that
England desired war and was responsible for it are, of
course, as the rest of the world knows, wholly without
foundation in fact," and because of the quotation from
Prince Lichnowsky indicting Germany.[135]

On the other hand, Modern History, by Hayes and Moon,
is given a clean bill of health because of its treatment of
this controversial subject. The critic, however, pointed out,
in fairness to the other writers criticized, that " in the
interval that has elapsed since the appearance of the other
texts . . . , certain new items of evidence had been brought
forward and the general war-fever had abated somewhat.
The authors of the new book therefore enjoyed certain
special advantages, which help, no doubt, to explain the
novel tone. . . ." [136]

Not only has the treatment of the origin of the War been
a source of criticism but also the divergent points of view
regarding German atrocities, reparations and the Treaty of
Versailles. On these points Professor Donald Taft in his
study " Historical Textbooks and International Differences "
has declared that American pupils are taught from two kinds
of textbooks, one group being " bitterly anti-German " and
the other attempting a fairness of judgment. Of this he cites
Guitteau's Our United States and Long's America as examples.[137] Much the same point of view is held by Isabel

[135] The Nation, loc. cit. Robinson, James Harvey, and Beard, Charles
A., History of Europe Our Own Times (Boston, 1921), pp. 543-544.
[136] The Nation, loc. cit. See Hayes, Carlton J. H., and Moon, Thomas
Parker, Modern History (New York, 1923).
[137] Taft, Donald R., " Historical Textbooks and International Differences " (Chicago, 1925). Guitteau, William Backus, Our United States
(New York, 1923). Long, William J., America (Boston, 1923).

Kendig-Gill in a pamphlet " War and Peace in United States History Text-Books," in which, in addition, she declares that " nowhere is there any fundamental analysis either of the political and economic situation out of which the war grew or of its spiritual and moral costs to the world." [138]

Following the close of the World War, the place of prominence held by the histories of Europe in the critic's eye was eclipsed by American histories. A desire to depict events favorable to the Allies was superseded by the apprehension that such a narrative would prove the undoing of American patriotism. This apprehension was mingled in the minds of many with the fear that the solid pillars of society were being threatened with radicalism and socialism. In this spirit, for example, attacks on history textbooks were inaugurated by the editor of *The Daily Courier* of Ottumwa, Iowa. On March 2, 1919, under the caption, " Get a New History," appeared an editorial attacking Muzzey's *An American History* because of its " socialistic trend " and its treatment of the period since the Civil War.[139] Two years later, due to the energy of the editor of the Ottumwa *Daily Courier*, Governor Nate Kendall of Iowa was asked by the

[138] Kendig-Gill, Isabel, " War and Peace in United States History Text-Books," National Council for Prevention of War, Washington, p. 10. The author quotes passages to prove her contention from Mace's *Beginner's History*, Muzzey's *An American History*, and Guitteau's *Our United States*. Also " Drugging the Young Idea," *The Freeman*, Vol. VII (August 22, 1923), pp. 556–557.

[139] *The* [Ottumwa, Iowa] *Daily Courier*, March 2, 1919, " With the persistency of a fanatic and the illogical deduction of a demagogue, Professor Muzzey makes the tariff and the trusts the principal defendants in the case which he brings against the United States of America. . . . His book is a clearly conceived and a closely written argument for socialism treating the various steps in the country's history from the standpoint of the socialist instead of the unbiased historian. . . ." As a result of this opposition, Muzzey's textbook was excluded from the Ottumwa schools. For the same reason the use of this history was discontinued in Leonia, New Jersey.

joint committee on Americanism of various patriotic and civic organizations to appoint a commission " to investigate anti-American and radical teaching in state owned institutions and the public schools." The action of the committee was prompted by the information " that there were good reasons to believe that some of the textbooks on American History used in our schools were wanting in national and patriotic spirit and sentiment; that they failed to instil devotion to American ideals, and pass[ed] over lightly events in American history which should . . . stimulate pride of country, patriotism and devotion to our institutions." [140] No action was taken by the Governor.

One of the most active organizations in the present-day movement to remodel the content of history textbooks has been the Sons of the American Revolution. In 1917 at the instigation of the Executive Committee of the National Society an examination of Muzzey's *An American History* was undertaken by Judge Wallace McCamant, later president-general of this organization. His verdict was unfavorable; and as a result the book was excluded from the public schools of Portland, Oregon, and Evanston, Illinois. Although a revised edition later appeared, this critic still believed Muzzey a " political partisan " and his history unsuitable for use in the public schools.[141] One of the most " grievous faults " which Muzzey committed, in the opinion of Judge McCamant, was in his discussion of the American Revolution, wherein he spoke " contemptuously of Hancock, Warren, Otis and the Adamses " in calling them " pa-

[140] *Iowa Legionnaire*, April 15, 1921.

[141] A pamphlet entitled *Muzzey's School History* written by Wallace McCamant, Chairman of the Committee on Patriotic Education of the National Society of the Sons of the American Revolution, July 27, 1922. See also *Official Bulletin of the National Society of the Sons of the American Revolution*, Vol. XVII (October, 1922), Washington, D. C.

triots " with quotation marks attached to the word.[142] He
was held equally culpable because the Revolutionary dispute
is said to have involved "a debatable question," a statement, which, in the critic's mind, should disqualify him from
writing a school history.[143] Yet a reading of the statement
in its context conveys a different meaning from that suggested by Judge McCamant, for Muzzey declares: " Until
the Declaration was published the Tories and Loyalists, of
whom there were tens of thousands in the American colonies,
were champions of one side of a debatable question, namely,
whether the abuses of the King's ministers justified resistance; but after the Declaration loyalty to the King of
Great Britain became treason to their country." The reviewer found other grievous faults in that " the author contemptuously refers to the speeches and papers of Henry and
the Adamses as ' their rhetorical warnings ' against being
' reduced to slavery ' "; that only one sentence is devoted to
Bunker Hill; that there is " no mention of the death of
Joseph Warren "; that there is " no reference to the gal-
lantry with which the Americans defended the rail fence
and the redoubt "; and only a brief mention of Lexington
and Ticonderoga. " Aside from four sentences," only
" seven pages " are devoted " to the Revolutionary War,"
when the " students in our public schools should be taught
that our free institutions were won by heroism and sacrifice." [144] Other omissions of " essential " facts were the
failure to describe the work of Marion, Sumter, Pickens and
Williams; no mention being made of Gansevoort, Anthony

142 *Ibid.*, p. 1. An examination of the textbook reveals the distasteful
quotation marks in the following passage: " Letters, pamphlets, petitions,
came in an uninterrupted stream from the Massachusetts ' patriots,' Hancock, Warren, Otis, and the Adamses."
143 Pamphlet, *op. cit.*, p. 2. See Muzzey, *op. cit.*, p. 115.
144 Pamphlet, *op. cit.*

Wayne or Stony Point, Light Horse Harry Lee or Paulus Hook, Bennington or John Stark.

Carrying the criticisms further, it was alleged that this history contains inaccuracies and unfair statements; that it is full of partisanship of a political character; that it gives a biased treatment of controversial subjects; and is pro-British.[145] It was the belief of the reviewer, moreover, that controversial subjects like the tariff have no place in a high school textbook, for " whatever the views of a citizen may be on this subject he should be permitted to send his children to school without having them taught that his own views on this question are unsound." Characterization of Mr. Wilson's policies, "particularly as set forth in his 'New Freedom' as an economic Declaration of Independence," also struck a discordant note. Class distinctions are also made conspicuous, the reviewer declared, as in such a statement as " Federalism, which stood in John Adams' phrase, for government by 'the rich, the well-born and the able ' "; and in " The failure of the South to get rid of slavery in the early decades of the nineteenth century must be set down to the domination of a class of rich, aristocratic planters." [146]

During the year 1923 the activities of the Sons of the American Revolution became diversified to the extent that their report on Patriotic Education dealt with several American histories. This report was actuated by the interest that had been shown in the " National Congress " meeting at Springfield in May, 1922, when that body expressed a deep interest in " the subject of American history textbooks " and resolved that the Committee on Patriotic Education " take needful measures to eliminate from our schools " all objectionable textbooks.[147]

---

[145] *Ibid.*, pp. 5–16.   [146] *Ibid.*, p. 13.

[147] Pamphlet entitled " The Sons of the American Revolution and the Histories in Use in Our Schools," p. 8.

In their review of American histories, the Committee found " a great deal of inaccuracy and considerable propaganda bearing on political questions which still divide the people." [148] They held as " fundamental defects and those which are most clearly subject to criticism at the hands of a patriotic society . . . inadequate and unsympathetic treatment of the American Revolution and a treatment of events in our recent history in such a manner as to inculcate loyalty to class rather than to country." [149] The Committee, furthermore, emphasized the importance of a study of an untainted American history, one teaching " a veneration of the great men of our past " as " the best antidote for radical and disintegrating propaganda." They maintained that " the chief purpose to be subserved in teaching American history is the inculcation of patriotism." [150] To devote only ten pages out of five hundred to a discussion of the Revolutionary War laid the author open to criticism by patriotic groups; and such inadequate treatment could not be excused on the ground that the book was written for advanced students who have gathered the necessary details in the elementary grades. The works of Fiske, Schouler, Trevelyan, and Lodge, although written for adults, discussed these details, which, in itself, was proof of their value to the Committee who were considering textbooks.

In the examination of history textbooks the Committee found " the McLaughlin and Van Tyne, O'Hara, Everett Barnes, Hart, James and Sanford, Muzzey and West histories objectionable in the treatment of the American Revolution." [151] The Muzzey, West and Burnham histories were described also as " open to criticism on the ground of class

---

[148] *Ibid.*, p. 1.   Also " Report of Committee on Patriotic Education " published separately and obtained from Judge Wallace McCamant, Portland, Oregon.

[149] *Ibid.*   [150] *Ibid.*, pp. 2–3.   [151] *Ibid.*, p. 3.

hatred." Because the objections to Muzzey's and West's books were based on more than one ground for complaint, separate criticisms were published by the Committee, which were " widely circulated." [152]

On the other hand, endorsement was accorded to Gordy's textbook and the Thwaites and Kendall history for grammar school use. For the high school the Committee recommended the amended edition of Guitteau's book and the Halleck history.[153]

As a result of their agitation, according to the Report, the Everett Barnes history had been amended and the author had removed from it the aspersions on John Hancock. The Committee wished to distinguish sharply, however, between this Barnes and " the old Barnes history which has always been sound in its Americanism." [154] They desired also to recommend "without qualification " the history of Dr. Edward Channing, who at their request had signified his willingness to make suggested changes in his textbook. With evident approval they quoted the following statement from William J. Long, "author of the latest history published by Ginn and Company " in which he said: "What I missed in our histories, especially those of recent date, was the spirit of devotion without which the mere facts of history have little interest or consequence to my boy and your boy." [155]

[152] *Ibid.*

[153] *Ibid.*, p. 6. Guitteau's *Our United States* and Halleck's *History of Our Country* are designed primarily for the junior high school, and not for the senior high school.

[154] *Ibid.*, p. 5. *Cf.* statement of Charles Grant Miller, page 211.

[155] Pamphlet, " The Sons of the American Revolution and the Histories in Use in Our Schools," p. 7. At their meeting at Swampscott, Massachusetts, in May, 1925, Judge McCamant again called the attention of the Sons of the American Revolution to the textbook situation, and urged them to use pressure to have the right kind of textbooks in the schools of their states. *Boston Herald*, May 19, 1925.

The efforts of the national group received the active support of many local units. Under the direction of "Compatriot S. T. Cameron of the District of Columbia Society " the Piney Branch Citizens' Association of Washington, D. C., opened fire on Muzzey's *An American History* for the reasons frequently assigned, and circulated, according to Judge McCamant, "a scholarly brief " that proved this textbook " hopelessly unfit for school use." [156]

Among the standards which the Piney Branch Citizens' Association set up for a textbook in American history were: that it should assume " an unquestioning attitude toward the sincerity, the aims or the purpose of the founders of this Republic or of those who have guided its destinies; that it should contain no material that tends to arouse political, racial, or religious controversy or hatred "; that it should " emphasize the principles and motives that were of the greatest influence in the formation and development " of the government; that " it must incite in the pupil ideals of patriotic and civic duty," as well as cultivating " an appreciation of the hardships endured and the sacrifices made in establishing and defending American ideals." [157]

No success attending their efforts to eliminate this textbook from the acceptable list in the Washington schools, the Piney Branch Association continued their attack. On April 25, 1923, a public hearing was given Professor Muzzey and his critics, at which " more than one hundred persons, including school officials, teachers, civic leaders and interested students . . . listened attentively to the arguments pro and

[156] *Ibid.*, p. 3.

[157] District of Columbia Board of Education Piney Branch Citizens' Association against Muzzey's School History (Washington, D. C., April 25, 1923), p. 2. [Washington, D. C.] *Sunday Star*, June 4, 1922. Muzzey's defense is criticized by the chairman of the Piney Branch Historical Committee in an issue of the *Star*, June 18, 1922.

con which continued for nearly four hours." [158] In defending himself, Professor Muzzey declared that Mr. Cameron had "garbled the facts and twisted phrases in a way" that was "absolutely unfair"; that he had taken "certain words and sentences and read them without the complete section," which, in many cases, put "an entirely different aspect upon them." [159] With Mr. Cameron, in criticizing adversely this American history, was Charles Edward Russell of the "Patriot League for the Preservation of American History." He regarded the book as "'a grave public menace,'" and declared that "the school children in the heart of China" were being taught "a more accurate account of the American revolution than those in the Washington schools." [160]

On the other hand, unqualified endorsement was given the textbook by Superintendent of Schools Frank W. Ballou. George J. Jones, head of the history department of the Washington high schools, emphasized "the destructive nature" of the attack and "pointed out that all of the teachers of American history in the local high schools vouch[ed] for its patriotism. . . ." [161] In support of Mr. Jones were Dr. George M. Churchill and Elmer L. Kayser, professors of American history at George Washington University, Dr. Charles E. Hill, professor of political science at the same university, Dr. Leo F. Stock, professor of history at the Catholic University, and Rear Admiral George W. Baird, former president of the Board of Education. [162]

In commenting upon this and other attacks directed against this textbook, Carson C. Hathaway in *The Dearborn Independent* for October 23, 1923, declared: "To Muzzey,

---

[158] *The* [Washington, D. C.] *Star*, April 26, 1923.
[159] *Ibid.*
[160] *Ibid.* The activities of the *Patriot League for the Preservation of American History* are treated in the section devoted to Charles Grant Miller and the Hearst newspapers.   [161] *Ibid.*   [162] *Ibid.*

history is a review of *what* happened and an important analysis of *why* it happened. To those who desire to be thrilled by the familiar stories of our national heroes, the text may not be satisfying. But perhaps there is enough thrill in even an unbiased treatment of American history to satisfy any thoughtful and patriotic American." [163]

In November, 1922, the Kentucky branch of the Sons of the American Revolution addressed a communication to nine educational institutions requesting the exclusion of Muzzey's *An American History* from the lists of approved textbooks, because of its " flippant, inaccurate and unsympathetic " content-matter.[164] Failure to inculcate " reverence for our Revolutionary fathers and their ideals " besides its " callous indifference " in the treatment of battles and heroes appeared to the Kentucky Sons characteristic of this book.

As a comment on their action, the *Louisville Times* editorially remarked:

" If the Sons of the American Revolution in Kentucky have discovered a public school text-book of history that is unfair to the national record that book is lonesome. The *Times* is not familiar with the work of Professor Muzzey of New York, which the society at its meeting last night denounced as ' unpatriotic, unfair, inaccurate, partisan, closely bordering on the socialistic and lacking in Americanism.' But for many years in the public schools of the United States courses have been full of text-books on history which committed most of these crimes in reverse order, by misstating all facts relating to the foreign controversies of the United States and the wars fought by this nation.

[163] Hathaway, Carson C., " Is Muzzey's American History Revolutionary? " *The Dearborn Independent*, October 20, 1923, p. 2.

[164] *Louisville Times*, November 9, 1922. Institutions to which the request was sent were the high schools of Owensboro, Ashland, Dayton, Maysville, Louisville, Collegiate School, Bowling Green, Kentucky State University, Hamilton College, Lexington, and Berea College, Berea.

" The Muzzey book may be all that is charged against it. If
so, it is remarkable that it was adopted in the Kentucky schools
after considerable investigation; that it was not complained of
during the inquiry into history text-books in New York; that the
University of Kentucky recommended it. . . .

" But unless the book is unfair and inaccurate it should be
defended against attack. The valor of ignorance is asserting
itself in all quarters of America. Calmly content for several
generations to study histories that were grossly unfair to every
other nation in the world, some portion of the American public
have lately gotten into the book-censoring business. . . .

" . . . The ancestors of the gentlemen who sat last night resented nothing more than censorship of all kinds. They wanted
to settle for themselves what they should read, eat, drink, wear
and do. The era of Jefferson and Franklin and Samuel Adams
was not the era of excision and paternalism." [165]

The *Courier-Journal* also, in an editorial on " Writing
History," stressed the new values which have developed in
the scientific presentation of history, causing " a fresh and
clarified perspective." To the *Courier-Journal* Muzzey's
textbook represented " the newer tendencies in historical
writing," and aimed wisely " to give the emphasis to those
factors in our national development, which appeal to us as
the most vital from the standpoint of today." The editorial
commended it for omission of facts which could easily be
found elsewhere, and because of its non-sectionalism." [166]

Action similar to that taken by the Kentucky chapter occurred in California, where not only the Sons of the American Revolution but the Sons of the Revolution instituted a
search for " anti-American " histories. Here the latter organization, under the leadership of Frank H. Pettingell, in
an effort to gain converts to their point of view, distributed

[165] *Ibid.*
[166] Louisville *Courier-Journal*, November 12, 1922.

to all school districts Charles Grant Miller's pamphlet *Treason to American Tradition.*[167] By the former organization two detailed reports regarding Muzzey's *An American History* were issued, the one expressing the opinion of a majority of a committee to investigate this book, and the other setting forth the views of a dissenting member.

The majority report revealed no criticisms which had not been presented in the National Report.[168] On the other hand, the minority statement included four points: first, that " fairness requires that if we are to pass upon the histories used in the schools, there should be an examination of those in general use, not merely one; second, if there is to be a critical examination of histories in use in the schools of this country, it should be by a committee composed of members sufficiently acquainted with the writing and teaching of history, that their report may be comprehensive and scientific, as well as patriotic; third, the majority report fails to consider thoroughly the purpose for which this history was written; and fourth, the history should be judged by its whole tone and spirit and purpose, and not by words and sentences isolated from their context." [169]

In analyzing the textbook and comparing statements with those cited in the majority report as reprehensible, the minority report accepted the principle adopted by some textbook writers, namely, that biographical history should

[167] This is the statement of Charles Grant Miller in the Chicago *Herald and Examiner,* March 5, 1922.

[168] The report is signed " September 8, 1922." The investigating committee were George Clark Sargent, E. L. Magee, E. J. Mott, W. P. Humphreys and Donozel Stoney. The adoption of the report " engendered a heated discussion " according to the *San Francisco Chronicle* of November 24, 1922.

[169] " Minority Report upon Muzzey's History of the United States to the Board of Managers of the California Society of the Sons of the American Revolution." (In manuscript.)

be left to the elementary grades and the study of institutional development to the secondary school.

As a result of this agitation, the Commissioner of Secondary Schools of California appointed a committee to investigate history textbooks. They reported that none of the books examined were found tainted by disloyal or unpatriotic sentiments, and that the attacks against history textbooks were due to a "revival of pro-German sentiment," to "an ineradicable Irish anti-British sentiment," to a "journalistic opposition to Great Britain," and "to an element of political reaction against the domestic legislation of recent years." [170]

In Ohio, also, the Sons of the American Revolution at their state convention in Cleveland in May, 1923, condemned Muzzey's *An American History* and adopted a resolution that no textbook should be used in the schools "which belittles the founders of our government or minimizes their achievements." [171]

During Education Week in 1922, the Idaho Society Sons of the American Revolution, under the leadership of Captain A. H. Conner, started an agitation against the *History of the American People* by Willis Mason West, resulting in the exclusion of this book from the Boise schools. Criticized in much the same manner as Muzzey's *An American History*, this textbook was held unfit to "be found in a single school

[170] *Report of the Committee of Five on American History Text-Books now in Use in California High Schools* (Sacramento, 1922). (In manuscript.) The committee appointed in April, 1922, reported in June. It was made up of E. D. Adams (chairman), Professor of American History, Stanford University; E. I. McCormac, Professor of American History, University of California; J. A. Nowell, Head of the History Department, Fresno Teachers' College; W. W. Mather, Head of the History Department, Ontario; A. H. Abbott, Professor of History, College of the Pacific, San José. They examined many of the commonly used American history textbooks.

[171] The *Cleveland Plain Dealer*, May 2, 1923.

in the United States of America." [172] To Captain Conner, the treatment of historical incidents, not only in the Revolutionary period and in the War of 1812, but in the Civil War and recent period, deserved severe condemnation. Objection was raised to the treatment accorded battles in the American Revolution and in the War of 1812, as well as that of controversial questions which have " no place in a history." [173] From the latter, Captain Conner adduced that " the author of this book is quite evidently a free trader." The discussion of the labor question, socialism, the direct primary, the initiative, the referendum, the League of Nations and other " controversial subjects," such as were found in this book " are out of place in a school history." Furthermore, it was charged that the book " excuses the South for its disgraceful treatment of Union soldiers in military prisons, (p. 566), states that Robert E. Lee ranks among the noblest figures in American history and practically accuses Grant of being in collusion with the ' Whiskey Ring.' " [174]

Captain Conner's criticism of West's discussion of the Civil War period gained ready converts to his point of view, and the Phil Sheridan Post Number 4 of the Grand Army of the Republic issued a denunciation of the textbook as " worse than a travesty on justice, and a slam in the face of true Americans." [175]

These and other efforts of the Sons of the American Revolution to censor history textbooks have resulted in their elimination from many lists of approved textbooks. Ac-

[172] Pamphlet " Should the ' History of the American People ' by Willis Mason West be used as a School Text Book? " p. 4. (Obtained by the author from A. H. Conner, Attorney-General of Idaho.) This attack of West's textbook was first published in the *Idaho Statesman*.

[173] *Ibid.*, pp. 3-4.

[174] *Ibid.*

[175] *Idaho Statesman*, December 9, 1922.

cording to F. W. Millspaugh, vice-president of the Tennessee chapter, "efforts to have certain books withdrawn from public schools in Tennessee and Alabama have been unvaryingly successful." [176]   Muzzey's history, according to Judge Wallace McCamant, was excluded from the schools of Adrian, Michigan, Murphreesboro and Nashville, Tennessee, Florence, Alabama, and a number of schools in Kentucky, and "all of the objectionable histories . . . from the schools of Indiana on a hearing before the textbook commission and as a result of the attack made upon them by the Sons of the American Revolution." [177]   According to Captain Conner, "Muzzey's history has been taken out of the schools of Burley, Coeur d'Alene, Idaho Falls, Nampa and Pocatello, and West's history has been taken out of Boise as a result of the activities of the National Society acting through the Idaho Society." [178]

Although many places have barred the books under suspicion, success has not everywhere attended the efforts of the Sons of the American Revolution.   This is accounted

[176] Letter under date of July 20, 1923, to the author. However, textbooks in Tennessee are selected by a board appointed by the governor.

[177] Letter under date of August 20, 1923, from Judge Wallace McCamant. A letter under date of July 11, 1923, from H. C. Weber, Superintendent of Schools at Nashville, Tennessee, stated that he was not informed regarding the results of a complaint against a textbook used in the Nashville schools which had been presented to the legislature. In Nashville, Tennessee, the High School used James and Sanford's *American History* for the past two years according to a statement from the Superintendent of Schools. In Adrian, Michigan, West's *History of the American People* was the textbook according to a "Directory of Adrian Public Schools, 1923–1924." W. F. Weisand, Superintendent of Schools of Nampa, Idaho, informed the author in a letter of November 19, 1923, that for the years 1923 and 1924, Beard and Bagley, *History of the American People* and Beard, *History of the United States* were used. Muzzey's history was still in use in November, 1923, according to the superintendents of schools at Burley, Idaho, and in Idaho Falls, Idaho. This information was obtained in personal letters from the Superintendent of Schools. It does not agree with Captain Conner's statement.

[178] Letter under date of September 8, 1923, from A. H. Conner.

for by Judge Wallace McCamant because of "the attempt made by the educators responsible for its [a book's] presence to defend their action," and because "the publishers of these objectionable books are strongly entrenched in educational circles. . . ." [179]

But others than "the educators" and "the publishers" have opposed the efforts of the Sons of the American Revolution in their attempts at textbook censorship. "Individual members" of the organization "in Rhode Island, New Jersey, the District of Columbia, Ohio, South Dakota and California have taken issue publicly with the work of . . . the [national] Committee." [180]   For example, the historian of the Passaic Valley (New Jersey) chapter, in reviewing Muzzey's textbook, asserted that "the whole trend of the book is to tell the logical course of events, and to explain the causes of events," and that there was "no ground" for Judge McCamant's observation that "the author has 'no abiding conviction in American fundamentals; no enthusiastic veneration for the great men who founded the Republic.'" [181]

Other dissenters from Judge McCamant's opinion were in general agreement with this statement, another member of the Sons of the American Revolution suggesting that "one must surmise that Judge McCamant came to the book determined to be displeased." [182]

A mutuality of interest with the Sons of the American

[179] Letter under date of August 20, 1923, from Judge Wallace McCamant.

[180] *Report of Committee on Patriotic Education* (S. A. R.), *op. cit.*, p. 7.

[181] Report of the Historian of Passaic Valley Chapter, S. A. R., on Muzzey's *American History*, December 15, 1922. (In manuscript.) Schuyler M. Cady historian. The report was approved by the chapter, February 12, 1923.

[182] *Official Bulletin of the National Society of the Sons of the American Revolution, December, 1922.*

Revolution in censoring school histories is seen in the action of the Sons of the Revolution at St. Louis in December, 1922. Aroused by an address of Roy F. Britton, president of the local chapter, a resolution to investigate history text-books used in the St. Louis schools was unanimously adopted. In Major Britton's report to the local chapter he expressed disapproval of Muzzey's *An American History* and Hart's *School History of the United States,* books which he himself had examined, as well as condemning Ward's edition of Burke's *Speech on Conciliation with America* and Guitteau's *Our United States,* which he had not examined. The last two books used in the St. Louis schools were also classed with the " de-Americanized " histories because " several men of prominence, apparently speaking with authority, as well as certain patriotic societies and newspapers have denounced" them.[183] McLaughlin and Van Tyne's *A History of the United States for Schools* and West's *History of the American People* were cited likewise as examples of the " revisionists' methods " according to men like Charles Grant Miller and Charles Edward Russell.[184] Major Britton's efforts received the approval of some of the newspapers of St. Louis for the " real service " he had rendered,[185] one editorial remarking that school histories should set forth that the American Revolution was " a tremendous exhibit of resolution and courage to set at naught the most powerful military and naval country of the time." [186]

Other patriotic organizations have likewise attested their

[183] *Report of Roy F. Britton to St. Louis Society of Sons of Revolution on American History Text-Books Used in St. Louis Schools,* December 16, 1922. (In manuscript.) Major Britton quoted from Charles Edward Russell's article " Behind the Propaganda Scenes " which appeared in *Columbia,* September, 1922.
[184] *Ibid.*
[185] *St. Louis Times,* December 18, 1922.
[186] *St. Louis Daily Globe Democrat,* December 18, 1922.

interest in the status of present-day history instruction. The Descendants of the Signers of the Declaration of Independence, on July 4, 1922, at their national convention, asserted an aversion to public school histories which would "misinterpret the men and measures, manners and methods and the great events of the Revolution and the subsequent periods leading up to the Constitution of 1787." [187] The Veterans of Foreign Wars in National Encampment on August 24, 1922, "indignantly" protested against the alleged un-American histories, and commended Charles Grant Miller for his "patriotic service" in exposing and checking "a sinister attempt to degrade our country's history." [188]

Similar action was taken by the New York State Department, Grand Army of the Republic, in 1923, in demanding the presentation of "true American history," [189] and by the National Society Daughters of the American Revolution in 1923.[190] The United Spanish War Veterans in annual convention deplored the "British propaganda" found in a school history,[191] and the Veterans of the Seventy-Eighth Division of the American Legion at Atlantic City, in September, 1923, passed resolutions for the suppression and removal from the schools of all unpatriotic textbooks and "particularly history books." [192]

These criticisms upon history textbooks impelled the

187 Quoted in a pamphlet of *The Patriot League for the Preservation of American History.*

188 Hirshfield, David, *Report on Investigation of Pro-British History Text-Books in Use in the Public Schools of the City of New York* (N. P.), p. 71.

189 *Ibid.*, p. 72.

190 *Ibid.*

191 *The New York Times*, September 15, 1921. The "school history" is not named.

192 *Ibid.*, October 1, 1923. The unity of opinion of various patriotic organizations was discussed in the *New York American*, November 4, 1923.

American Legion to undertake, in 1922, the writing of an American history. This project received the endorsement of more than fifty national patriotic societies, but the preparation of the textbook was first entrusted to Charles F. Horne, professor of English in the College of the City of New York and editorial director of the American Legion. According to Mr. Horne, the Legion had as a purpose " an absolutely honest history . . . in no sense boastful or extravagant." [193] In the statement of their principles, the Legion expressed a desire that their history " speak the truth, so that no child learns afterwards to distrust it. But in telling the truth it must be careful to tell the truth optimistically. It will mention the blunders of the past so that the child learns to be careful; but it must dwell on failure only for its value as a moral lesson, must speak chiefly of success. . . ." [194]

The Legion, among other things, likewise set up as a principle for their textbook the inspiration of patriotism. Upon " every page a vivid love of America " must be preached. It was their conviction that such a book should " encourage patriotism, strengthen character, stimulate thought and impress the worth of Truth." [195]

In 1925, *The Story of Our American People* expressed in a tangible form the aims of the Legion. Two volumes offer solace to those whose sensibilities have been wounded by the treatment accorded events in the American histories most commonly used in the public schools. For the pupil is taught that " this is the land of hope," a land that " even strangers love," — looked upon by " the poor folk and oppressed of other lands . . . as a kind of paradise, . . . where work brings its best reward, the one region where

[193] Statement obtained from Charles F. Horne, New York City, December, 1923. See Appendix for complete statement of principles.
[194] *Ibid.*
[195] *Ibid.*

Peace seems assured, the land of Opportunity . . ." to which even " the leaders of other countries " turn " as a land of Power, able to help them in their political troubles, yet not grasping at their rights." [196]

To the pupil is revealed " a Divine Purpose " controlling the history of America for, although " perhaps the oldest continent in the world," America lay " unused " until the time when " civilization should prove worthy of it." It was " by natural processes " that " the world of Europe was sifted and sorted that there might be planted here some of its richest seed," a people who might well be " called a ' chosen race ' of Europeans." Among this number were some " made desperate by Europe's dreary lack of opportunity "; sometimes there were " folk convicted as criminals, but laws have not always judged men as God judges them, and the governments of those days were apt to be harsh and narrow." [197]

Many of the points " omitted " from other school histories are found here. Not a few of our heroic characters such as Betsy Ross, Nathan Hale, Molly Pitcher, " Mad Anthony " Wayne, John Paul Jones, and Haym Salomon are given recognition. Nor are there missing such slogans as " Don't give up the ship." [198]

The pupil is led through " the Second War for Independence, a story of outworn patience and of mistakes which

[196] Horne, Charles F., *The Story of Our American People* (2 v., New York, 1925), p. 1. The work is not issued for general publication as yet, according to a foreword.

[197] *Ibid.*, Chapter I. In connection with this last statement the textbook adds that " some of the convicts sent here were indeed evil-minded rascals; but many were men we would have applauded for their so-called crimes." *Ibid.*, p. 10. Illustrations of a " Divine Purpose " in American events are found elsewhere, for example Burgoyne's surrender, 1777, " brought to our people a sense of awe, of direct aid from Heaven." (Vol. I, p. 377.) See also Vol. I, p. 439.

[198] *Ibid.*, pp. 365, 371, 390, 394, 396, 404, Vol. II, p. 94.

ended in unexpected fortune; " through the war with Spain, "a people's war "; and finally through the World War, in which we were " no feeble foe to match even the terrible German colossus." [199]

In a letter to *The New York Times* Professor Claude H. Van Tyne, under the caption " A Questionable History," declares the title of this history to be " so bombastic that it might as well be ' The Marvelous Story of Us.' " He points out that the pamphlet which accompanies the book lists not only the organizations which are said to have gone over the material and to have given it their approval, but also school-men and historians " of wide repute." " I will not say as to the schoolmen," said Professor Van Tyne, " but as to historians I have looked over the entire list which is given and I find not one historian of repute in it. . . . There is also added an imposing array of senators . . . some chairmen of great national political parties, who, of course, endorse the scheme out of pure policy. . . . That which was a cloud no bigger than a man's hand when Charles Grant Miller began his infamous attack upon the histories written by men who really knew the facts has become a menacing storm, threatening truth wherever it is found." [200]

According to Frank C. Cross, National Director of the Americanism Commission in 1925, the American Legion believed that " much of the agitation and complaint regarding school textbooks in history has apparently come from prejudiced sources — from men and institutions that are themselves propagandists. . . ." The Legion, furthermore, he

---

[199] *Ibid.*, Vol. II, pp. 80–118; 348–358; 415–444.

[200] *The New York Times*, July 24, 1925. Professor Van Tyne also said: " I have noticed many manifest errors and dubious statements as I ran hastily over the part devoted to the American Revolution, but the main trouble is in its organization, and its sense of proportion. . . . One virtue it has which I had not expected. It is not bitterly anti-British."

declared, do not believe that the authors who have been generally attacked are " unpatriotic or that their books are written as the result of organized propaganda." Yet they felt that some of the authors had " laid themselves open to just criticism because they have sometimes made statements from the point of view of a critic or investigator rather than from that of a teacher," that " some of these authors are at fault in placing before immature pupils the blunders, foibles and frailties of prominent heroes and patriots of our Nation." The Legion also took exception to the introduction of " matters of controversial nature without giving adequate space . . . for presentations of the essential facts on both sides." [201]

Through the activities of such patriotic groups have arisen agitations similar to that in Dubuque, Iowa, where the local post of the Veterans of Foreign Wars sponsored a history textbook attack.[202] Under the direction of a committee composed of a representative of the Ladies' Grand Army of the Republic, the American Legion, the Veterans of Foreign Wars, the Spanish-American War Veterans, the Parent-Teacher Association, and the Superintendent of Schools, McLaughlin and Van Tyne's *A History of the United States for Schools* was cast out of the public schools.

Still others than the patriotic societies of the United States have censored the content of history textbooks. Among these are the National Association for the Advancement of Colored People, who have advocated the inclusion in all school histories of some account of the place and achieve-

[201] Personal correspondence, December, 1925, with Frank C. Cross, National Director of the Americanism Commission, American Legion. Mr. Cross gave this information because of an inquiry as to the extent and manner in which the Legion had become interested in the teaching of American history and the Constitution. See Appendix.

[202] *The Des Moines Register*, February 27, 1923.

ment of the negro in this country's development.[203] The Ethical Society of Davenport, Iowa, would seek a substitute for West's *History of the American People* because it does not depict sufficiently the contributions of countries like Germany to the United States.[204]

The New Jersey State Council of the Junior Order of United American Mechanics, "representing 80,000 members in its 1922 Convention" endorsed the work of the Patriot League for the Preservation of American History and demanded an "unimpaired" American history.[205]

Similar action was taken by the Knights of Pythias in their Grand Lodge meeting in Trenton, New Jersey, in September, 1923, in unanimously accepting a report on history textbooks used in the New Jersey schools and adopting a resolution condemning "*A School History of the United States* by Albert Bushnell Hart; *A History of the United States* (1919) by John F. O'Hara; Burke's *Speech on Conciliation with America* (1919) by C. H. Ward; *An American History* Revised (1920) by D. S. Muzzey; *Builders of Democracy* by Edwin Greenlaw; *Our United States* (1919) by William Backus Guitteau; McLaughlin and Van Tyne's *History of the United States for Schools*, revised 1919; *History of the American People* (1918) by Willis Mason West; *Short American History by Grades* and later condensed into one volume and *American History for Grammar Grades* (1920) by Everett Barnes."

They further pledged their "unflagging support to the Patriot League for the preservation of American History

203 *The Christian Science Monitor*, August 31, 1923.

204 Communication of the Ethical Society to the School Board, Davenport, Iowa, May 24, 1923. (In manuscript.) The communication refers to Charles Grant Miller's pamphlet *Treason to American Tradition* for details.

205 Hirshfield, *Report*, p. 74.

in its plans to drive from our schools all treason texts that have a tendency to deprive the generations yet to come of the sacred heritages that were won by the unmatchable sacrifices of our forefathers." The Committee recommended also a campaign of publicity against the condemned histories and the appointment of committees in each " subordinate Lodge " through whom these books were to be " thrown out and their use prohibited." [206]

In March, 1923, *The New Age* called the attention of Masons to the criticisms raised by patriotic organizations and by Charles Grant Miller against American histories. Since most of the " distinguished patriots," who were either omitted from the textbooks or who were slightly mentioned "with some slurring or critical allusion," were " Masons," *The New Age* urged parents to look into the kind of histories their children were using.[207]

In 1924 " forty-three " patriotic and fraternal organizations of New Jersey united in endorsing the Williams school history bill, designed to legalize the censorship of histories in that state. These included the American Legion, the Descendants of the Signers of the Declaration of Independence, the Sons of the American Revolution, the Steuben Society of America, the Grand Army of the Republic, the United Spanish War Veterans, the Knights of Columbus, the Veterans of Foreign Wars, the Daughters of the American Revolution, the Junior Order United American Mechanics, the Knights of Pythias, and the Patriotic Order

[206] *Report of Special Committee on School Histories and Text Books Adopted by Grand Lodge Knights of Pythias September 20, 1923.* It was also recommended that a copy be sent to the State Board of Education and that the Supreme Representatives be instructed to present the matter before the Supreme Lodge.

[207] " Concerning School Histories," *The New Age,* March, 1923, pp. 156–157.

Sons of America.[208]   An exhaustive discussion of the text-books commonly attacked was issued by the New Jersey Unit of the Patriot League in February, 1924. According to this pamphlet the Guitteau, the Muzzey, the Barnes, the McLaughlin and Van Tyne histories had been revised to meet the objections raised against them, but not to the entire satisfaction of their critics.[209]

Set off against the advocates of a highly nationalized history are those interested in promoting the spirit of internationalism. With this desire Robert Andrews Milliken suggested the re-writing of history through the Committee of the League of Nations on Intellectual Coöperation. The work as projected purported not to be an attempt to reform each nation's textbooks but to present an impartial world history, neither neglecting nor overestimating the achievements of distinct national groups.[210]   The same sentiment is responsible for the advocacy of an abolition of partisan textbooks tending to foster bitterness and hostility among nations, which was sanctioned in June, 1923, by the Federation of the League of Nations Society.[211]

INVESTIGATIONS BY MUNICIPAL AND SCHOOL AUTHORITIES

The endeavors of those who have constituted themselves textbook censors have borne fruit in many towns and cities of the United States. They are the source of the well-known New York City investigation of history textbooks. In October, 1920, Superintendent William L. Ettinger appointed

---

[208] This bill is discussed on page 104.

[209] " Patriotic Organizations Appeal for School History Bill," The New Jersey Unit, The Patriot League (Newark, New Jersey, February 22, 1924), p. 12. This pamphlet sets forth the criticisms commonly raised against the histories.

[210] The Des Moines Register, April 24, 1923.

[211] The Christian Science Monitor, June 27, 1923.

Associate Superintendent Edgar D. Shimer and a committee to investigate attacks made on histories used in the public schools. In November, 1921, the Committee presented a unanimous report on the fundamental principles that should govern the preparation of textbooks on history for the city schools. During November and December, 1921, and into January, 1922, the Committee held open session weekly to listen to charges against histories, at which L. R. MacEagain of the Irish Patriotic League, Charles Grant Miller, Patrick J. Lang, Mrs. E. J. Cramer of the Daughters of the American Revolution, Mrs. M. R. Jacobs, Abraham Wakeman,[212] and Edward F. McSweeney of the Knights of Columbus appeared.[213]

On May 12, 1922, the comprehensive report of the Committee was adopted by the Board of Education. This document is concerned chiefly with three matters: the establishment of a set of fundamental principles and reasonable standards for the writing of school histories, a detailed consideration of the charges made against textbooks, and certain conclusions reached as a result of the inquiry.

In the formulation of the " General Principles " by which a history textbook should be written, the Committee was doubtless guided by a letter of October 28, 1920, from Superintendent Ettinger, in which he suggested that " a distinction should be drawn between the obligation to cleave closely to the line of historical truth, such as is incumbent upon the historian writing for adult readers and the discretion properly conceded to an author of school texts who

---

[212] *The New York Times*, December 3, 1921. Charles Grant Miller at this time is reported by the *Times* to have said that Hart's history contained nothing objectionable to Americans, but that the preface was bad.

[213] *Ibid.*, December 10, 1921. In this section not all the places in which history investigations have been carried on have been mentioned. Only typical and outstanding cases are given. See pages 253, 259, 265, 273.

writes for immature minds incapable of and disinclined to make fine distinctions but instinctively inclined to worship at the shrine of all that is loyal, heroic, and self-sacrificing." Mr. Ettinger believed it unwise to present to children facts concerning the infirmities of men who had been inspirational forces in national life. He objected, furthermore, to forces which tended to destroy a reverence for the institutional life of the country.[214]

In setting forth the " General Principles " for guidance in writing history textbooks, the Committee denied to the author " absolute freedom in the selection or in the interpretation of historical material " because " predetermined aims and standards predetermine selection and interpretation." Furthermore, the Committee felt there should not be included in a textbook statements of a derogatory character concerning American heroes. Material which would tend to " arouse political, racial, or religious controversy, misunderstanding, or hatred " they also wished excluded.[215]

In the investigation, examination was made of many of the best known textbooks in American history and government including those by Barnes, Guitteau, Hart, Magruder, McLaughlin and Van Tyne, Morris and West. In all of these books the Committee found statements which were objectionable to them, their chief disapproval arising from the discussions of our relationship with England, especially in the American Revolution and in the War of 1812; the incorporation of controversial topics in the textbook; the failure to inculcate patriotism; the emasculation of accounts

---

[214] *Report on History Text-Books used in the Public Schools of the City of New York*, p. 6. An abbreviated form of this report was published in *The Historical Outlook*, Vol. XIII (October, 1922), pp. 250-255.

[215] *Report, op. cit.*, p. 14. The " General Principles " are set forth in more detail in the Appendix of this study.

of wars for the purpose of encouraging peace; and derogatory statements concerning our national heroes.

In speaking of the American Revolution, the *Report* declared: " Throughout . . . there should be but one aim: to impress upon the pupils the sublime spectacle of thirteen weak colonies spread along fifteen hundred miles of sea coast, poorly equipped and poorly disciplined, giving battle to the strongest military and naval power in the world. In addition the Colonists were surrounded by hostile Indians and in their midst was a large body of Tories working at times openly, at times secretly, but, at all times against them. . . . The pupil must be taught that if liberty is to continue ' to dwell in our midst ' he must be prepared, should occasion arise, to make similar sacrifices." [216] Authors of textbooks, the *Report* indicated, should " refrain from such characterizations as ' War Hawks ' or from cynical, sarcastic or sneering remarks concerning the prosecution of the war." It was also felt that such a statement as Barnes made — " The war was a mistake. It was a case in which anger overcame judgment " — would be the generator of an unfortunate attitude in the pupils.[217] Nor should writers indulge in controversial discussions because " The public schools are maintained by the public funds. The taxpayers are of various creeds and political beliefs " and it is necessary to respect their feelings.[218]

Criticism was directed toward several textbooks because they failed " to inculcate patriotism by bringing to the attention of the pupils the best in the lives, words and deeds of our patriots." According to the Committee too much attention was given " to the utterance and achievements of the heroes of other countries." To those who would offer disagreement to such a statement because it meant a " nar-

[216] *Ibid.*, p. 20.   [217] *Ibid.*, p. 25.   [218] *Ibid.*, p. 25.

row-visioned patriotism " tending to accentuate racial consciousness, they offered the suggestion that " in the elementary grades, our primary concern is to acquaint the pupils with the deeds and words of our own heroes, and the traditions of our own land." [219] Even though derogatory statements regarding our national heroes might be statements of fact, they asserted that " truth is no defense to the charge of impropriety," for it " is a solemn and sacred obligation " to preserve " unsullied the name and fame of those who have battled that we might enjoy the blessings of liberty." [220]

The conclusion of the Committee included, besides the criticism indicated in the discussion of the *Report* given above, the statement that no evidence of intentional disloyalty had been found on the part of the authors of the textbooks although their attitude toward the founders of the Republic in some cases was " entirely reprehensible." Nor was there evidence to support the charge that the textbooks had been written as " a result of unwholesome propaganda " although some of the writers frankly stated that they believed " there ought to be more friendly relations between Great Britain and the United States, and that they had written their histories from that standpoint." [221]

Another investigation of the history textbooks used in the New York City schools was projected in December, 1921, under the auspices of the Hylan city administration. On December sixth, Mayor John F. Hylan instructed David Hirshfield, Commissioner of Accounts, to make " a thorough investigation . . . with regard to the new history readers and text-books alleged to contain anti-American propa-

[219] *Ibid.*, p. 26.
[220] *Ibid.*, p. 23.
[221] *Ibid.*, p. 170. Willis Mason West is mentioned. *Ibid.*, p. 160.

ganda, which have been introduced into the schools of this city." [222] To the Mayor it was a matter of considerable concern that the school children of that city should be " inoculated with the poisonous virus of foreign propaganda which seeks to belittle American patriots." [223]

The inquiry was begun December tenth, at which time J. J. Shields, an insurance agent, and Charles Grant Miller were consulted by Mr. Hirshfield. [224] According to *The New York Times*, Mr. Hirshfield did not wish to employ experts in his investigation, preferring men of " sound judgment " who were " open to conviction." [225]

In the course of the examination of the books under criticism, Mr. Hirshfield held " five public hearings during the period from February 3 to April 18, 1922, to which all those interested were invited." [226] Among those who spoke were Alvin E. Owsley, National Commander of the American Legion, who raised objections to history teaching in which " children do not understand the facts " of American history; Joseph T. Griffin; [227] Colonel H. B. Fairfax, representing the Veterans of Foreign Wars, who was surprised at the intimation in school textbooks that Paul Revere's ride was a myth; Julius Hyman, who felt that Jewish heroes like Haym Salomon and Aser Levi should be given a place in histories; [228] and William Pickens, a negro, who wished his-

---

[222] *The New York Times*, December 7, 1921. Hirshfield, *op. cit.*, p. 7.

[223] *Ibid.*, p. 8.

[224] *The New York Times*, December 11, 1921.

[225] *Ibid.*, December 8, 1921. Mr. Hirshfield is alleged to have said that the investigation had been planned for several months but had been " postponed to forestall the cry that it was to get Irish votes." *Ibid.*

[226] Hirshfield, *op. cit.*

[227] Joseph T. Griffin, the author of *American History Must It be Rewritten to Preserve Our Foreign Friendships?* Cited in the discussion of the Knights of Columbus movement.

[228] Haym Salomon, mentioned in the diary of Robert Morris as " my

tory textbooks to record the fact that the first man killed in the Boston riot was Christmas Adams [Crispus Attucks] a negro, that 5,000 negroes fought in Washington's army, 250,000 in the Civil War and 400,000 in the World War.[229]

On the other hand, Mr. Francis M. Kinnicut of the English-Speaking World and Mr. Telfair Minton of the Loyal Coalition spoke in defense of the histories under attack.[230] According to Mr. Hirshfield, " representatives of the textbook publishers " were also present but " none spoke " in defense of their books.[231]

In his investigation, Mr. Hirshfield examined Muzzey's *An American History*, West's *History of the American People*, Hart's *School History of the United States*, McLaughlin and Van Tyne's *A History of the United States for Schools*, Guitteau's *Our United States*, Barnes' *Short American History by Grades*, and Barnes' *American History for Grammar Grades*.[232]   All of the books were found guilty of " promoting more friendly relations and mutual understanding with Great Britain " to the extent that the " school children are now being taught not the consecrated maxim, ' Taxation without representation is tyranny,' but, quite to

---

little Jew friend on Front Street," is credited with lending $400,000 to the colonists, becoming bankrupt.   Aser Levi, a Dutch Jew, was not permitted by Peter Stuyvesant to serve in the militia, but by an appeal to Holland finally, was able to do so.   *The New York Times*, February 4, 1922.

[229] *Ibid.;* also *The Standard Union* [Brooklyn, New York], February 3, 1922.   The negro killed in the Boston riot was Crispus Attucks.   Among others who appeared at the hearings were Charles Grant Miller, Charles Edward Russell, Warren B. Fisher of the United American War Veterans, Thomas P. Tuite of the Vanderbilt Post G. A. R. and of the Star Spangled Banner Association, Judge Wallace McCamant, Mrs. Marie J. Stuart of the National Association for the Advancement of Colored People, and Major David Banks of the Military Order of Foreign Wars.

[230] Hirshfield, *op. cit.,* p. 9.

[231] *Ibid.,* p. 10.

[232] Ward's edition of Burke's *Speech on Conciliation with America* was also examined.   The latest editions of the textbooks were reviewed.

the contrary, that ' in England's taxation of the colonies there was no injustice or oppression,' and that the real reason independence was sought, was because after England had at great cost crushed out autocracy in the Western Hemisphere, the colonists no longer needed the protection of the mother country, and were unwilling to pay their fair share of the costs incurred." [233]

Mr. Hirshfield's appraisal is not unlike that of all other critics who allege that pro-British agencies are in control of the writing of American history. " A determined purpose to disregard the Declaration of Independence, breed disrespect for the Constitution of the United States and American institutions and belittle the great men and women responsible for the establishing of the United States of America " is seen in the writings of many educators who are charged with a willingness " to be subsidized into sympathy with the Carnegie design of ' the reunited states, the British-American Union.' " [234]

In addition to the grievances urged against the historians in their treatment of Anglo-American relations, Mr. Hirshfield objected to the characterization accorded such " great leaders " as Jackson, Monroe and Clay by McLaughlin and Van Tyne, who with " other history revisionists show a peculiar fondness for this unfair method of estimating the characters of American leaders." [235] Among other criticisms directed against Muzzey's history was that of inaccuracy,[236]

[233] Ibid.
[234] Ibid., p. 67. Mr. Hirshfield charged certain financial leaders of the country like George E. Roberts and Frank A. Vanderlip with abetting movements for Anglo-American concord. The National Security League in its program for " ' the special training of school teachers to interpret the United States Constitution in the public schools ' " and to " secure legislation in the various states which will make this teaching compulsory throughout the country " was described as another agency under pro-British influence.
[235] Hirshfield, op. cit., pp. 38–40.   [236] Ibid., pp. 18–19.

and West's textbook was condemned because it was written by an "outright propagandist endeavoring zealously to promote the British design of an Anglo-American union." [237]

In the discussion allotted by the Report to Guitteau's *Our United States* and the Barnes histories, Mr. Hirshfield pointed out changes made by these authors in revisions which have appeared since these books were first criticized. These changes led Mr. Hirshfield to remark that "the promptness with which 'modern historical scholarship' may shift itself to any attitude required is truly amazing." [238] Mr. Barnes, especially, he charged with "mobility" of judgment, but declared that Barnes "is only a Brooklyn school principal and is not considered in scholastic circles of colleges and historical associations, like some of the other complained-of historians, who have been seduced into a sycophantic acceptance of English authority on all things American." [239]

The statements in the Hirshfield Report regarding school histories bear a striking similarity to those of Charles Grant Miller. Indeed, with but insignificant exceptions the Hirshfield attacks on McLaughlin and Van Tyne's *A History of the United States for Schools*, Guitteau's *Our United States*, Barnes' *Short American History by Grades* and his *American History for Grammar Grades* are couched in the same language as that employed by Charles Grant Miller in his articles in the Hearst newspapers. Furthermore, the section of the Report devoted to "British Propaganda Agencies are Active in America," is substantially a verbatim re-publica-

[237] *Ibid.*, p. 20.

[238] *Ibid.*, p. 44. Guitteau's history was criticized for his discussion of the League of Nations in addition to other points objectionable to Mr. Hirshfield. It was held that such discussions are inappropriate, inasmuch as it is still an "unsettled political question" which will be "an issue in some form or other in the coming presidential campaign." *Ibid.*, p. 47.

[239] *Ibid.*, pp. 57–58.

tion of an article which appeared October 15, 1922, in the
Chicago *Herald and Examiner*.[240] A comparison of the
statements under the name of David Hirshfield and those
under that of Charles Grant Miller tends to verify a statement in the *New York Tribune* which ascribes the authors-
ship of the Hirshfield Report to Charles Grant Miller.[241]
Indeed, the *Tribune* in a series of articles beginning November 5, 1923, discussed in detail the Hirshfield Report and
asserted that it is " a substitute paper for a document turned
in by a reputable scholar and expert who had been expressly
commissioned at considerable expense to the city to make a
thorough survey of the books in question." [242] According
to the *Tribune*, " coincident with holding some public hearings " the Commissioner of Accounts " employed Joseph
Devlin, a recognized lecturer and writer on historical and
educational subjects, to examine the complained-of histories." [243] Mr. Devlin, " a staunch supporter of Tam-
many " and of Mayor Hylan, is said to have included in his
report on history textbooks an exoneration of the " Brit-
icized " historians, characterizing them as one hundred per

240 This is entitled " Propaganda seeks to Distort American History.
British Workers are Being Backed by a Heavily Financed Machine. Pur-
pose of the Changes in Textbooks Range All the Way from Cultivation of
'More Friendly Relations' to the Fulfillment of the Carnegie Prophecy of
the Reunited States, the British-American Union and the Cecil Rhodes
Design." The articles in the Chicago *Herald and Examiner* in which the
McLaughlin and Van Tyne history was criticized appeared July 24, 1921,
and January 14, 1923. The Hirshfield report adopts the same phraseology.
Guitteau's textbook was attacked in an article of November 20, 1921, and
the Barnes histories in an article of July 17, 1921.

241 *New York Tribune*, November 5, 1923. The *Tribune* published this
statement from Miller: " The printed Hirshfield report is substantially as
I wrote it except for illiteracies and pictures." The *Tribune* asserted that it
had possession of fac-similes of special pay roll vouchers signed " David
Hirshfield, Commissioner of Accounts " for **Charles Grant Miller** and
Joseph Devlin, for expert work.

242 *Ibid.*

243 *Ibid.*

cent American whose loyalty to the United States could not be questioned.[244]   Although better compilations of American history could be imagined by Mr. Devlin, he asserted that the historians were not guilty of the charges made, — charges designed " to help keep bigotry, dissension and distrust between this country and England." [245]

Besides the books which the Hirshfield Report condemned as lacking in Americanism, Mr. Devlin examined *A History of the United States* by John P. O'Hara, *A History of the United States of America* by Charles Morris, *American Government* by Frank A. Magruder, *Builders of Democracy* by Edwin Greenlaw, *History of the United States* by Charles A. Beard and Mary R. Beard, and *The Making of Our Country* by Smith Burnham.[246]   The Magruder and Greenlaw textbooks, Mr. Devlin pointed out, were not histories, and the only cause for complaint which he could find against the latter was the inclusion of "Hymn of Love for England."   The former was described as a " plain work on civics and government, not dealing with history at all and free from one-sided opinion."   Regarding the Morris and Burnham histories, Mr. Devlin found no objection.   The authors of the Beard textbook, however, he felt should be asked to " cut out all apologies for the conduct of England," and the O'Hara volume, although " very well compiled," was open to charges of bias and a pro-Catholic viewpoint.[247]

Of those histories which the Hirshfield Report had condemned, Mr. Devlin found only one which justified the

[244] *Ibid.*, November 6, 1923.
[245] *Ibid.*
[246] *Ibid.*, November 11, 1923.   The O'Hara history was criticized in an article by Charles Grant Miller in the Chicago *Herald and Examiner*, July 3, 1921.   See page 210.
[247] *Ibid.*   These histories, according to the *Tribune,* were not on the authorized list for use in the New York City schools.

charge of a pro-British point of view. This textbook —
The History of the American People by Willis Mason West
— had been banned from the New York City schools. The
McLaughlin and Van Tyne history, the Devlin Report declared, should be revised in such a way that it would arouse
more "pride in American breasts for the part the forefathers of our country played in freeing it from England,"
but it was not found culpable in many of the respects commonly alleged.

The employment of Mr. Devlin for the purpose of investigating history textbooks was denied by Mr. Hirshfield.
The only connection which Mr. Devlin had with the history
inquiry, according to Mr. Hirshfield, was to "list all the
textbooks, particularly as to authorship and the number of
textbooks by different authors used in the same grade of
work." Later when "Mr. Devlin took it upon himself to
write a history report and had the audacity to submit same
to me, I dismissed him at once," declared the Commissioner
of Accounts.[248]

In refutation of Mr. Hirshfield's denial regarding his part
in the history inquiry, Mr. Devlin asserted that he began
his investigation of history textbooks on December 21, 1921,
as "an expert" through the direction of Mr. James McGin-
ley, Hirshfield's "chief of staff," and continued the work
for seven months when "the investigation was brought to a
close" due to lack of funds.[249] "Nearly a year after these
opinions had been submitted by Mr. Devlin and shelved,"
stated the *Tribune,* "the Hirshfield-Miller version appeared. . . ."[250]

[248] *Ibid.*, November 5, 1923.   [249] *Ibid.*, November 23, 1923.

[250] *Ibid.*, November 5, 1923. Devlin was paid $2000 for his work, and
Miller received $562.50 for his work from February to May, 1923, as a
"special expert in history text-book investigation," according to the
Tribune.

The Devlin Report " being the opposite of what his employers wanted," remarked *The New York Times,* " . . . the job was turned over to one Charles Grant Miller, who joyously and promptly turned out, and in, a report of just the right — meaning the desired — kind, and that is the one, says the Tribune, which Mr. Hirshfield signed and published, greatly horrifying a part of the metropolitan population and as much amusing the rest of it." [251]

The Hirshfield Report stimulated much discussion throughout the country. In New York, Superintendent of Schools William L. Ettinger declared " that the very idea of the Commissioner of Accounts investigating such a subject as the teaching of history in the public schools was highly amusing," and that the Report was " belated and unnecessary inasmuch as the school authorities had already condemned seven of the eight histories condemned by Hirshfield." [252]

The press in all sections of the United States devoted their columns to the Report and to the teaching and writing of history. The *Atlanta Journal,* under the caption of " Politician vs. Historian," remarked that " Mr. Hirshfield's views . . . are of no consequence. But the general reaction to his ganderish expression of them is highly interesting and altogether wholesome." The *New York World,* according to the *Journal,* suggested that " ' the standing of the historians whom he attacks is better than his own '; while the Buffalo News comments: ' Instead of leaving history to educators who are reputed to know something about it, the politicians

[251] *The New York Times,* November 6, 1923.

[252] *Ibid.,* June 5, 1923. *An American History* by David S. Muzzey was the eighth history in the Hirshfield list. At the time of the investigation under the auspices of the schools there had been no complaint against this book according to Superintendent Ettinger.

are arrogating to themselves the right to determine what texts shall, and what texts shall not, be used.' " [253]
" The New England view is well reflected by the Hartford Times," declared *The Journal*, in saying that " ' if we are teaching history and not mythology we want our children to acquire a critical capacity which shall enable them to appraise the world they live in by an intelligent application of the knowledge of the past . . . if a child has been trained to believe that between the years 1776 and 1885 all Americans were supermen, the appearance of a Hirshfield must come with something of a shock.' " [254] Similar sentiment was expressed by the *Baltimore Sun* which asserted that Mr. Hirshfield's " jazzy little turn on the public stage would hardly deserve notice at all if it were not for the lamentable tendency of a few excitable citizens whom it represents." [255]

To the [Fort Wayne, Indiana] *News Sentinel* " there is something in that name Hirshfield that sounds significant," [256] and to the *Milwaukee Journal* " the very intemperance " of Mr. Hirshfield's charges suggested that he was " not without his own prejudices." [257] The *Dubuque Telegraph-Herald* ascribed Mr. Hirshfield's fears to " an overstimulated imagination " or to " the close connection of his chief, Mr. Hylan, with William Randolph Hearst," who " is doing his best to stir up ill-feeling between the United States and Great Britain." [258]

The reaction of historians was reflected by James Truslow Adams in his article " History and the Lower Criticism " in *The Atlantic Monthly* for September, 1923, in which he

[253] *The Atlanta Journal*, June 27, 1923.
[254] *Ibid.*
[255] *Ibid.* The *Baltimore Sun* is also quoted by *The Atlanta Journal*.
[256] *The News Sentinel*, June 6, 1923. Editorial.
[257] *The Milwaukee Journal*, June 9, 1923. Editorial.
[258] *Dubuque Telegraph-Herald*, June 14, 1923.

described the advance made in historical scholarship during the generation before the War. "Since then, however," he declared, "the forces of reaction and obscurantism seem to have been let loose and to have gathered fresh strength. . . . Partly because it [history] uses the language of the common man, the common man constitutes himself a judge of its truth, and we have the spectacle of a municipal commissioner of accounts attacking the validity of the scholar's work while a town chamber of commerce defends it."

"What then of the future?" queried Mr. Adams. "Is the writing of popular history to be an effort to discover and to disseminate among the people the true story of mankind in the past, or is it to be written as an ethical or political tract, to further the passionate conflicts of the present?" The desire of the historian to portray the truth and to be just in his estimates, is to Mr. Adams a surety that "the patriot need fear no danger to the ideals and inspiration to be derived from an ever more painstaking scrutiny of the history of the colonies and of the nation. The historian who most loves truth is most likely to love his country."[259]

Other cities have passed through experiences similar to that of New York, but less publicity has attended the investigations. On October 23, 1922, the City Council of Boston "unanimously passed an order requesting the School Committee to give a hearing for the consideration of certain objections made to the use in the public schools . . . of 'School History of the United States,' revised 1920, by Albert Bushnell Hart; Burke's 'Speech on Conciliation,' edited by C. H. Ward 1919, and 'American History,' by D. S. Muzzey."[260]

259 Adams, James Truslow, "History and the Lower Criticism," *The Atlantic Monthly*, Vol. CXXXII (September, 1923), pp. 308–317.

260 *City of Boston, Proceedings of School Committee*, December 18, 1922, p. 180.

In compliance with this request the School Committee "personally examined the books under discussion with considerable care. . . ." They also had prepared "a careful and dispassionate review under the direction of all of the Board of Superintendents of all or substantially all of the criticisms made against these books and brought to their attention, and a refutation of these criticisms which, in the opinion of the Committee, justice to the authors demands." [261]

Although the Committee were not "in entire sympathy and agreement with all the statements which the books contain," nor in complete accord regarding the emphasis placed upon "certain events in our national history," yet they felt that " such differences " were not " sufficient to warrant the condemnation of the books nor the impeachment of the sincerity and good faith of the authors." [262]

A " hearing " regarding the textbooks under examination was arranged for and held by the School Committee and the City Council on November 15, the latter being represented by one member. " In the course of the hearing," stated the Report, " irrelevant and extraneous matters were brought to the attention of the School Committee to which it listened with scant patience." What the School Committee regarded as " unwarranted and ill-founded attacks were made upon the authors of these books," whereas to the Committee " the real and only question at issue " was whether their [Muzzey's and Hart's] histories contain material to which reasonable and proper objection may be made." [263]   In the opinion of the Committee " no historian had ever succeeded in writing a book which met satisfactorily every point of view, nor does any history place an equal amount of emphasis upon all the topics which it discusses." Besides, " it is clearly impossible

[261] *Ibid.*   [262] *Ibid.*   [263] *Ibid.*

that one brief volume should give adequate treatment to all the steps incident to the origin and growth of a great nation." [264]

The Committee also deplored " the course pursued by the critics of these books in tearing from their context detached sentences and omitting explanations and summaries which are essential to a grasp of the authors' real meaning." Such a procedure, they believed, would permit a critic to find an " opportunity for criticism of any book that ever has been written on the subject of history, and indeed on many other subjects as well." [265]

After having given " due consideration to the matter," the School Committee therefore were of the opinion " that the criticisms against these two books " did not justify " their exclusion from the Authorized List." [266] A dissenting opinion, however, was issued, which, " while in agreement " with the Report, nevertheless set forth the view that the Board of Superintendents should ask for certain changes in the books when they were revised.[267]

In the comprehensive reviews of Hart's *School History of the United States* and Muzzey's *An American History,* the Committee pointed out that the chief sources of the criticisms were taken from " Mr. Charles Grant Miller, — Treason to American Tradition; Mr. Wallace McCamant, — Review of Muzzey's American History; Mr. James A. Watson, — Speech before the Boston City Council and interview reported in the Boston Globe of October 24, 1922, . . . and from the ' Report on History Text Books used in public schools of the City of New York, 1922.' "

---

[264] *Ibid.*
[265] *Ibid.*
[266] *Ibid.*, p. 181. Signed by David D. Scannell and Frances G. Curtis.
[267] *Ibid.* Signed by Richard J. Lane.

In examining each statement which had been quoted to prove that these textbooks were Anglicized editions, the Committee showed that the " apologetic attitude toward England " charged by the critics could not be so considered when quotations were taken in their entirety.

In concluding their reviews, the Committee declared, " Both writers have shown a striking sense of proportion, great skill in focusing attention upon what is vital, and commendable courage in calling attention to weaknesses and mistakes in our history, some of which still need to be corrected. The few defects of these books are insignificant as compared with their many excellencies. Both books mark an advance in the writing of history texts for school use. Both are worthy contributions to the study and teaching of American history. Neither of them should be excluded from our schools." [268]

Because of alleged un-Americanism West's *History of the American People* was banned from the approved lists of textbooks in Alta, Iowa, and Jackson, Minnesota.[269]   The McLaughlin and Van Tyne history received like treatment in Battle Creek, Michigan.[270]   From the San José (California) Carnegie Library Hart's *Formation of the Union,* his *National Ideals Historically Traced,* and Van Tyne's *American Revolution* were removed by orders of the library board, who declared them " un-American and unfit for reading, particularly by school children." [271]   *The Study of the Nations* by Harriet Tuell was prohibited in the schools of Somerville, Massachusetts, because of alleged pro-British

[268] *Ibid.,* p. 191. The Report is given in part in the Appendix.

[269] Letter from S. G. Reinertson, Superintendent of Schools, Jackson, Minnesota, and formerly Superintendent at Alta, Iowa, under date of March 25, 1923.

[270] Chicago *Herald and Examiner,* March 5, 1922.

[271] *The New York Times,* May 1, 1923. Also *The Survey,* Vol. L (April 15, 1923), p. 68.

leanings. The attacks against this book culminated in a bill in the Massachusetts Senate, in 1921, forbidding its use in any school of the commonwealth, but the bill died in committee.

PUBLIC OPINION REGARDING THE CENSORSHIP OF
HISTORY TEXTBOOKS

These endeavors to censor history textbooks have occasioned much discussion by the press, by educators and others. To *The New York Times* " however commendable these efforts to find and set forth the historical truth may be, and however honorable and sincere the motive, it must be admitted by all that this is not the way to ' rewrite history.' " [272]

To the [New York] *Evening Globe* " the controversy over school histories is largely between defenders of doctrine and defenders of free inquiry, between those who do not believe that children can be trusted with the truth and those who believe that they can. Most of the modern histories have been written by scholars inspired by the scientific spirit and, therefore, no more tender with myths about history than a modern bacteriologist with myths about disease. . . . A true American history need not rob us of the story of Paul Revere or the reverence for George Washington, but it will teach that personal anecdotes are not the life of a nation, that great men as well as mean men flourish in every generation. . . ." [273]

The reaction of teachers engaged in the public schools is much the same as that of the press. The continued agitation regarding histories carried on in Washington, D. C., led the

[272] *The New York Times,* September 12, 1921.
[273] The [New York] *Evening Globe,* February 22, 1922.

High School Teachers' Association to adopt the following resolutions:

"It is resolved that the questioning of the Americanism of teachers of history in American schools is resented, that the teachers themselves should be the judges of the content of the courses, and that the object of teaching history is to give the truthful picture of the past, with due regard to the age of the pupil for whom the work is intended, and therefore the truth should not be distorted for any purpose whatever; both sides of a controversial question should be presented from an academic point of view so that the students of history shall be trained in habits of open-minded tolerance." [274]

Further evidence of a rebellion against the censorship attempted over history textbooks was manifested at the annual meeting of the Association of History Teachers of the Middle States and Maryland in May, 1923, when a series of resolutions was unanimously adopted "deploring an agitation based on either ignorance or malice, or which has for its object the promotion of animosities between classes of nations; . . . ." [275]   In October, 1923, the Washington State Teachers' Association resolved:

"1. That decisions regarding textbooks should be made by those scientifically trained; 2. That teachers who show a lack of judgment in the interpretation of texts, or whose loyalty is questioned, should be disciplined, or dismissed by their own school board. There should be no blanket charge against the whole corps. 3. That no unbiased committee of examiners has, on investigation, substantiated the attacks made on History teaching in American schools. 4. That examination will show that the groups making these attacks have no understanding of the distinction between grade and high school history, no conception of

[274] *The Dearborn Independent,* October 20, 1923.
[275] Adopted May 5, 1923. Columbia University, New York.

the methods of teaching, nor of the necessary content of an American history.　5. That a cursory examination of the attacks appearing in newspapers and originating with organizations prove much of their charge is based on half quotations and a wrenching of sentences from their context.　These display an entire lack of the American quality of fair play." [276]

The objection of historical scholars toward present-day censorship of history textbooks voiced itself at a meeting of the American Historical Association in December, 1923, when the following resolutions were adopted:

" *Whereas,* there has been in progress for several years an agitation conducted by certain newspapers, patriotic societies, fraternal orders, and others, against a number of school text-books in history and in favor of official censorship, and

" *Whereas,* this propaganda has met with sufficient success to bring about not only acute controversy in many cities but the passage of censorship laws in several states, therefore

" *Be it resolved* by the American Historical Association, upon the recommendation of its Committee on History Teaching in the Schools and of its Executive Council, that genuine and intelligent patriotism, no less than the requirement of honesty and sound scholarship, demand that text-book writers and teachers should strive to present a truthful picture of past and present, with due regard to the different purposes and possibilities of elementary, secondary and advanced instruction; — that criticism of history text-books should therefore be based not upon grounds of patriotism but only upon grounds of faithfulness to fact as determined by specialists or tested by consideration of the evidence; — that the cultivation in pupils of a scientific temper in history and the related social sciences, of a spirit of inquiry and a willingness to face unpleasant facts, are far more important objectives than the teaching of special interpretations of particular events; —

[276] Adopted October 25, 1925.

and that attempts, however well meant, to foster national arrogance and boastfulness and indiscriminate worship of national ' heroes ' can only tend to promote a harmful pseudo-patriotism; and

" *Be it further resolved,* that in the opinion of this Association the clearly implied charges that many of our leading scholars are engaged in treasonable propaganda and that tens of thousands of American school teachers and officials are so stupid or disloyal as to place treasonable text-books in the hands of children is inherently and obviously absurd; — and

" *Be it further resolved,* that the successful continuance of such an agitation must inevitably bring about a ruinous deterioration both of text-books and of teaching, since self-respecting scholars and teachers will not stoop to the methods advocated." [277]

The sentiment of other educators is much the same as that of writers of history and the history teacher. Professor William C. Bagley has declared that " an official public or governmental censorship over history text-books would be a calamity of the first magnitude." [278] To Dean Percy R. Boynton " the hue and cry about American histories for schools is a piece of post-war hysteria." [279] In general, the attitude of educators can be summarized in the words of

[277] *The American Historical Review,* Vol. XXIX (April, 1924), p. 428.
[278] Giddings, Franklin, " Are we getting better text-books? " *The Independent,* Vol. I (June 3, 1922), pp. 5–9.
[279] *Ibid.* The following comment on the attitude of historians and educators toward the censorship of histories appeared in the *New York American,* November 4, 1923: " It has been insolently asserted by speakers for foreign propaganda agencies and by some college professors and school men that the interpretation of American patriotism should be left to ' higher historical scholarship ' and that ' ignorant ' and narrowly nationalistic American patriotic organizations should keep their hands off. We contend, on the contrary, that we who have followed the flag for American ideals know what these ideals are; we cherish them for what they are and will maintain them in our schools as zealously as we have maintained them in battle-line."

Dr. Payson Smith of Massachusetts: " The public school does not owe to business interests or to special interests or to labor interests of any kind that there shall be constructed in the minds of the young people attitudes and opinions designed to be definitely and specifically helpful to those interests. . . . It is not a legitimate part of the public school program to deal in any phase of propaganda. Let the doors of the school-house once be opened to the appeals of those who want . . . any subject taught from the special viewpoint of a group of people and they must remain open until the schools will be so crowded with the teachings of the propagandists that there will be no time or opportunity left for doing the work which is the primary responsibility of the schools." [280]

[280] Dr. Payson Smith in an address on " Schools should be Uninfluenced," *The Christian Science Monitor*, November 2, 1921.

Doubtless it is pertinent to call attention to the work of peace organizations in the analyses of history textbooks by which it has been shown that heroes and achievements of war have received much more space than heroes and achievements of peace. See *War and Peace in United States History Text-Books* by the National Council for Prevention of War, Washington, D. C., and *An Analysis of the Emphasis upon War in Our Elementary School Histories,* by the Association for Peace Education, Chicago.

APPENDICES

A. The Lusk Laws of New York regarding Instruction in Patriotism and Citizenship, the Flag, Text-Books, and Qualifications for Teachers.

B. *Report of Committee of Five on American History Textbooks Now in Use in California High Schools.*

C. New York City — Board of Education, *Report of the Committee to Investigate . . . History Textbooks in Use in the Public Schools of the City of New York. . . .*

D. City of Boston, Proceedings of School Committee, *Report of and Review on Certain Text Books in History Used in the Schools, and Order Relating Thereto.*

E. *Report of the Proceedings of the Convention of the American Federation of Labor,* Cincinnati, June, 1922, "Investigation of Text Books."

F. Wisconsin Law of 1923 affecting History Textbooks.

G. (Statement regarding Principles) *The American Legion School History.*

H. *Report of the American Bar Association,* Vol. XXIX (1924), *Committee on American Citizenship,* "Our Citizenship Creed."

A. THE LUSK LAWS OF NEW YORK REGARDING IN-STRUCTION IN PATRIOTISM AND CITIZENSHIP, THE FLAG, TEXTBOOKS, AND QUALIFICATIONS OF TEACHERS [1]

4. PATRIOTISM

Article 26-C

Instruction in Patriotism and Citizenship

Section 705. Courses of instruction in patriotism and citizenship. In order to promote a spirit of patriotic and civic service and obligation and to foster in the children of the state moral and intellectual qualities which are essential in preparing to meet the obligations of citizenship in peace or in war, the regents of the university of the state of New York shall prescribe courses of instruction in patriotism and citizenship, to be maintained and followed in all the schools of the state. The boards of education and trustees of the several cities and school districts of the state shall require instruction to be given in such courses, by the teachers employed in the schools therein. All pupils attending such schools, over the age of eight years, shall attend upon such instruction.

Similar courses of instruction shall be prescribed and maintained in private schools in the state, and all pupils in such schools over eight years of age shall attend upon such courses. If such courses are not so established and maintained in a private school, attendance upon instruction in such school shall not be deemed substantially equivalent to instruction given to pupils of like age

---

[1] *Revolutionary Radicalism Its History, Purpose, and Tactics with an Exposition and Discussion of the Steps Being Taken and Required to Curb It*, Vol. III, pp. 2430–2434.

in the public schools of the city or district in which such pupils reside. (Added by L. 1918, ch. 241, in effect April 17, 1918.)

706. Rules prescribing courses; inspection and supervision; enforcement. The regents of the university of the state of New York shall determine the subjects to be included in such courses of instruction in patriotism and citizenship, and the period of instruction in each of the grades in such subjects. They shall adopt rules providing for attendance upon such instruction and for such other matters as are required for carrying into effect the objects and purposes of this article. . . .

5. THE FLAG

Article 27

The flag

710. Purchase and display of flag. It shall be the duty of the school authorities of every public school in the several cities and school districts of the state to purchase a United States flag, flagstaff and the necessary appliances therefor, and to display such flag upon or near the public school building during school hours, and at such other times as such school authorities may direct.

711. Rules and regulations. The said school authorities shall establish rules and regulations for the proper custody, care and display of the flag, and when the weather will not permit it to be otherwise displayed, it shall be placed conspicuously in the principal room in the school house.

712. Commissioner of Education shall prepare program. 1. It shall be the duty of the Commissioner of Education to prepare, for the use of the public schools of the state, a program providing for a salute to the flag and such other patriotic exercises as may be deemed by him to be expedient, under such regulations and instructions as may best meet the varied requirements of the different grades in such schools.

2. It shall also be his duty to make special provision for the observance in the public schools of Lincoln's birthday, Wash-

ington's birthday, Memorial day and Flag day, and such other legal holidays of like character as may be hereafter designated by law when the Legislature makes an appropriation therefor.

713. Military drill excluded. Nothing herein contained shall be construed to authorize military instruction or drill in the public schools during school hours.

6. TEXTBOOKS

Article 25, Section 674. Textbooks containing seditious or disloyal matter. No textbook in any subject used in the public schools in this state shall contain any matter or statements of any kind which are seditious in character, disloyal to the United States or favorable to the cause of any foreign country with which the United States is now at war. A commission is hereby created, consisting of the commissioner of education and of two persons to be designated by the regents of the university of the state of New York, whose duty it shall be on complaint to examine textbooks used in the public schools of the state, in the subjects of civics, economics, English, history, language and literature, for the purpose of determining whether such textbooks contain any matter or statements of any kind which are seditious in character, disloyal to the United States or favorable to the cause of any foreign country with which the United States is now at war. Any person may present a written complaint to such commission that a textbook in any of the aforesaid subjects for use in the public schools of this state or offered for sale for use in the public schools of this state contains matter or statements in violation of this section, specifying such matter or statements in detail. If the commission determine that the textbook against which complaint is made contains any such matter or statements, it shall issue a certificate disapproving the use of such textbook in the public schools of this state, together with a statement of the reasons for its disapproval, specifying the matter found unlawful. Such certificate of disapproval of a textbook, with a detailed statement of the reasons for its disapproval, shall be duly forwarded to the boards of education or other boards or authorities having jurisdiction of the public schools of the cities, towns or school districts of this state, and after the receipt of such certificate the use of a textbook so disapproved shall be discontinued in such city, town or school district.

Any contract hereafter made by any such board of education or other school authorities for the purchase of a textbook in any of such subjects, which has been so disapproved, shall be void. Any school officer or teacher who permits a textbook in any of such subjects, which has been so disapproved, to be used in the public schools of the state, shall be guilty of a misdemeanor. (Added by L. 1918, ch. 246, in effect April 17, 1918.)

7. QUALIFICATIONS OF TEACHERS

Article 20, Section 550. Qualifications of teachers. No person shall be employed or authorized to teach in the public schools of the state who is

1. Under the age of eighteen years.

2. Not in possession of a teacher's certificate issued under the authority of this chapter or a diploma issued on the completion of a course in a state normal school of this state or in the state normal college.

3. Not a citizen. A person employed as a teacher on April 4, 1918, who was not a citizen, may continue in such employment provided he or she, within one year from such date, shall make application to become a citizen and within the time thereafter prescribed by law shall become a citizen. The provisions of this subdivision shall not apply to alien teachers who are citizens of countries that were allied with this country in the prosecution of the war with Germany and who were employed as teachers in this state on or prior to April 4, 1918, provided such teacher make application to become a citizen before the first day of September, 1920, and within the time thereafter prescribed by law shall become such citizen. (Amended by L. 1918, ch. 158, and L. 1919, ch. 120, in effect March 31, 1919.)

551. Minimum qualifications of teachers in primary and grammar schools. No person shall hereafter be employed or licensed to teach in the primary and grammar schools of any city or school district authorized by law to employ a superintendent of schools who has not had successful experience in teaching for at least three years, or in lieu thereof has not completed:

1. A course in one of the state normal schools of this state or in any approved college, prescribed by the commissioner of education. (Subdivision 1 amended by L. 1920, ch. 155, in effect April 5, 1920.)

2. An examination for and received a life state certificate issued in this state by a superintendent of public instruction or the commissioner of education.

3. A course of study in a high school or academy of not less than three years approved by the commissioner of education or from some institution of learning of equal or higher rank approved by the same authority, and who subsequently to the completion of such course has not graduated from a school for the professional training of teachers having a course of not less than two years approved by the commissioner of education or its equivalent.

568. Removal of superintendents, teachers and employees for treasonable or seditious acts or utterances. A person employed as superintendent of schools, teacher or employee in the public schools, in any city or school district of the state, shall be removed from such position for the utterance of any treasonable or seditious word or words or the doing of any treasonable or seditious act or acts while holding such position. (Added by L. 1917, ch. 416, in effect May 8, 1917.)

B. REPORT OF COMMITTEE OF FIVE ON AMERICAN HISTORY TEXTBOOKS NOW IN USE IN CALIFORNIA HIGH SCHOOLS [2]

STANFORD UNIVERSITY, CALIFORNIA,
June, 1922.

MR. A. C. OLNEY,
Commissioner of Secondary Schools,
State Board of Education,
SACRAMENTO, CALIFORNIA.

DEAR SIR: In April, 1922, you were directed by the State Board of Education to appoint a Committee of five educators with instructions " to examine the textbooks on American History in use in the Junior High Schools, High Schools, and Junior Colleges of California and to report on those, if any, which treat any part of American history in a disloyal or unpatriotic manner or which minimize the best patriotism of American tradition."

The committee appointed consisted of E. D. Adams (Chairman), Professor of American History, Stanford University; E. I. McCormac, Professor of American History, University of California; J. A. Nowell, Head of History Department, Fresno Teachers' College; W. W. Mather, Head of History Department, Ontario; and A. H. Abbott, Professor of History, College of the Pacific, San José. The textbooks examined were:

West, *History of the American People,* 1918, Rev. 1920. Allyn & Bacon.
Hart, *New American History,* 1921. American Book Company.
Fish, *The Development of American Nationality,* 1919. American Book Company.

[2] *Report of the Committee of Five on American History Textbooks Now in Use in California High Schools* (Sacramento, 1922).

McLaughlin, *A History of the American Nation*, 1919. D. Appleton & Company.

Forman, *Advanced American History*, 1922. The Century Company.

Muzzey, *An American History*, 1920. Ginn & Company.

Fite, *History of the United States*, 1919. Henry Holt & Company.

Becker, *Beginnings of the American People*, 1915. Houghton Mifflin Company.

Dodd, *Expansion and Conflict*, 1915. Houghton Mifflin Company.

Johnson, *Union and Democracy*, 1915. Houghton Mifflin Company.

Paxson, *The New Nation*, 1915. Houghton Mifflin Company.

Ashley, *American History*, 1921. Macmillan Company.

Bassett, *Short History of the United States*, 1921. Macmillan Company.

Beard, *History of the United States*, 1921. Macmillan Company.

Channing, *Students' History of the United States*, 1915. Macmillan Company.

Thompson, *History of the United States*, 1917. B. H. Sanborn & Company.

Haworth, *The United States in Our Own Times*, 1920. Scribner's Sons.

REPORT

In the opinion of your Committee none of these texts treat " any part of American history in a disloyal or unpatriotic manner." All of the authors may be credited with a desire to assist in inculcating a loyal and patriotic Americanism. . . . Before attempting that judgment it has seemed necessary to agree upon a statement setting forth what we consider to be the essentials of " the best patriotism of American tradition. . . ."

Possibly our effort to summarize and state these essentials has no place in this report, since it was in effect but a preliminary step necessary to a common point of view in examining the texts. Nevertheless our summary is here offered both as an indication of our procedure and as containing the points upon which the texts were judged.

In our opinion the " best patriotism of American tradition," when conveyed by history textbooks should directly aid in establishing certain principles and ideals in the pupil's mind. The more important of these we will list as follows:

(1) Pride in America and a Sense of Nationality.

A belief that America has developed a high type of political and social organization. But recognition that these are not now and never have been perfect and that they are a result of growth, largely anticipated by the framers of our government, to meet changing conditions. This requires a critical treatment of history, pointing out both excellencies and defects, whether in men or in events. It should help the pupil to develop a habit of just criticism, but also, what is equally important, a habit of giving high approval where merited.

(2) A Sense of Individual Liberty.

The recognition that America has contributed to world development the theory that human happiness is best secured by guarding individual liberty and by seeking to provide in the highest degree possible an equal opportunity to win that happiness. The history text should develop the origins with us of this ideal, in religious controversies, political quarrels with the mother country in colonial times, industrial development, and in political and social changes at home.

(3) A Respect for Private Property.

Inherited from old world institutions but emphasized more than by other nations from our earliest times. This is a bedrock American principle, but as developed in the United States emphasis always has been placed on the opportunity to acquire property as essential to individual liberty seeking happiness, not alone on the right to defend and to protect it. It is a principle essential to the American conception of, and contribution to, a progressive betterment of Society. . . .

(4) A Belief in Democratic Self-Government by Majority Rule.

This asserts the Jeffersonian doctrine that rule by the majority, while not insuring perfection, is more likely to approach it than any other form of rule, and more likely to preserve individual happiness under law. America, more than any other nation, made the contribution of the ideal of democracy by majority rule to the theory of political government. . . .

(5) Obedience to Law.

Since it has its sanction in majority rule, thus providing a reasonable limitation on individual liberty.

(6) A Desire for Justice.

It has long been, and still is, a marked attribute of America, and history texts should expound it. They should show its manifestations (or at times the lack of it), (a) in the spirit of compromise that minorities may not be oppressed by majorities; (b) in our relations with other countries; (c) in our industrial disputes. Especially in foreign relations the text should seek to present fairly the view opposed to American contention in order that the justice of our action may be weighed.

(7) A Will to Defend these Principles.

This is an essential result of American history teaching which should bring out the sacrifice, devotion and patriotism of Americans in the past as regards: (a) our relations with other nations; and (b) our domestic relations, either political, religious or social. But in neither field should old and dead controversy be treated in such a way as to perpetuate animosities. . . .

Finally, the text should seek to be strictly unbiased as regards both expression and content. It should narrate truthfully the important facts of American history in such a way as to make clear the principles and ideals which have been developed in America and for which she stands.

Examining the texts submitted, it can not be said that any one of them neglects, absolutely, these principles of " the best patriotism of American tradition." . . .

Your committee wishes further to point out the progressive nature of history teaching in the schools of California. The high school does not attempt to cover the same ground in American History courses as the elementary, nor in the same manner. It is left to the elementary schools to emphasize especially the biographical element, while the high school texts develop the institutional side of our nation's growth. Hence we commend the omission by some authors of many names of those who have contributed something worth while to American progress, but whose deeds and significance can best be presented by the elementary school text. This leaves room for the high school text to include those matters of social and economic development which are essential to give our young people the proper historical background for understanding our present complex problems.

Your committee finds no text wholly objectionable under the instructions of the State Board of Education. This is not to say, however, that in our opinion the texts are equally worthy. They vary in exactness of statement, in clearness of presentation, in grasp of principles, and, what is more serious, in fairness of language and view. . . .

With this report approving all of the texts submitted to us, further comment may be regarded as superfluous. It seems to us, however, that we have a duty in directing your attention to the apparent sources of some of the attacks on various texts. During the recent World War you appointed a committee (upon which two of the members of your present committee also served) to examine all history texts in use in the California schools with instructions to report whether they " were pro-German or were unduly friendly to our allies." All of the American history texts then reviewed were reported as approved, but with some minor criticisms made privately to the publishing firms or authors. It appears to your present committee that many of the attacks now being made on certain texts are emanating from persons or organizations dissatisfied with the friendly relations established between America and our allies in the great war, and desirous of destroying that better understanding created by the war. Some of the attacks appear to be due to a revival of pro-German sentiment; some to an ineradicable Irish anti-British sentiment; some to an element of political reaction against the domestic legislation of recent years; some of journalistic opposition to Great Britain. Generally the method used in such attacks is to print sentences objected to without including the context. This deprives the reader of the opportunity to judge whether the criticism is just or not. Such criticism is in itself unfair and unscientific. A book must be judged by its general tone and spirit rather than by isolating words or phrases from their context and thus conveying a false impression of the author's meaning.

The point which we would make is, that attacks of this nature, though requiring consideration, are not worthy of serious respect, since usually they conceal real motives under the mantle of

" traditional American patriotism." It is an age of propaganda and in substance most of these attacks are propaganda, having an ulterior purpose. Honest criticism by one who sincerely feels that a text fails to teach American patriotism should always be listened to and his criticisms weighed. But propaganda criticism deserves no respect either by school boards or the authors of texts. As to such propaganda assertion that any American history text now in use in California high schools and junior colleges " treats any part of the American history in a disloyal or unpatriotic manner, or minimizes the best patriotism of American tradition," your committee reports in the negative.

(*Signed*) E. D. Adams, *Chairman*
E. I. McCormac
A. H. Abbott
J. A. Nowell
W. W. Mather

C. REPORT OF THE COMMITTEE TO INVESTIGATE . . . HISTORY TEXTBOOKS IN THE PUBLIC SCHOOLS OF THE CITY OF NEW YORK,[3] 1922

GENERAL PRINCIPLES

The formulation of aims and standards by the Commissioner of Education denies, by necessary implication, that the writer of a textbook for use in the public schools has absolute freedom in the selection or in the interpretation of historical material. Predetermined aims and standards predetermine selection and interpretation.

The textbook must contain no statement in derogation or in disparagement of the achievements of American heroes. It must not question the sincerity of the aims and purposes of the founders of the Republic or of those who have guided its destinies.

The textbook must contain no material which tends to arouse political, racial, or religious controversy, misunderstanding or hatred.

The textbook must contain no material tending to arouse misunderstanding or hatred between the United States and any other nation.

The selection of material must be restricted to that which contributes most directly and essentially to the attainment of the legitimate objectives of the public school system as formulated by the State Commissioner of Education.

The writer must be prepared at all times to " come out in the open and cheerfully and unhesitatingly stand up and make known to the entire community," the aims and the ideals, the purposes and the motives, which actuated him in the selection of his material and in his interpretation thereof.

[3] New York City Board of Education, Report on *History Textbooks used in the Public Schools of the City of New York* (New York, 1922).

312

SPECIFIC AIMS

1. To acquaint the pupils with the basic facts and movements, political, industrial, and social, of American history.

2. To emphasize the principles and motives that were of greatest influence in the formation and development of our government.

3. To establish ideals of patriotic and civic duty.

4. To awaken in the pupil a desire to emulate all praiseworthy endeavor.

5. To emphasize the importance of weighing permissible evidence in forming judgments.

6. To present the ethical and moral principles exemplified in the lives of patriotic leaders.

7. To inspire in the pupil an appreciation of the hardships endured and the sacrifices made in establishing and defending American ideals.

8. To develop in the pupil a love for American institutions and the determination to maintain and defend them.

9. To bring the light of reason and experience to bear on radical or alien theories of economic and political systems.

10. To enable the pupil to interpret the present in terms of the past and to view intelligently the functions and the value of existing institutions.

DISCUSSION OF GENERAL PRINCIPLES AND SPECIAL AIMS

In order to give a clearer and more definite idea of the scope and intent of the general principles and special aims formulated by the Committee we submit herewith a discussion of said general principles and special aims.

A. *The Primary Problem in Writing a History Textbook Is Propriety Of Selection of Material*

. . . As the pages of a textbook are limited, no material should be used unless it is essential and of the highest educational value.

The child's time must not be taken up with facts which do not measure up to this standard.

B. *The Textbook Writer Is Not A Historian*

Strictly speaking the textbook writer is not a historian. The historian writes for the open market. He has the privilege of selecting and organizing his material in accordance with his own views. He may be an impartial writer or he may be a partisan. The textbook writer has not this freedom. He is subject to the limitations imposed upon the teacher. . . .

It is for the teacher to determine what material is needed. It is for the textbook writer to supply it. Unfortunately, an examination of the prefaces in various textbooks shows that some textbook writers do not take this view. . . .

We believe that a textbook writer who seeks to influence our international relations is a propagandist. Under our constitution it is for the federal government, in the first instance, to determine what our foreign relations shall be. The children in attendance in our public schools must not be used directly or indirectly to influence official action in such matters.

C. *The Burden Of Proof Rests Upon Him Who Makes A Derogatory Statement*

As a rule derogatory statements have little or no educational value. . . . Only when a man has been guilty of an act of great moral turpitude is a discussion of his act likely to lead to beneficial consequences. Nero's cruelty and Arnold's treason are illustrations. . . .

D. *Probable Reason For The Presence Of Much Of The Material To Which Objections Have Been Made*

Probably the factor principally responsible for the presence of objectionable material in the textbooks under investigation is that the writers have not divided their material into topic-units, and have not formulated aims, sufficiently extensive in scope to permit marshalling the facts in due subordination. . . .

E. *Emasculated Accounts Of Wars In Order To Encourage Peace*

Objection has been made to the treatment in some of the textbooks of the wars in which we have been engaged. The objections are to the effect that the accounts are emasculated. In reply it is strenuously urged that " the surest way to end war, is to sing the praises of peace and to say little of war and the heroes of war." . . .

War in defense of freedom or in vindication of righteousness, justice and equity should be vividly portrayed, and the praises of its heroes should be joyously sung. Thus only can we raise a citizenry willing to die for the country.

F. *Our Heroes*

Objection has been made that some of the textbooks contain statements in derogation of our national heroes. In reply it has been urged that the statements are true, and that attention should be called to the weaknesses of our heroes or we will esteem them too highly.

Truth is no defense to the charge of impropriety. . . .

The assurance that posterity will hold our heroes in grateful remembrance is one of the most powerful incentives to heroic achievement. To preserve unsullied the name and fame of those who have battled that we might enjoy the blessings of liberty, is a solemn and sacred obligation. . . .

G. *Propaganda*

It has been charged that some textbooks contain propaganda. In reply some have alleged that all who make the charge are persons opposed to friendly relations with Great Britain. The reply cannot be sustained, as appears from the following editorial in " *The American Legion Weekly* " of October 7, 1921:

" The country has known for some time that school textbooks on American history are being revised on the theory that the elimination or correction of obvious untruths or distorted truths concerning England's relations with this country, notably during the Revolutionary War, would promote the cause of international friendship. . . . If the purpose of some of the authors was not to give the lasting impression to the school children of this country that the Revolutionary War was an unjustifiable war, that is likely to be the effect of their work. . . . It will be regretted if what appeared to be a meritorious undertaking has been exploited with propaganda which every fair-minded American must resent." . . .

H. *Controversial Topics*

As far as possible, the writer of a textbook should avoid controversial topics. The public schools are maintained by the public funds. The taxpayers are of various creeds and political beliefs. Their feelings must be respected. . . .

I. *Patriotism*

It is objected that some of the textbooks make no attempt to inculcate patriotism by bringing to the attention of pupils the best in the lives, words, and deeds of our patriots; and that in some of the books, too much attention is given to the utterances and achievements of the heroes of other countries.

In reply, it is urged that true patriotism does not require that we magnify our country at the expense of others; that a " narrow-visioned " patriotism means that the Englishman will become more English, the German, more German; and the American, more American. . . . Patriotism is not " egotism." To make certain that the pupils in the elementary grades are thoroughly familiar with our own heroes before we introduce them to the heroes of other lands is neither " narrow-visioned " nor evidence of " international hatred." . . .

D. REPORT OF AND REVIEW ON CERTAIN TEXT BOOKS IN HISTORY USED IN THE SCHOOLS, AND ORDER RELATING THERETO [City of Boston] [4]

The following was presented:

On October 23, [1922] the City Council unanimously passed an order requesting the School Committee to give a hearing for the consideration of certain objections made to the use in the public schools of this city of " School History of the United States," revised 1920, by Albert Bushnell Hart; Burke's " Speech on Conciliation," edited by C. H. Ward 1919; and " American History," by D. S. Muzzey. The preface to the Ward edition of Burke's " Speech on Conciliation " was found to be in certain respects objectionable, and the book therefore has been dropped from the list.

In compliance with this request the School Committee appointed for a hearing the late afternoon of Wednesday, November 15, and in response to a further request that the hearing be in the evening rather than in the afternoon in order to meet the convenience of the members of the City Council, the hour was changed to 8 o'clock P.M. on that day. The City Council was represented at the hearing by one of its members.

The School Committee believes that extreme care is taken to avoid the inclusion upon the so-called Authorized List of any unfit or improper books for use in the public schools, and whenever in the past it has appeared that any books to which reasonable objections may be made have been so included prompt steps have been taken to discontinue the use of such books. This course will be followed in the future as carefully as in the past.

The School Committee welcomes all honest and fair-minded criticism of any of its acts, and particularly when such criticism

[4] City of Boston, *Proceedings of School Committee*, December 18, 1922.

is helpful and constructive. It does not welcome criticism that seeks merely to tear down or destroy and does not substitute for the object of attack something that is better and more useful. .

The members of the Committee have personally examined the books under discussion, with considerable care, both before and after the hearing. They feel, therefore, that they are reasonably well acquainted with the contents of the books and with the objections that have been urged against them. They have also had prepared a careful and dispassionate review under the direction of the Board of Superintendents of all or substantially all of the criticisms made against these books and brought to their attention, and a refutation of these criticisms which, in the opinion of the Committee, justice to the authors demands. The review is hereto appended.

Neither this report, nor the accompanying review should be construed as indicating that the members of the Committee are in entire sympathy and agreement with all the statements which the books contain, nor that proper and balanced emphasis has been placed in all instances upon certain events in our national history. Opinions on this point must necessarily and widely differ and cannot be brought into absolute reconcilement, but such differences certainly are not sufficient to warrant the condemnation of the books nor the impeachment of the sincerity and good faith of the authors.

In the opinion of the Committee, also, there are in the books examples of what might be called " loose writing," one single instance of which must suffice.

Professor Hart says " the only way to find out what races composed the white population (in 1790) is to examine the family names and they show that about five-sixths were descended from English ancestors; one-twelfth were Scotch, Scotch-Irish, and Irish; . . . ; [sic] about one-twentieth were Germans, and about one-fiftieth were Dutch."

We think this is not a correct historical statement to make. True, reliable statistics are, of course, hard to obtain, but it is surely not correct to say that the only way to find what races composed the white population at that time is to examine the family names. For instance, the names of two hundred members of the Charitable Irish Society of this city, a society formed in 1737, have been called to our attention, who were members of that society prior to 1790 and most of them prior to 1770, and who would not, if Professor Hart's standard obtained of judging from names alone, very likely be considered by him as Irish.

In the course of the hearing irrelevant and extraneous matters were brought to the attention of the School Committee to which it listened with scant patience. The question at issue was the fitness or the unfitness of two books for use in the public schools. In the course of the hearing, what the School Committee regards as unwarranted and ill-founded attacks were made upon the authors of these books. The life of Professor Hart, the service of his two sons in the World War, and his ancestry forbid any suspicion of his loyalty and patriotism. The life of Professor Muzzey and his ancestry, with its record of honorable service in the Civil War, in the War of 1812, and at Lexington, equally forbid any belief that he would be subservient to foreign influence. Any hint or suggestion that either of these gentlemen was influenced to promote British propaganda especially by pecuniary recompense is unthinkable. Nor is their reputation and standing as reliable historians to be impugned by such criticism as is now levelled against them.

The real and only question at issue is whether their histories contain material to which reasonable and proper objection may be made. It goes without saying that no historian has ever succeeded in writing a book which met satisfactorily every point of view, nor does any history place an equal amount of emphasis upon all the topics which it discusses. One history may deal mainly with the social and economic growth of a nation; another with its military or naval exploits; another may dwell at length upon the personal achievements of its great figures; another upon its political development. It is clearly impossible that one brief volume should give adequate treatment to all the steps incident to the origin and growth of a great nation. Therefore, the list authorized for use in the public schools contains not merely a single book, but many histories all differing in their treatment of the subject, and these books are, of course, largely supplemented by the personal instruction and guidance of the teacher.

If the books in question contain so much that is objectionable and unpatriotic, it is singular that some of our great body of intelligent and patriotic teachers have failed to discover these grave defects, and that the books have had so little apparent effect upon the loyalty of the pupils who have had access to them.

The School Committee also deplores the course pursued by the critics of these books in tearing from their context detached sentences and omitting explanations and summaries which are essential to a grasp of the authors' real meaning. The critic who pursues such a course may easily find opportunity for criticism of any book that ever has been written on the subject of history, and indeed on many other subjects as well.

In the course of the hearing certain passages in these books were attacked on the ground that they gave an unfavorable impression concerning the character and actions of a few of the great party leaders of the time; but it must not be forgotten that in such instances the authors have merely noted the opinions of opposing party leaders.

Unquestionably, the pupils in our schools are perfectly well aware of the severe, pointed and frequently virulent criticism that is constantly being directed against men now in public life. Acquainted with this criticism, is it reasonable to expect them to believe that the leaders of our country in past years were really super-men or demi-gods, and not equally subject to the weaknesses and frailties that surround human life today? Even the revered Abraham Lincoln was the target, in his time, of abuse and vilification. Nor did Washington himself escape the calumnies of some of his contemporaries.

As to the omission of what the critics regard as adequate mention of former national heroes, such as Nathan Hale, Anthony Wayne, Putnam, Sumter, Pickens, Marion, Stark, Sullivan, Knox,

Commodore Barry, Sergt. Jasper, Light Horse Harry Lee, Molly Pitcher and Betsy Ross: It should not be forgotten that the exploits of these patriots, important, brilliant and picturesque as they were have been repeatedly emphasized in the course in history during the earlier years of the pupils' school life while these two books are adapted to use of older pupils.

The School Committee would gladly express its opinion item by item on the various specific criticisms that have been made against these books were it not for the fact that to do so would unduly lengthen this report. They are covered in detail in the accompanying review.[5]

The main and controlling question at present issue is this: Does either of these books contain matter which is unpatriotic, disloyal or calculated to falsely impress the minds of the pupils to whom they are made accessible? If they do, their further use in the schools should not be permitted. If they do not, there is not good and sufficient reason to justify their exclusion and the consequent reflection upon the sincerity and good faith of their authors.

It should not be forgotten moreover that these books are in constant process of revision and correction as errors and misstatements are discovered, and this is true probably of the works of all historians of standing and repute.

It may be pointed out also that those who advance these criticisms do not suggest the titles of other books which they would regard as unobjectionable. On this point they are absolutely silent.

The School Committee, therefore, having given due consideration to the matter, is of the opinion that the criticisms against these two books are not sufficient to justify their exclusion from the Authorized List, and directs that the City Council be so informed.

DAVID D. SCANNELL.
FRANCES G. CURTIS.

[5] The review is not included in this Appendix.

The undersigned, while in agreement with the foregoing report, is, nevertheless, of the opinion that the Board of Superintendents should see that in any future revision of these two books certain statements therein contained, which this report and the accompanying review do not approve, are omitted or modified by the authors or publishers.

RICHARD J. LANE.

E. REPORT OF THE PROCEEDINGS OF THE CONVEN-
TION OF THE AMERICAN FEDERATION OF
LABOR, CINCINNATI, JUNE, 1922. EIGHTH DAY
PROCEEDINGS [6]

*" Investigation of Text Books " under the Committee on
Education and the Executive Council*

The committee is exceedingly glad to report the completion of
the survey of text books and social studies under the direction
of the permanent Committee on Education and the Executive
Council by O. S. Beyer, Jr. This significant piece of work is now
in the hands of that committee. Its scope is indicated by the
title, " Social Studies in the Public Schools."

The report is divided into six sections and a supplement, as
follows:

PART I — *Influences at Work in Public Education:*
1. The Threat to Public Education.
2. Who is Responsible?
3. Safeguards and Remedies.

PART II — *Nature and Extent of Instruction in Social Studies:*
1. Importance of the Social Studies.
2. Content of the Course.
3. Extent to Which They are Being Taught.

PART III — *Survey of Social Science Text Books:*
1. The Importance of the Text Books.
2. Growth of the Social Studies.
3. Nature of the Tests Applied to the Text Books.
4. Summary of the Findings.
5. Chief Criticisms of Text Books.

[6] American Federation of Labor, *Report of the Proceedings of the Convention of the American Federation of Labor at Cincinnati, June 22, 1922,
Eighth Day Proceedings* (Washington, D. C., 1922).

6. Text Books in Use.
7. The Selection of Text Books.
8. Subjects of Investigation Outside of Classroom.
9. Topics Discussed in Current Events.
10. The Inclusion of the Labor Movement in Courses of Study.

PART IV — *Conclusions.*

PART V — *Recommendations:*
1. With Regard to This Report.
2. With Regard to Future Action.

PART VI — *Appendices:*
A. The Number of Schools Using Each Specified Text in Civics.
B. The Number of Schools Using Each Specified Text in Economics.
C. The Number of Schools Using Each Specified Text in Sociology.
D. Observation, Investigation, etc., Carried on Outside the School for Economics Course by Number of Schools.
E. Observations, Investigations, etc., Carried on Outside of School for Civics Course by Number of Schools.
F. Typical Subjects Discussed in Current Events by Number of Schools.

Supplementing — Evaluating of Specific Text Books in History, Civics, Economics and Sociology:
1. Type of Book.
2. General Consideration.
3. Specific Considerations.
4. Detail Evaluation of Text Books.
   a. Civics.
   b. History.
   c. Economics.
   d. Sociology.

Part I of the report reveals that a serious threat is menacing our public education system, which, however, is not working itself out so much against the means of education, such as the courses of study and the text books used, as against the human part of our educational system, namely, the great body of teachers. Responsibility for this threat devolves mainly upon a group of extra-educational associations, such as the National Association of Manufacturers, National Industrial Conference Board, " America First " Publicity Association, and others. Their influence, however, is being partially counteracted by public-spirited, progressive educational organizations. Safeguards and remedies are at the disposal of the organized labor movement individually and in coöperation with the progressive educational associations to reform the situation. This section concludes with a description of the many organizations active in the field of public education endeavoring to exert an influence upon it.

Part II brings out the true significance of the social studies in relation to the history, achievements, aims and ideals of the labor movement. It emphasizes, based upon scientific data, the place of the labor movement in the social sciences. Its great significance in modern society is thus clearly established. The opinions and judgments of our most eminent progressive educators are cited in support of these findings, having been secured by special inquiry. This section also reveals that the extent to which these studies which properly deal with the labor movement are being taught is entirely inadequate. Progress, however, has been made in recent years in the extension of the social sciences in our public schools. Nevertheless, very much still must be done. In fact, the whole public educational system, if the ideals of humanity as expressed by the labor movement, are to receive adequate consideration in public education, will require reconstruction around the social studies.

Part III deals with the importance of the text book in teaching the social studies. It describes the basis upon which the tests were formulated by means of which the text books covered in this report were evaluated. The summary of these evaluations are [sic] then presented, together with a résumé of the chief criticisms of the texts scrutinized. In all, 123 text books — 47 histories, 47 civics, 25 economics, and 4 sociologies — were evaluated. The tests bring out that one-half of the books (55 per cent) are of the newer type, dealing with the broader aspects of government and the social and industrial life of the people, rather than with forms of organization, military events and abstract theories. Still, a larger proportion (60 per cent) recognized to a greater or less degree the power for growth in our institutions; are dynamic rather than static in their methods of treatment. In dealing with questions of particular interest to labor there is a great divergence in concept as well as in method of treatment. The older formal texts either omit these subjects entirely or treat them so unsatisfactorily that for all practical purposes they might just as well be omitted. Some of the more modern ones deal with them briefly and perfunctorily, but on the whole the newer type of text does attempt to give the labor movement in the problem of industry adequate and just consideration. Failure to do so is apparently due to ignorance of the author or to a hesitancy to deal with this difficult subject, rather than to a deliberate attempt to keep the facts of industry out of the schools. Although numerous cases of error, misleading statements, misplaced emphasis, discrimination against unions, and use of obsolete material, may be pointed out. The survey finds no evidence that text books are being used for propaganda purposes. The publishers, the report considers, are undoubtedly deserving of a great deal of credit for keeping schoolbooks free from propaganda, and to this spirit of fair-play and desire for truth it considers that the organized labor movement may look for help in the correction of erroneous, misleading or unfair statements which mar the pages of otherwise excellent texts.

Concerning the text books in use, the report points out that not only is an increasing supply of the better books becoming available, but there is also a steadily increasing demand for them. The investigation made also reveals the fact that, especially in civics and history, the modern or more approved text is being used to a larger extent than the less satisfactory. Subjects discussed or investigated in supplementary courses of study such as Current Events, the report indicates, pay a great deal of attention to problems and matters of special interest to labor. . . .

F. WISCONSIN LAW OF 1923 AFFECTING HISTORY TEXTBOOKS [7]

AN ACT To create section 40.36 of the statutes, relating to textbooks used in the public schools.

The people of the state of Wisconsin, represented in senate and assembly, do enact as follows:

SECTION 1. A new section is added to the statutes to be numbered and to read: 40.36 (1) No history or other textbook shall be adopted for use or be used in any district school, city school, vocational school or high school which falsifies the facts regarding the war of independence, or the war of 1812 or which defames our nation's founders or misrepresents the ideals and causes for which they struggled and sacrificed, or which contains propaganda favorable to any foreign government.

(2) Upon complaint of any five citizens filed with the state superintendent of public instruction that any history or other textbook which is being used in any district school, city school, vocational school or high school contains any matter prohibited by subsection (1) of this section, the state superintendent shall fix a time for a public hearing upon such complaint, which shall be not more than thirty days from the date of filing said complaint, and shall be conducted either by the state superintendent or the assistant state superintendent, or by one of the state inspectors of schools, to be designated by the state superintendent, and which hearing shall be held at the county seat of the county where the complainants reside. Notice of such hearing shall be given at least ten days prior to the date thereof through the public press and by registered mail to the complainants, the school board interested and to the publishers of such textbook.

[7] *Laws* of Wisconsin, 1923, chapter 21

(3) Within ten days after such hearing the state superintendent shall make a finding upon such complaint. If he finds that any textbook contains matter prohibited in subsection (1) of this section, he shall make note of such finding in the list of textbooks which he is required by paragraph (b) of subsection (1) of section 40.35 annually to publish and to transmit to all county and city superintendents. No such textbook shall thereafter be placed on the list of textbooks which may be adopted, sold or exchanged in this state.

(4) Every school board, board of education, board of vocational education, or county board of education which has control over the textbooks used in any district school, city school, vocational school, or high school, shall cause any textbook which the state superintendent has found contains matter prohibited in subsection (1) of this section to be withdrawn from use in such school prior to the opening of the school year following the publication of such finding of the state superintendent. No state aid under the provisions of sections 20.25, 20.26, 20.27, 20.28, 20.29, 20.33 and 20.335 of the statutes shall be paid for the support of any district school, city school, vocational school or high school during any year in which any such textbook is used in such school after the finding of the state superintendent.

SECTION 2. This act shall take effect upon passage and publication.

G. THE AMERICAN LEGION SCHOOL HISTORY OF THE UNITED STATES IS TO FOLLOW THESE LINES:[8]

1. It is meant for a textbook to teach history, not literature nor the meaning of words. Hence, it must be simple, easily read in the upper grades of Grammar Schools, that is, by boys and girls from twelve to fifteen. It must fit their intelligence. AVOID INFLATED WORDS: EXPLAIN UNKNOWN IDEAS.

2. It must inspire the children with patriotism, must preach on every page a vivid love of America. It must BELIEVE in our land, and make others believe in it. It must believe in democracy. SPEAK WARMLY; HAVE ENTHUSIASM.

3. It must build up character. It must emphasize that our ancestors accomplished great deeds, and thus strengthen the children to attempt brave deeds themselves. It must tell of noble things and praise them. Hence it should preserve the old patriotic legends, though pointing out where these are legends rather than facts. PRESERVE THE LEGENDS; PRAISE NOBLE DEEDS.

4. It must speak in an earnest spiritual strain, believing in God; and not being afraid to mention Him, though of course never in a sectarian way. It must not rouse religious or racial hatred or distrust. It must create a confidence in righteousness and decency. ENCOURAGE FAITH; BUILD HIGH SELF-RESPECT.

5. It must speak the truth, so that no child learns afterward to distrust it. But in telling the truth it must be careful to tell truth optimistically. It will mention the blunders of the past so the child learns to be careful; but it must dwell on failure only for its value as a moral lesson, must speak chiefly of success. EMPHASIZE EFFORT AND SUCCESS, NOT FAILURE.

6. It must be non-partisan. It must give each State and Section full space and value for the achievements of each, not cen-

[8] Horne, Charles F., Editorial Director, THE AMERICAN LEGION, *The American Legion School History* (30 Church Street, New York, 1923).

tralize on any one section. It must give each political party praise for what the party has accomplished, but praise none unduly by belittling others. CARRY NO PROPAGANDA.

7. It must INTEREST the children. Too little emphasis has perhaps been laid on this point. A few facts made living will last with the child; a mass of unattractive detail is soon forgotten. Keep lists of things for an appendix. DEAL WITH PEOPLE RATHER THAN THINGS.

8. As it is to be studied by as many girls as boys, it must interest girl students. It must bring out the womanly side, must mention women, their inspiration to their men, their deeds of devotion as well as their material accomplishments. ENLARGE THE WOMAN PART.

9. As the students have already heard of Columbus, Washington, etc., the text must allow for this. It must avoid repeating obvious things; but it must gather all the child's odds and ends of historical knowledge into one complete view, a sustained narrative. MAKE A COMPLETE PICTURE.

10. In brief, the book is intended to encourage patriotism, strengthen character, stimulate thought and impress the worth of TRUTH.

Arrangement and Make-Up

The book will be so arranged that it can be furnished in two volumes (dividing at the year 1789) to fit the seventh and eighth years of school work as usually organized.

The paragraph headings are to be in themselves a brief outline of the story; and no other material, such as notes, etc., shall be allowed to break the narrative flow.

Mechanical make-up is to follow the established text book standards as to size, spacing, typography, color and paper to prevent eye-strain. The binding is to be attractive and durable; and the illustrations will be a special feature.[9]

9 See the Principles of the American Legion as announced in 1925 by the Director of Americanism. These follow on the next page. The attitude of the Legion toward history textbooks as given by Mr. Cross, the Director, is included.

*Statement of Principles of the American Legion for the Writing
of their American History Textbook, as well as their Attitude toward present-day Textbooks* [10]

1. To acquaint the pupils with the basic facts and movements, political, industrial and social, of American History.

2. To emphasize the principles and motives that were of greatest influence in the formation and development of our government.

3. To establish ideals of patriotic and civic duty.

4. To awaken in the pupil a desire to emulate all praiseworthy endeavor.

5. To emphasize the importance of weighing permissible evidence in forming judgments.

6. To present the ethical and moral principles exemplified in the lives of patriotic leaders.

7. To inspire in the pupil an appreciation of the hardships endured and sacrifices made in establishing and defending American ideals.

8. To develop in the pupil a love for American institutions and the determination to maintain and defend them.

9. To bring the light of reason and experience to bear on radical or alien theories of economic and political systems.

10. To enable the pupil to interpret the present in terms of the past and to view intelligently the functions and the value of existing institutions.

In brief, the attitude of The American Legion toward current history texts is set forth by the following report on history investigation:

The committee on history investigation, at the time this report was written, had about half completed their investigation.

Much of the agitation and complaint regarding school textbooks in history has apparently come from prejudiced sources —

[10] Received from Frank C. Cross, National Director Americanism Commission, American Legion, December, 1925.

from men and institutions that are themselves propagandists and who use this method of checking their own un-American sentiments.

The formal complaints published after " investigation " have been by men apparently incompetent to sit in judgment on historical data. For example, the Commissioner of Accounts of New York City. We believe that there are a sufficient number of thoroughly competent educational experts who can pass on such matters without calling in a Commissioner of Accounts.

We do not believe that such men as Muzzey of Columbia University, West of the University of Michigan [sic], Hart of Harvard, McLaughlin of Chicago University, Van Tyne of the University of Michigan, Guitteau, Director of Schools, Toledo, are unpatriotic or that their books were written as the result of organized propaganda.

We believe, however, that the authors have laid themselves open to just criticism because of the fact that they have sometimes made statements from the point of view of a critic or investigator rather than from that of a teacher. Their work is thus perhaps legitimate for the advanced student and investigator but not in our opinion for the public school pupil.

We believe also that some of these authors are at fault in placing before immature pupils the blunders, foibles and frailties of prominent heroes and patriots of our Nation. History should be taught with a view to inspiring our boys and girls with love of country and admiration for noble ideals. If a pupil is led to believe that a great National hero was guilty of weakness and crime he is likely to excuse such failings in himself and others. School texts should not belittle men who have given their lives for their country even if it should be discovered by experts that they have been subject to ordinary human frailties.

We believe too that some of the writers have been guilty of introducing matters of controversial nature without giving adequate space (which in the nature of the case they could not do) for presentation of the essential facts on both sides. In some instances the author's own personal views in such subjects seem

to be exploited. An example is the treatment of the tariff in some
of the text books.

Material is sometimes presented to give critical results of recent
historical research, rather than to influence good citizenship. The
list of fundamental principles of The American Legion History
given above states our ideas of the matter which should be presented and the method of its presentation.

With regard to subjects that may be internationally controversial, such as the American Revolution, it should be borne in
mind that a good majority of the colonists supported the Revolution and had firm faith in the rectitude of their conduct and that
almost all of our people have since believed that they were right,
and we do not believe that it is in the interest of good citizenship
to have that faith called in question.

We believe that much of the criticism against so-called pro-
Anglican statements is prompted by pro-German sentiments. For
example the objection to referring to England as the mother
country. The Colonists themselves used this term. The objection
seems to be purely captious and in a line with a recent agitation
to create another language than the English as the language of
America.

While we do not believe in glorifying war we believe that some
of our great National victories and our National heroes should
be written up in a more inspirational manner than is done in some
histories. We are confident that this will be accomplished in The
American Legion History now being written.[11]

[11] According to a statement in the *Boston Herald*, May 7, 1926, the
Legion withdrew its support, June, 1925, due to opposition within its membership, when it abrogated its contract with the United States History
Publishing Company. As a result, they were "to receive no financial benefit from the sale of the history; permission, however, was granted to the
company to carry on its title page the fact that the book was prepared at
the suggestion of the American Legion." A letter to the author, May 13,
1926, from the Assistant National Director, Americanism Commission, however, declares: "The Legion has not retracted in its position relative to this
history. . . . The only change made is that the National Executive Committee annulled the arrangement whereby the Legion was to receive a per-
centage from the sale of these books. The United States History Publishing
Company is a private concern."

H. AMERICAN BAR ASSOCIATION, *Report* (1924).

Committee on American Citizenship, " Our Citizenship Creed." [12]

1. I am living under a government — and am myself a part of such government — wherein at least an elementary knowledge of the nature and principles of this Government must be generally diffused among the great mass of its citizens. I therefore believe it to be my duty to inform myself on American history, the foundations of our Government as embodied in the United States Constitution, and the application of the principles therein contained to present-day problems.

2. Since ours is a government of, for, and by the people, it is by the very same token a government of and by public opinion. It is, therefore, my duty, as a good American citizen, to help form public opinion in the community in which I live in order that all citizens may hold intelligent, just, and humane views on governmental questions and endeavor to have such views embodied in our laws.

3. Since popular government is shaped in the first instance by the exercise of suffrage, it is one of my primary duties as a good American citizen to cast my ballot in all local, state and national elections and to urge my fellow-citizens to do the same.

4. Since ours is " a government of laws and not of men," and since an orderly government can exist only through laws justly administered and impartially enforced, I declare it to be my duty as a good citizen to serve as a juror whenever summoned, and to use my influence in every proper way to the end that lawyers, judges and jurors so conduct the administration of justice as to entitle the law and the courts to popular approval and support.

[12] *Report of the Forty-Seventh Annual Meeting of the American Bar Association* . . . 1924, p. 271.

5. I believe that we Americans have the best government that has ever been created — the freest and the most just for all the people — and that it is my duty to uphold and defend this Government at all times. I believe that just as the " Minute Man of the Revolution " was ready upon a moment's notice to defend his rights against foreign usurpation, it is my duty as a patriotic American to be a " Minute Man of the Constitution," ready at all times to defend the long-established and cherished institutions of our Government against attacks, either from within or without, and to do my part in preserving the blessings of liberty for which my revolutionary forefathers fought and died.

6. I believe that as a good American citizen I must maintain continuously a civic consciousness and conscience; that my country needs my active service in times of peace no less than in war; that patriotism must be a constituent part of my religion; that no prouder boast can emanate from my lips than truly to declare, " I am an American citizen," and that as an American citizen the Constitution of the United States ought to be as actual a part of my life and of my religion as the Sermon on the Mount.

BIBLIOGRAPHY

BIBLIOGRAPHY

(Statutes Omitted)

BOOKS

Atwood, Harry F., *Back to the Republic.* Laird and Lee, Inc., Chicago, 1918.

Atwood, Harry F., *Safeguarding American Ideals.* Laird and Lee, Chicago, 1921.

Jefferson, Thomas, *The Writings of Thomas Jefferson.* Paul Leicester Ford, ed. 3 v. G. P. Putnam's Sons, New York, 1894.

Journal of the Twenty-Second Annual Session of the National Encampment, Grand Army of the Republic . . . 1888. Minneapolis, 1888.

Journal of the Twenty-Sixth National Encampment, Grand Army of the Republic . . . 1892. Albany, New York, 1892.

Journal of the Twenty-Eighth National Encampment, Grand Army of the Republic . . . 1894. [N. P.]

Journal Twenty-Ninth Encampment, Grand Army of the Republic . . . 1895. [N. P.]

Journal of the Thirty-First National Encampment of the Grand Army of the Republic . . . 1897. Lincoln, Nebraska, 1897.

Journal of the Thirty-Second National Encampment of the Grand Army of the Republic . . . 1898. Philadelphia, 1898.

Journal of the Thirty-Third National Encampment of the Grand Army of the Republic . . . 1899. Philadelphia, 1899.

Journal of the Thirty-Fourth National Encampment of the Grand Army of the Republic . . . 1900. Philadelphia, 1900.

Journal of the Thirty-Fifth National Encampment of the Grand Army of the Republic . . . 1901. St. Louis, 1901.

Journal of the Thirty-Sixth National Encampment of the Grand Army of the Republic . . . 1902. Minneapolis, 1903.

Journal of the 37th National Encampment of the Grand Army of the Republic . . . 1903. Philadelphia, 1903.

Journal of the Thirty-Eighth National Encampment of the Grand Army of the Republic . . . 1904. Chicago, 1904.

Journal of the Thirty-Ninth National Encampment (Grand Army of the Republic) . . . 1905. Boston, 1905.

Journal of the Fortieth National Encampment of the Grand Army of the Republic . . . 1906. Philadelphia, 1906.

Journal of the Forty-First National Encampment of the Grand Army of the Republic . . . 1907. Zanesville, Ohio, 1907.

Journal of the Forty-Third National Encampment of the Grand Army of the Republic . . . 1909. [N. P.]

Journal of the Forty-Fourth National Encampment of the Grand Army of the Republic . . . 1910. [N. P.]

Journal of the Eighteenth Annual Encampment of the Grand Army of the Republic, Department of Kansas, 1899. Topeka, Kansas, 1899.

Proceedings of the Convention for Organization and Adoption of the Constitution of the United Confederate Veterans . . . 1889. New Orleans, 1891.

Minutes of the United Confederate Veterans, Vol. I (1889–1897). New Orleans.

Minutes of the Fourth Annual Meeting and Reunion of the United Confederate Veterans . . . 1894. [N. P.]

Report of the United Confederate Veterans Historical Committee . . . 1894. New Orleans.

Minutes of the Fifth Annual Meeting and Reunion of the United Confederate Veterans . . . 1895. [N. P.]

Minutes of the Sixth Annual Meeting and Reunion of the United Confederate Veterans . . . 1896. New Orleans, 1897.

Minutes of the Seventh Annual Meeting and Reunion of the United Confederate Veterans . . . 1897. New Orleans, 1898.

Minutes of the Eighth Annual Meeting and Reunion of the United Confederate Veterans . . . 1898. New Orleans, 1899.

Minutes of the Ninth Annual Meeting and Reunion of the United Confederate Veterans . . . 1899. New Orleans, 1900.

Minutes of the Eleventh Annual Meeting and Reunion of the United Confederate Veterans . . . 1901. New Orleans.

Minutes of the Twelfth Annual Meeting and Reunion of the United Confederate Veterans . . . 1902. New Orleans.

Minutes of the Thirteenth Annual Meeting and Reunion of the United Confederate Veterans . . . 1903. New Orleans.

Minutes of the Fourteenth Annual Meeting and Reunion of the United Confederate Veterans . . . 1904. [N. P.]

Minutes of the Eighteenth Annual Meeting and Reunion of the United Confederate Veterans . . . 1908. New Orleans.

Minutes of the Nineteenth Annual Meeting and Reunion of the United Confederate Veterans . . . 1909. New Orleans.

Minutes of the Twentieth Annual Meeting and Reunion of the United Confederate Veterans . . . 1910. New Orleans.

Report of the United Confederate Veterans Historical Committee . . . *Twenty-First Annual Reunion* . . . 1911. *New* Orleans.

Minutes of the Thirty-Second Annual Meeting and Reunion of the United Confederate Veterans . . . 1921. New Orleans, 1921.

MacDonald, William, *Documentary Source Book of American History, 1606–1913*. The Macmillan Company, New York, 1916.

Mann, Horace, *Annual Reports on Education.* Horace B. Fuller, Boston, 1868.

Nelles, Walter, ed., *Espionage Act Cases with Certain Others on Related Points.* National Civil Liberties Bureau, New York, 1918.

Revolutionary Radicalism Its History, Purpose and Tactics with An Exposition and Discussion of the Steps Being Taken and Required To Curb It, Being the Report of the Joint Legislative Committee Investigating Seditious Activities. Filed April 24, 1920, in the Senate of the State of New York. 4 v. J. B. Lyon Company, Albany, 1920.

Report of the Forty-Fifth Annual Meeting of the American Bar Association Held at San Francisco, California, August 9, 10 and 11, 1922. The Lord Baltimore Press, Baltimore, 1922.

Report of the Forty-Sixth Annual Meeting of the American Bar Association Held at Minneapolis, Minnesota, August 29, 30 and 31, 1923. The Lord Baltimore Press, Baltimore, 1923.

Report of the Forty-Seventh Annual Meeting of the American Bar Association Held at Philadelphia, Pennsylvania, July 8, 9 and 10, 1924. The Lord Baltimore Press, Baltimore, 1924.

Russell, William Howard, *My Diary North and South.* T. O. H. P. Burnham, Boston, 1863.

Trachtenberg, Alexander, ed., *The American Labor Year Book 1919–1920.* The Rand School of Social Science, New York, 1920.

Wister, Owen, *A Straight Deal or the Ancient Grudge.* The Macmillan Company, New York, 1920.

Textbooks

A Syllabus of the World War for Use in the High Schools of the City of New York. Adopted by the Board of Superintendents. Department of Education, The City of New York, 1918.

Ashley, Roscoe Lewis, *Modern European Civilization.* The Macmillan Company, New York, 1920.

Barnes, Everett, *American History for Grammar Grades.* D. C. Heath and Company, New York, 1920.

Berry, Margaret K., and Howe, Samuel B., *Actual Democracy.* Prentice-Hall, Inc., New York, 1923.

Bullock, Charles J., *Elements of Economics.* Silver, Burdett and Company, Boston, 1913.

Burch, Henry Reed, *American Economic Life.* The Macmillan Company, New York, 1921.

Chambers, Henry Edward, *A School History of the United States.* American Book Company, New York, 1898.

Davidson, William M., *A History of the United States.* Scott, Foresman and Company, Chicago, 1903.

Estill, Harry F., *The Beginner's History of Our Country*. Southern Publishing Company, Dallas, Texas, 1919.

Evans, Lawton B., *The Essential Facts of American History*. Benjamin H. Sanborn and Company, Chicago, 1920.

The Franciscan Sisters of the Perpetual Adoration, *A History of the United States for Catholic Schools*. Scott, Foresman and Company, Chicago, 1914.

Goodrich, Samuel Griswold, *The First Book of History for Children and Youth*. Jenks, Palmer and Company, Boston, 1848.

Greg, Percy, *History of the United States from the Foundation of Virginia to the Reconstruction of the Union*. 2 v. West, Johnson and Company, Richmond, 1892.

Guitteau, William B., *Our United States*. Silver, Burdett and Company, Boston, 1919, 1923.

Hart, Albert Bushnell, *A School History of the United States*. American Book Company, New York, 1920.

Hassard, John R. G., *A History of the United States of America*. Catholic Publication Society of America, New York, 1878.

Hayes, Carlton J. H., and Moon, Thomas Parker, *Modern History*. The Macmillan Company, New York, 1923.

Hazen, Charles Downer, *Modern Europe*. Henry Holt and Company, New York, 1923.

Horne, Charles F., *The Story of Our American People*. 2 v. United States History Publishing Company, New York, 1925.

Horton, Rushmore G., *A Youth's History of the Great Civil War in the United States*. Van Evrie, Horton and Company, New York, 1866.

Hughes, R. O., *Text-Book in Citizenship*. Allyn and Bacon, Boston, 1923.

James, James Alton, and Sanford, Albert Hart, *American History*. Charles Scribner's Sons, New York, 1915.

Lee, Susan Pendleton, *New School History of the United States*. B. F. Johnson Publishing Company, Richmond, Virginia, 1899.

Long, William J., *America*. Ginn and Company, Boston, 1923.

McCarthy, Charles H., *History of the United States*. American Book Company, New York, 1919.

McLaughlin, Andrew C., *History of the American Nation*. D. Appleton and Company, New York, 1919.

McLaughlin, Andrew C., and Van Tyne, Claude Halstead, *A History of the United States for Schools*. D. Appleton and Company, New York, 1911.

Montgomery, David, *The Beginner's American History*. Ginn and Company, Boston, 1899.

Muzzey, David Saville, *An American History*. Ginn and Company, Boston, 1920.

O'Hara, John P., *A History of the United States*. The Macmillan Company, New York, 1919.

Robinson, James Harvey, *Medieval and Modern Times*. Ginn and Company, Boston, 1918.

Robinson, James Harvey, and Beard, Charles A., *History of Europe Our Own Times*. Ginn and Company, Boston, 1921.

Robinson, James Harvey, and Beard, Charles A., *Outlines of European History*, Part II. Ginn and Company, Boston, 1916.

Stephenson, Nathaniel Wright, *An American History*. Ginn and Company, Boston, 1913.

Southworth, A. T., *The Common Sense of the Constitution of the United States*. Allyn and Bacon, Boston, 1924.

Thompson, Waddy, *History of the People of the United States*. D. C. Heath and Company, New York, 1919.

Venable, W. H., *A School History of the United States*. Von Antwerp, Bragg and Company, New York, 1872.

Webster, Hutton, *Modern European History*. D. C. Heath and Company, New York, 1920.

West, Willis Mason, *American History and Government*. Allyn and Bacon, Boston, 1913.

West, Willis Mason, *History of the American People*. Allyn and Bacon, Boston, 1918.

West, Willis Mason, *Ancient World*. Allyn and Bacon, Boston, 1913.

Whelpley, Samuel, *A Compend of History from the Earliest Times, comprehending a general view of the present state of the world with respect to civilization, religion and government.* American Stationers' Company, Boston, 1837.

MAGAZINES

Adams, James Truslow, " History and the Lower Criticism," *The Atlantic Monthly,* Vol. CXXXII (September, 1923), pp. 308–317.

Adams, W. I. Lincoln, " Right and Wrong Ways of Teaching History," *Current History,* Vol. XVI (July, 1922), pp. 550–551.

Barnes, Harry Elmer, " Seven Books of History Against the Germans," *The New Republic,* Vol. XXXVIII (March 19, 1924), pt. II, pp. 10–15.

Barnes, Harry Elmer, " The Drool Method in History, *"The American Mercury,* Vol. I (January, 1924), pp. 31–38.

Chafee, Zechariah, " Freedom of Speech," *The New Republic,* Vol. XVII (November 16, 1918), pp. 66–69.

De Bow's Review of the South and West. v. 1–32 old series, v. 1–4 new series. J. D. B. De Bow, ed., New Orleans, 1846–1867.

Deshon, George, " A Novel Defence of the Public School," *The Catholic World,* Vol. L (February, 1890), pp. 677–687.

Eagleton, Clyde, " The Attitude of Our Textbooks Toward England," *Educational Review,* Vol. LVI (December, 1918), pp. 424–429.

" The K. of C. Historical Commission," *The Fortnightly Review,* Vol. XXX (December 1, 1923), pp. 457–458.

" History and Fiction as International Trouble-Makers," *The Literary Digest,* Vol. LXXX (July 7, 1923), pp. 36–37.

Editorial, " Teacher-Baiting: The New Sport," *The Nation,* Vol. CXII (April 27, 1921), p. 613.

" Concerning School Histories," *The New Age,* March, 1923, p. 156.

" Civil Liberty in the United States," *The World Tomorrow,* Vol. VIII (June, 1925), p. 186.

" Drugging the Young Idea," *The Freeman*, Vol. VII (August 22, 1923), pp. 556–557.

" Accepted Fable," *The Freeman*, Vol. VII (June 27, 1923), pp. 366–367.

" The Anti-Catholic Spirit of Certain Writers," *The Catholic World*, Vol. XXXVI (February, 1883), pp. 658–667.

" The Teacher Among Free Men," *The New Republic*, Vol. XXVI (March 2, 1921), pp. 8–9.

" Charges against New York City Teachers," *School and Society*, Vol. VI (December 22, 1917), p. 733.

" Freedom of Teaching in the New York City Schools," *School and Society*, Vol. IX (February 1, 1919), pp. 142–143.

" The Meeting of the American Historical Association at Columbus," *The American Historical Review*, Vol. XXIX (April, 1924), p. 428.

" Other Heresies," *The New Republic*, Vol. XVIII (April 12, 1919), pp. 330–331.

" The War is Over in Iowa," *The Survey*, Vol. XLVIII (September 15, 1922), p. 712.

" More Educational Inquisition," *The New Republic*, Vol. XVII (January 11, 1919), pp. 305–307.

" New York's Disloyal School Teachers," *Literary Digest*, Vol. LV (December 8, 1917), pp. 32–33.

Editorial, *The Survey*, Vol. L (April 15, 1923), p. 68.

Giddings, Franklin H., " Are we getting better textbooks? " *The Independent*, Vol. I (June 17, 1922), pp. 5–8.

Giddings, Franklin H., " Are we getting better textbooks? " *The Independent*, Vol. I (June 3, 1922), pp. 6–9.

Hamilton, Gail, " Catholicism and Public Schools," *North American Review*, Vol. CXLVII (1888), pp. 575–580.

Harré, T. Everett, " Shadow Huns and Others," *The National Civic Federation Review*, Vol. IV (February 15, 1919), pp. 12–16.

Hathaway, Carson C., " Is Muzzey's American History Revolutionary? " *The Dearborn Independent*, October 20, 1923, p. 2.

Herskovitz, Melville J., and Willey, Malcolm M., "What Your Child Learns," *The Nation*, Vol. CIX (September 17, 1924), pp. 282–284.

The Iowa Legionnaire, April 15, 1921.

Jacowitz, Jacob, "History Textbooks Under Fire," *Journal of the National Education Association*, Vol. XI (March, 1922), pp. 117–118.

Lew, Timothy T., "China in American School Text-Books," Spl. Suppl. to *The Chinese Social and Political Science Review*, Vol. VI–VII (July, 1923).

McAndrew, William, "American Liberty More or Less," *The World's Work*, Vol. XLVII (December, 1923), p. 180.

McClure, S. S., "Some Delusions about Ireland," *McClure's Magazine*, Vol. LII (June, 1922), pp. 93–103.

McSweeney, Edward F., "The Anger of the Anglophiles," *Columbia*, Vol. I (April, 1922), pp. 10–21.

Randall, A. W. G., "Pan-Germanic Education and French 'Decadence,'" *Contemporary Review*, Vol. CVIII (1915), pp. 589–599.

Reddin, John H., "The American History Contest," *Columbia*, September, 1921.

"Root out Revolutionary Radicalism," *The National Civic Federation Review*, Vol. V (September 25, 1920), pp. 3–4, 21.

Russell, Charles Edward, "Behind the Propaganda Scenes," *Columbia*, Vol. II (September, 1922), pp. 5–6.

Miss Rutherford's Scrap Book, Valuable Information about the South, Vol. I (January, 1923). Athens, Georgia.

Schuyler, Robert Livingston, "History and Public Opinion," *Educational Review*, Vol. LV (March, 1918), pp. 181–190.

"Social Studies and the Public Schools," *School Review*, Vol. XXVII (1919), pp. 205–212.

Sisson, Edward A., "The Historical Education of the American Citizen," *Journal of the National Education Association*, Vol. XI (February, 1922), pp. 56–57.

Stephens, H. Morse, "Nationality and History," *The American Historical Review*, Vol. XXI (January, 1916), pp. 225–237.

Sweet, W. W., " Religion in Our School Histories," *The Christian Century*, Vol. XLI (November 20, 1924), pp. 1502–1504.

The S. S. Bulletin, Publication of the Steuben Society, New York, 1922.

" War in the Textbooks," *The Nation*, Vol. CXIX (September 17, 1924), p. 277.

NEWSPAPERS

The Atlanta Journal, June 27, 1923.

Boise, Idaho: *Idaho Statesman*, December 9, 1922.

Boise, Idaho: *Evening Capital News*, June 14, 1922.

Boston, Massachusetts: *The Christian Science Monitor*, May 17, 1920, November 2, 1921, June 27, 1923, August 31, 1923. *Boston Herald*, May 19, 1925, May 7, 1926.

Brooklyn, New York: *The Standard Union*, February 3, 1922.

Cedar Rapids, Iowa: *The Cedar Rapids Republican*, May 30, 1922.

Chicago American, January 22, 1920.

Chicago: *Herald and Examiner*, January, 1918 to June, 1924.

The Chicago Daily Tribune, June 23, 1922.

The *Cleveland Plain Dealer*, May 2, 1923.

The Des Moines Register, April 6, 1922, February 27, 1923, April 24, 1923, November 23, 1924.

Dubuque Telegraph-Herald, June 14, 1923.

Fort Wayne, Indiana: *The News Sentinel*, June 6, 1923.

Louisville, Kentucky: *The Courier-Journal*, November 12, 1922.

Louisville, Kentucky: *The Louisville Times*, November 4, 1922, and November 9, 1922.

The Milwaukee Journal, June 9, 1923.

The New York American, July 2, 1922, October 8, 1922, October 22, 1922, November 4, 1923.

New York: *Evening Globe*, February 22, 1922.

New York: *The Gaelic American*, March 11, 1922.

New York: *The Globe and Commercial Advertiser*, May 15, 1922.

The New York Times, January, 1914 to December, 1925.

The *New York Tribune*, November, 1923.
Ottumwa, Iowa: *The Daily Courier*, March 2, 1919.
Philadelphia: *The Evening Bulletin*, March 1, 1922.
St. Louis, Missouri: *The St. Louis Daily Globe Democrat*, December 18, 1922.
St. Louis, Missouri: *The St. Louis Star*, December 20, 1922.
St. Louis, Missouri: *The St. Louis Times*, December 18, 1922.
San Francisco Chronicle, November 24, 1922.
The Seattle Star, September 30, 1918.
Washington, D. C.: *Star*, June 4, 1922, April 26, 1923.
Washington, D. C.: *The United States Telegraph*, October 5, 1836.

PAMPHLETS AND DOCUMENTS

American Bankers Association, Commission on Public Education. Pamphlets and statements *in re* Textbooks. New York.
American Federation of Labor, *Report of the Proceedings of the Convention of the American Federation of Labor, June 22, 1922, Eighth Day Proceedings.* American Federation of Labor, Washington, D. C., 1922.
Report of American Federation of Labor Committee on Education on Social Studies in the Public Schools. American Federation of Labor, Washington, D. C., 1923.
American Federation of Labor, *Official Record of the American Federation of Labor in the Struggle to Bring Knowledge to the Masses,* " Education for All." American Federation of Labor, Washington, D. C., 1922.
City of Boston, *Proceedings of School Committee,* December 18, 1922. [N. P.]
California State Board of Education, Special Bulletin No. 4, Series of 1918, *Concerning Textbooks in History.* Sacramento, 1918.
California State Department of Education, Bulletin No. 4-A, *Teaching the United States Constitution and American Ideals.* Sacramento, 1918.
Report of the Committee of Five on American History Text-

books now in Use in California High Schools. California State Printing Office, Sacramento, 1922.

Clum, Woodworth, " America is Calling," Better America Federation of California, Los Angeles.

Chafee, Zechariah, " Freedom and Initiative in the Schools," *The Public and the Schools,* New York, 1919.

Conner, A. H., *Should the " History of the American People " by Willis Mason West be used as a School Text Book?* [N. P.]

Constitution Anniversary Association, *Bulletin,* No. 9, No. 10, Chicago.

The English-Speaking Union, Bulletin No. 7, June, 1923. New York.

[Communication of the] *Ethical Society to the School Board, Davenport, Iowa, May 24, 1923.* (In manuscript.)

Report of the Committee from the Fathers of Soldiers League to the Board of Education, Des Moines, Iowa, 1918. (In manuscript.)

Griffin, Joseph T., *American History Must It be Rewritten to Preserve Our Foreign Friendships?* [N. P.]

Hart, Albert Bushnell, " School Books and International Prejudices," International Conciliation, Bulletin No. 32. New York, January, 1911.

Hirshfield, David, *Report on Investigation of Pro-British History Text-Books in Use in the Public Schools of the City of New York.* [N. P.]

Jaegers, Albert, *A Brief Sketch of the Life and Character of Baron von Steuben.* Jacob Leisler Unit, Steuben Society, New York, 1922.

Kendig-Gill, Isabelle, " War and Peace in United States History Text Books," National Council for the Prevention of War, Washington.

Report of Special Committee on School Histories and Text Books Adopted by Grand Lodge Knights of Pythias September 20, 1923. [N. P.]

Report of the Committee on Social Studies of the Commission on the Reorganization of Secondary Education of the National

Education Association, " The Social Studies in Secondary Education." Bulletin, 1916, No. 28, Bureau of Education. Washington, 1916.

McCamant, Wallace, *Muzzey's School History*, Report of the Chairman of the Committee on Patriotic Education of National Society Sons of the American Revolution. [N. P.]

McCamant, Wallace, *Report of Committee on Patriotic Education*. [Sons of the American Revolution]. May 9, 1923. [N. P.]

McSweeney, Edward F., *America First*. Boston, [Edward F. McSweeney] 1922.

Miller, Charles Grant, *Treason to American Tradition: A Study of Eight Altered School Histories*. Sons of the Revolution in the State of California. Los Angeles, 1922.

Miller, Charles Grant, *Treason to American Tradition, The Spirit of Benedict Arnold Reincarnated in United States History Revised in Text-Books. An Exposure of Ten Anglicized School Histories*. The Patriot League of America, New York, 1922.

Montana State Council of Defense, *Bulletin of the Montana State Council of Defense, April 22, 1918*. Butte, Montana, 1918.

National Industrial Conference Board, *A Case of Federal Propaganda in Our Public Schools*. National Industrial Conference Board, Boston, 1919.

National Security League, Pamphlets. The National Security League, New York.

National Society of the Sons of the American Revolution, *Official Bulletin of the National Society Sons of the American Revolution*. Vol. XVII (October, 1922), No. 2. Washington, D. C.

Report to the Nashville Congress, Sons of the American Revolution, 1923, *The Sons of the American Revolution and the Histories in Use in Our Schools*. [N. P.]

Official Bulletin of the National Society of the Sons of the American Revolution, December, 1922. [N. P.]

New York City Board of Education, *Report of the Committee*

to Investigate . . . *History Textbooks Used in the Public Schools of the City of New York.* Board of Education, New York, 1922.

State Department of Education, 1921, *American History and Patriotic Programs for all Schools of Oklahoma.* [N. P.]

Patriotic Organizations Appeal for School History Bill, New Jersey Unit, The Patriot League. Newark, New Jersey, February 22, 1924.

Forty-Ninth Annual Report of the State Board of Education . . . of Rhode Island, January, 1919.

Report of Roy F. Britton to St. Louis Society, Sons of Revolution. December 16, 1922. (In manuscript.)

Report of the Historian of Passaic Valley Chapter S. A. R. on Muzzey's American History. December 15, 1922. (In manuscript.)

Minority Report upon Muzzey's History of the United States to the Board of Managers of the California Society of the Sons of the American Revolution. (In manuscript.)

Resolutions of the Association of History Teachers of the Middle States and Maryland. Adopted May 5, 1923. Columbia University, New York.

Ridder, Victor, *The Germans in America, A Comprehensive Review of their Share in Founding, Developing and Safeguarding the United States.* Uga Publishing Company, New York, 1922.

Rutherford, Mildred Lewis, *A Measuring Rod to Test Text-Books and Reference Books in Schools, Colleges and Libraries.* Athens, Georgia, 1922.

Rutherford, Mildred Lewis, *The Truths of History.* Athens, Georgia, 1921.

Taft, Donald R., *Historical Textbooks and International Differences.* The Association for Peace Education, Chicago.

" Hearings Before the Subcommittee of the Committee on the Judiciary," 65th Congress, 2d Session on S. 3529 (February 23–April 13, 1918) A Bill to Repeal the Act Entitled " An Act to Incorporate the National German-American Alliance "

approved February 25, 1907. Government Printing Office,
Washington, 1918.

District of Columbia Board of Education, *Piney Branch Citizens'
Association Against Muzzey's School History.* Washington,
D. C., April 25, 1923.

Board of Education, Washington, D. C., Ernest Greenwood,
Chairman, *Report of the Special Committee on Muzzey's
American History.* 1923.

Congressional Record, 68th Congress, 2d Session, Vol. LXVI, No.
77, pp. 5396–5398. Washington.

House Report, No. 12033, Public Bill, No. 595, 68th Congress, 2d Session, "An Act Making Appropriations for
the Government of the District of Columbia and Other
Activities Chargeable Wholly or in Part Against the Revenues of Such District for the Fiscal Year Ending June 30,
1925."

*Toward the New Education: The Case Against Autocracy in Our
Public Schools.* The Teachers' Union of the City of New
York.

*The Trial of the Three Suspended Teachers of the De Witt Clinton
High School.* Teachers' Defense Fund, New York.

Dotey, Aaron I., *The Exploitation of the Public School System
of New York.* Teachers' Council, New York.

Department of Education of the City of New York, *In the Matter of the Trial of Charges of Conduct unbecoming a teacher
and to the prejudice of good order, efficiency and discipline
preferred against Benjamin Glassberg.* The Teachers'
Union, New York.

BOOKS (*Secondary*)

Bourne, William Oland, *History of the Public School Society of
the City of New York.* William Wood and Company, New
York, 1870.

Brown, Elmer Ellsworth, *The Making of Our Middle Schools.
An Account of the Development of Secondary Education in*

the United States. Longmans, Green and Company, New York, 1907.

Carlton, Frank Tracy, *Economic Influences upon Educational Progress in the United States, 1820–1850.* University of Wisconsin, Madison, 1908.

Cubberley, Ellwood P., *Public Education in the United States.* Houghton Mifflin Company, Boston, 1919.

Inglis, A. J., *The Rise of the High School in Massachusetts.* Columbia University Publications, New York, 1911.

Johnson, Henry, *Teaching of History in Elementary and Secondary Schools.* The Macmillan Company, New York, 1915.

Littlefield, George Emery, *Early Schools and School Books of New England.* Club of Old Volumes, Boston, 1904.

O'Brien, Michael J., *A Hidden Phase of American History.* Dodd, Mead and Company, New York, 1919.

Russell, William F., *The Early Teaching of History in the Secondary Schools of New York and Massachusetts.* McKinley Publishing Company, Philadelphia, 1915.

Schrader, Frederick Franklin, " *1683–1920.*" Concord Publishing Company, New York, 1920.

Werner, M. R., *Brigham Young.* Harcourt, Brace and Company, New York, 1925.

INDEX

Abbott, A. H., committee work of, 264, 306
Abolition, textbooks in support of, 138
Abraham, reference to, 138
Adams, Christmas, death of, 282
  (see also Attucks, Crispus)
Adams, E. D., committee work of, 247, 264, 306
Adams, James Truslow, article by, 289
Adams, John,
  attitude toward education, 4
  inauguration of, 63
  reference to, 212, 213, 254, 255, 256
Adams, Samuel,
  reference to, 254, 262
  relative of, 222
Adrian (Michigan), schools of, 266
Agricultural Chemistry, study of, 18
Agriculture, development of, 12
Alabama,
  Americanization laws in, 105
  curriculum in, 83
  laws relative to education, 16, 17, 22, 25, 26, 28, 39, 47
  requirement for teachers in, 55
  schools of, 266
  teaching of patriotism in, 95
  textbooks in, 41, 67, 69, 73, 98, 100
Alabama *Code*, reference to, 16
Alabama Patriotic Society, establishment of, 95
Alexander, Magnus N., 204
Algebra, teaching of, 6
Alien teachers, laws relative to, 304
Aliens, restrictions on, as teachers, 34, 35, 86, 88
Allen, Ethan, mention of, 211, 218
Allied Powers, citizens of, employment of, as teachers, 87

Allies,
  praise of, 245
  reference to, 253
Alsace-Lorraine, reference to, 242
Alta (Iowa), schools of, 293
America,
  accomplishments of, 18
  attitude of England toward, 237
  British in, 284
  Catholic Church in, 177, 178
  Colonists in, 160, 212
  " Defamation " of, 210
  development of, 184
  economic conditions in, 71
  founders of, 135
  freedom of, 287
  friendship of, 235
  influence of Irish in, 230
  liberty in, 209
  opportunities of, 12, 271
America, Speech on Conciliation with, 209, 213, 268
America First, 226
" America First " Publicity Association, responsibility of, 325
America is Calling, writing of, 194
American Allies, 247
American Association for International Coöperation, 220
American Bankers Association, 203
American Bar Association,
  report relative to textbooks, 334, 335
  work of, 185, 186, 188, 192
American Car Company, member of, criticises textbook, 202
American Citizenship, report of committee on, 185, 334, 335
American colonies, settlers in, 255
" American Creed," teaching of, 56
American Democracy, Problems in, 77
American Economic Life, 202

355